THE GREAT AMERICAN DEER HUNT

THE GREAT AMERICAN DEER HUNT

HOW SUCCESSFUL HUNTERS BAG TROPHY
DEER AND KEEP THEIR FREEZERS FULL

LARRY GRUPP

PALADIN PRESS · BOULDER, COLORADO

The Great American Deer Hunt:
How Successful Hunters Bag Trophy
Deer and Keep Their Freezers Full
by Larry Grupp

Copyright © 1992 by Larry Grupp

ISBN 0-87364-677-0
Printed in the United States of America

Library of Congress Catalog Number: 92-60209

Published by Paladin Press
P.O. Box 1307
Boulder, Colorado 80306, USA.
(303) 443-7250

Direct inquires and/or orders to the above address.

Illustrations by Bill Border

CONTENTS

PREFACE

State fish and game officials tell us that the average committed deer hunter will bag fifteen to twenty-five deer of both sexes during an entire lifetime of hunting! Records show that in many places in the United States, deer hunters who really work at it by going out as often as they can and attempting to hunt as smart as they can shoot no more than one deer every two to three years. To keep his interest up, the average deer hunter finds he must make do vicariously with a party kill on a yearly basis. Usually this is sufficient to keep the adrenaline flowing.

In spite of these frequent long, dry spells when the average hunter simply walks through the woods without seeing a shootable critter, deer hunting remains the most popular big game shooting done in North America. In 1990, an estimated twenty-five million hunters spent at least part of one day trying to bag a deer.

Unless one is fortunate enough to hunt with a skilled old-timer who is good at both bagging deer and giving instructions, the average hunter statistically cannot become a good, consistent deer hunter in his lifetime. Kill statistics work mightily against him—there simply are not enough successes to make on-the-job training a realistic alternative. Twenty-five kills are not enough to demonstrate to a hunter the impact of herd movements, weather conditions, environmental changes, hunting clothes, rifles, and—most important—the reaction of deer to common hunting practices and malpractices.

A similar situation exists when evaluating a rifle's relative merit as a deer getter. We all know hunters who swear that their 7mm mag, .30-30, .264 Magnum, and so on are the best deer rifles ever placed on the face of the Earth. They believe this even though it is virtually impossible to evaluate a particular rifle or caliber until the owner has used it to kill at least five or six deer. That is about a third of the average deer hunter's lifetime quota.

As a result, the average deer hunter only *thinks* he knows if his trusty .294 Squashemflat is really doing the job in heavy brush or across deep canyons. Most of what he knows comes from outdoor writers who may or may not have killed more than the average in their lifetime. Deer hunters tend to quote their favorite writer as an expert when in real life this guy may have shot only few more deer than they have. His only claim to fame may be the ability to weave an exciting tale.

The director of the nation's largest outdoor book club once told me that its best-selling books were on deer hunting. During the fall season, every hunting magazine carries its obligatory monthly article on chasing old *odocoileus virginianus*. Neophytes know that their sport, while difficult to master, is powerfully addictive. They spend hour upon hour reading about deer hunting as well as reliving the few kills they have made with their hunting partners. Theirs is a genuine attempt at craft improvement, something that may elude the wives and girlfriends who must sit through it all.

After a year or two of discussion, the limited feedback that an incident or two can yield is beat to death. Books on deer hunting, the fledgling hunter now finds, invariably are written by people with graphic writing skills and an inexhaustible supply of supporting pictures as opposed to those who have actually killed a great number of deer. A few genuinely skilled deer hunters still write about the subject, but many of them are passing from the scene.

The bit of experience the deer hunter may have acquired, along with a questioning mind, may lead him to conclude that a strong hint of bullshit clings to most of what is popularly written regarding deer hunting. How do the writers know a .25-20, for instance, is not a good deer cartridge when they have not killed, as the case may be, the obligatory six deer with it?

What to do about the dilemma?

Many years ago, business and law schools were faced with a predicament similar to that confronting deer hunters. Among their graduates were a number of tycoons who were experts at putting together business deals. These men and women wanted to teach eager young students how they did it, but they were constrained by their inability as teachers. Like most superskilled deer hunters, they also lacked the line of bull-shit needed to successfully put their experiences down in writing.

In this case, a solution finally appeared. Some really smart teachers developed the case study approach to teaching business, law, and financial management. They found that the tycoons could relate their real-life experiences to the teacher/writers, who wrote them down verbatim as case studies. Each experience was refined and distilled so that the reader could easily pick out the important concepts. Students, they found, could add years of experience by reading cases that emphasized the important basics.

In that regard, if we could get some of the old-timer deer getters to sit down and relate specific cases when they actually bagged deer, it might be helpful to the average deer hunter. As is true with the business and law school case studies, how the deal was lost could also be instructive so long as the successes outnumbered the failures. For deer hunting, what was needed were accurate accounts enumerating weather and ground conditions, rifles and calibers, clothing and equipment, movement of deer, movement of various members of the hunting party, ranges of shots, length of the hunt, and other vital information integrated into a no-nonsense case study that others could read and analyze for their own benefit. The forty unadorned case studies that follow are the result of that approach.

Fortunately, there are still a number of deer hunters throughout our land who can kill a deer virtually every time they go out. At the very least, someone in their party gets a deer during every hunt. Invariably, these superskilled deer hunters live in remote rural areas. They are generally characterized as being poor, with tattered old equipment. Many actually live subsistence lives, and most have few friends who are not pissed off at them because of their tag-filling activities, knowing that when they go out with these hunters, one way or another their season is going to come to a screeching halt. In states where more than one deer is allowed, they find that their pleasant afternoon interludes are quickly constrained by a lack of freezer space.

While checking with the expert deer finders, I discovered that most actually were meat hunters, interested mainly in the contest and in filling the freezer—i.e., they usually shot whatever deer they coaxed into their sights. This should not be a bar to the trophy hunter interested only in big bucks. He simply can pick and choose from the old-timers' systems, confident he will see more shootable deer.

With these concepts in mind, I have put actual deer hunts into case study style for deer hunters to evaluate. In every case, the reader is promised an unembellished account of what actually happened out in the field. Everyone is free to draw their own conclusions based on the many kills and a few spectacular misses. No hypothetical six-paragraph discussions will follow on the supposed merits of one primer over another in rifle rounds, or how beautiful it was to be out that day. Only a no-nonsense account of the actual hunt is included. Each hunter must apply the lesson of that hunt to his own area.

Happy and successful deer hunting to all.

ACKNOWLEDGMENTS

While putting this book together was the work of one person, it could not have been completed successfully without the input of many. By the very nature of the project, these contributors come from a variety of diverse backgrounds. A few were statisticians and analysts who seldom, if ever, hunt deer.

As one would suppose, most of the contributors to this book were older men and women who have killed a lot of deer. Most of the men were farmers, ranchers, or of a similar background. Try as I might, I found few women who consistently and gladly killed deer. They may be out there, but I failed to connect with them.

Unfortunately, the type of people who should be providing input into the volume in front of you generally are not those for whom writing about hunting comes easily or naturally. Especially gifted deer hunters usually do not brag or even talk about their activities outside a limited circle. They abhor additional hunting pressure on their territory, and they definitely do not want the spotlight of social notoriety thrown on them. Some have suffered or heard of those who have suffered at the hands of brain-dead animal-rights activists. Rather, their view of wild game is that of a crop that must be managed. Their only wish is to continue to pursue their activities in relative obscurity.

But within their circle of trusted friends and relatives, skilled deer hunters *will* discuss their successes and, if one is very patient, their failures. By doing so, they follow the ancient tradition of their cult in that they are excellent raconteurs of their adventures. Putting an incident down on paper, however, is another matter entirely. Yet, as the list that follows demonstrates, some are very cerebral people who, for reasons of their own, wish to remain in the background.

Not recognizing as many of these people as possible would, I feel, be the greater travesty. As is common in these circumstances, one often does not know where to begin or end. What follows then is not based on importance or anything other than the order in which these people's names came to mind.

Marion Wilcox, an independent old-line farmer who, with his many brothers, first showed me that good drivers who know the country can always get a critter. We started my learning process forty years ago on foxes, acquiring the knowledge that one must always know the territory as well as the minds of his hunting partners. Mind reading is not critically important today with the use of walkie-talkies. Nonetheless, it was important to know the country back when the Wilcoxes hunted because they essentially had to read their partners' minds with regards to how they'd move. This is still a consideration today even when using two-way radios.

Sam Wilder, the old Dean of Deer Hunters, has probably killed more deer than any other living person. Fifty-eight years ago, at the age of eleven, he dropped his first whitetail using a .25-20 bolt-action. Wilder recalls carrying the .25-20 because all the "good" big-bore rifles were taken up by the "real" hunters in the group. Since that time, Mr. Wilder has hunted deer in a score of states, often covering six or eight in the same season. His diversity of knowledge added materially to what follows.

Dr. Ted Terrel proved that he, at least, can take his rifle into the bush alone at any time and, without help, kill a deer. Dr. Terrel achieved his remarkable deer hunting ability as a result of his rural upbringing as well as his following deer for a full year on horseback. He earned his Ph.D. by living with deer, but he has never let a formal education obscure his practical nature. Terrel is a deer hunter who always seems to be in the right place at the right time.

Jim Thiemens, chief forester for Potlatch Corporation, was a constant source of information regarding species, food, yarding habits, and migration patterns of deer. Coincidentally, Thiemens is one of the best blacktail deer hunters around today.

Another forester, *Pete Black*, deserves recognition for his tracking ability and for his general talent at reading deer sign in the woods. Often, Mr. Black pointed out sign as big as a billboard that we failed to take note of.

Erik Grupp, a helicopter crew chief who grew

up shooting deer for the table, now spends more time in the air than on the ground, where he can keep better track of the quarry he has spent half a lifetime pursuing. Around Grupp, one never doubts where the deer are. He always knows.

We must mention *Maurice McConkie Tanner*, U.S. State Department guru/philosopher, now retired, who—when told at the age of fifty-two that deer hunting is addictive and required huge amounts of cerebral effort—went out and proved both to be true. Although Tanner first killed a deer at age fifty-three, he proved that successful hunters never walk through the woods with their minds in neutral. Tanner proved to me that the basic thesis of this book is correct—that one can learn by the case-study approach.

Mention must be made of my late *Uncle Dugan*, half Ojibwa Indian, who forgot more about deer hunting than any other person who has ever lived. No one knows how many deer he killed in his lifetime. I would like to have used some of his tales, but because of the basic nature of Indian hunters, they are not suited to a book for general distribution. His concepts and philosophical threads do, however, run through this entire volume.

Admittedly, the previous list is a glittering array of deer-hunting talent. Yet my deepest, most heartfelt thanks must go to the Muppet. Although her direct, overt involvement is tough to discover, it would never have been done without her.

Dozens of farmers, loggers, ranchers, lawyers, college professors, wildlife experts, and others contributed mightily to this effort. Some know how to hunt deer, and some know only what they read in books. Others are statistical and spatial geniuses. All of these people helped immensely. The fact that they are not thanked individually should not denigrate their contributions. Each case study they took so much time and patience to explain was important, and I thank them all.

INTRODUCTION

Harvard, Idaho, lies about ninety miles south and east of Spokane, Washington. A tiny little community of two hundred, Harvard was named by an early surveyor who apparently had attended Harvard University. In deference to other Ivy League schools, there are also a Yale and a Princeton as well as a Vassar in the immediate area.

Harvard is an area characterized by small lots of patchy, cleared farmland lying immediately adjacent to State Highway 6. About three-quarters of a mile from the two-lane blacktop, high rolling hills dominate the landscape. Unless one must climb them in a hurry, they are not mountains. Residents refer to them as a prelude to the Rocky Mountains.

At one time, these hills supported large, merchantable white-pine timber. Fires in the 1920s and extensive logging in the 1930s decimated the large old growth. Today, cold winters of varying lengths force farmers in the area to raise grass, hay, barley, oats, Christmas trees, and saw logs.

Continuous tree culling mixed with stock grazing has created a continuum of fringe area that is wildly conducive to whitetail deer production. Some of the largest concentrations of deer in North America inhabit the hills around Harvard. Yet the region is not notorious for really huge bucks, keeping it out of the national spotlight as one of the primo deer-hunting destinations. Few records have been set here other than perhaps the sheer numbers taken by the many local hunters who annually comb the region's hills.

The Harvard Circle, however—an area of about fifty miles' radius around Harvard, Idaho—is a place where virtually every hunter gets a deer every year. This alone sets it apart from other areas, where usually one in three hunters bag a deer. Game officials estimate the statewide success ratio to be about 75 percent annually. Within the Harvard Circle, the kill is reported at or above 95 percent!

Resident farmers, ranchers, loggers, and others who work out on the land know the country better than the insides of their pockets, and as a result they take a lot of deer. Under the circumstances, one would expect that. Yet other successful hunters include high school girls, teachers, professors, lawyers, store clerks, and mechanics who have but a few days a year to be afield. Success among this unlikely group is similarly high, due in part to the many deer.

Another curious characteristic may contribute to the high deer kill around Harvard. Rural people in the area are still subject to the ancient raconteur tradition, wherein they draw their entertainment not passively from sitting in front of the tube but from reliving accounts of the chase over and over again. A less rural population might be fearful of arousing antihunter sentiment. Schoolchildren do not dwell on the uncool. But during hunting season, How The Deer Was Got is a constant topic of conversation.

It's the chicken-and-the-egg syndrome: do the many deer in the area provide the high kill rates, or is it because the local people enjoy hashing and rehashing their hunts over and over again, thus passing down, from generation to generation, what works and what does not?

There are, living in the Harvard Circle, master deer getters who can and often do take specific deer on the last day of the season. They are sufficiently confident that they can go out hunting every day, knowing that on the last day they can pick the buck or big grinding doe they want for the locker. All shoot for food, and all are addicted to deer hunting. In preparation for this book, I ran into one old-timer who swore he saw fourteen shootable deer the last day of the season.

No one seems prepared to claim that the many deer killed created the raconteur tradition, or that the raconteur tradition created the excellent deer hunters. Most have never given the subject a moment's consideration. As with hens and eggs the world over, all we can do is observe the results.

Part of these results has been refined into this case-study approach to hunting. Although many, if not most, of the Harvard Circle old-timers have never heard of case studies, it is, in fact, what has developed from their approach to deer hunting. It is also the method they use to teach their youngsters how to take deer successfully.

Invariably, these studies emphasize truly important aspects of deer hunting such as weather and ground conditions, clothing appropriate to

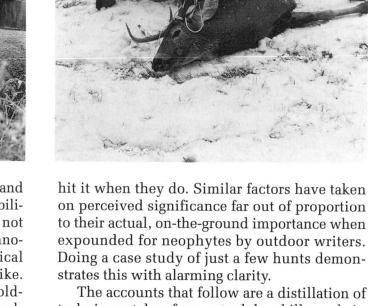

the type of hunt, knowledge of the country and the deer's habits, and, most important, the ability to think one's way into a hunt. They do not place a great deal of emphasis on new technological wrinkles, faddish methods, physical stamina, caliber of rifles, luck, and the like. Taking rifle calibers as an example, these old-timers do not care what make, model, and caliber one is using to hunt deer. They know all will kill deer if the users can see the critter and then

hit it when they do. Similar factors have taken on perceived significance far out of proportion to their actual, on-the-ground importance when expounded for neophytes by outdoor writers. Doing a case study of just a few hunts demonstrates this with alarming clarity.

The accounts that follow are a distillation of techniques taken from actual deer kills made in the four corners of the United States using the Harvard Circle psychology.

CHAPTER 1
SEEDLING-EATING DEER

HUNT CHECKLIST

Weather
Crisp at night, with daytime highs in the upper forties.

Terrain
Gently rolling, essentially flat farmland with few prominences.
Scrub- and brush-covered area, not farmed.

Wind Direction
Out of the north, 8 to 10 knots.

Conditions Previous Day
Frost at night as days grew colder, but no major change.

How Hunter Moved
Walked from farmhouse to Christmas tree plantation, where he waited
patiently for buck to expose itself.

Clothes
Camouflage sweatshirt, cotton work pants, leather field boots.

Rifle Caliber and Scope
.308 bolt-action with 4X scope.

Sex of Deer
8-point (eastern count *) buck.

Time of Day
Very first light.

Length of Hunt
About 1 1/2 hours.

Length of Shot
40 yards.

How Deer Moved
Deer fed into Christmas tree plantation to place where hunter was on stand.

Skill of Hunter
Hunter had killed numerous deer in his lifetime.

* Traditionally, hunters east of the Mississippi River count the points on both antlers,
while those west of the river count only one side.

The owner of 240 acres of mostly cleared, farmable land observed that deer were eating seedlings in his 5-acre Christmas tree plantation. They clipped the tender new pines off at ground level, reducing the stand by 60 to 80 percent. He observed that this was an ongoing situation and not the work of a solitary group of roving foragers.

Tracks amongst the decimated seedlings indicated that several deer were frequenting the area. Two active buck scrapes in the plantation suggested that one or more mature, breeding bucks were also around. There did not appear to be another food source nearby that would attract them.

The land itself was gently rolling, with no extreme landform greater than forty feet top to bottom within eight hundred yards of the farm. Intermittent patches of scrubby, second- and third-growth maple, ash, cherry, and oak covered the region. The soil itself was fairly heavy clay, with occasional rock outcrops giving rise to odd patches of brush in otherwise farmable fields.

The farmer often drove to more traditional areas in his state and adjoining states to hunt deer. He was an active hunter, but he had never killed a deer on his own land. In this case he decided that, due to deer depredations, he was now experiencing greater damage than pleasure afforded by the psychological value of seeing the deer around his place.

A thin line of third-growth ash, maple, and oak approximately thirty feet tall bordered the plantation, separated by a ring of open area covered by grass and weeds approximately twenty feet wide. On the other side, a bare alfalfa field sharply marked the edge of what any self-respecting deer would call semicover. To the far east, about two hundred feet from the plantation, a heavier stand of scrub comprising perhaps twenty acres provided the only real cover close to the Christmas trees. It was possible to see through the third growth at virtually any point, but the larger, easterly woodlot was sufficiently dense to hide a number of deer.

Weeds and grass grew waist high in the tree plantation except in a ring around the seedlings, where they had been killed by chemicals and plowing. Planting was on twenty-foot center grids. However, at least 70 percent of the seedlings were now in a deer stomach.

On the basis of his infrequent sightings of the deer as well as their tracks around the seedlings, the hunter could not determine which cover the deer used as shelter. He guessed it was the larger wooded tract to the east, but it could have been any number of small woodlots lying beyond.

It was the last week in October, several days after deer season opened in that region. The weather had been crisp in the morning, dropping to the high thirties, with some evidence of frost forming in the wet grass in dips and depressions. Temperatures the day of the hunt were in the low forties, and forecasts promised slightly overcast, gray skies with winds running eight to ten knots out of the north. It was a repeat of prior days, with no significant change in sight. A bit of mist rose from the damp weeds and grass swirling in the gentle breeze. The hunter had no problem keeping track of wind direction.

First light that time of year was about 6:10 A.M. At 5:00 A.M., he pulled on a cotton camouflage sweatshirt, an old green military field hat, and old, tattered cotton work pants and started his walk to the Christmas tree plantation. He wore common three-quarter-length leather work boots. Other than a belt knife and three extra rounds for his .308 Remington 660, he took nothing extra.

The time of day, the overcast, and the light mist all contributed to a dark morning. It was possible to walk silently to the plantation only because the farmer knew the paths and trails perfectly. He walked due east on a little-used dirt road for five hundred yards till he reached a lane heading north into the tree plantation. After he turned onto the lane, the gentle wind was in his face, but it was garbled a bit by the surrounding trees. No buildings, fences, or landforms were available as reference points.

About two hundred yards out on the lane, the land rose gently about twenty feet to the tree plantation. He followed the road up the slight rise but did not enter the noisy, waist-high grass and weeds.

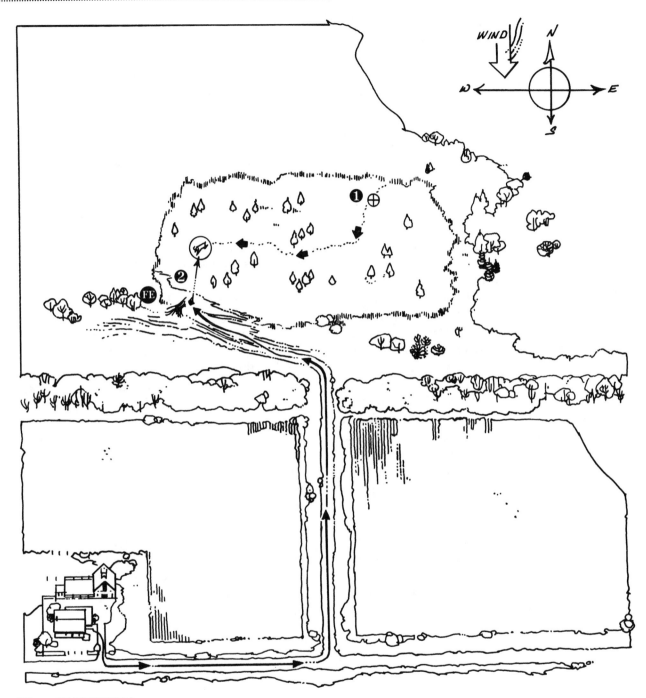

FE - FALLEN ELM
1 - DEER FIRST SIGHTED AT DAWN
2 - HUNTER SHOOTS BUCK

The hunter inched around the plantation to his left, staying on the edge of the patch. He crept slowly and quietly in the dim morning gray for perhaps another sixty yards and stopped in front of an ancient elm snag. Dead, rotting limbs were strewn grotesquely about the area under the elm.

He thought about sitting down on one of the limbs till dawn, but the high weeds would have obscured his view. He elected to stand as silently as possible.

In the gray, prelight conditions exacerbated by the rising wisps of mist, the hunter had to use lots of imagination to determine if a deer lurked in the tree farm ahead of him. Winds were still steady across the field from the north, carrying his scent harmlessly south.

Now and then he thought he heard a noise, but it was still too dim to tell what caused it. He remained motionless for about ten minutes. He soon decided that either his eyes were acclimating to the dark or it was getting light enough to see. In reality, both conditions were at work.

He thought he saw movement to his right—a large brown to gray form moving through the high grass. After another minute or two, he saw the horizontal back line of a deer as it faded in and out of the grass and weeds. It was moving from right to left and a bit toward the hunter's location.

When he first saw the critter, it was about a hundred yards away. Gradually it worked its way west toward the edge of the field where the hunter stood stone still. He sensed that the deer intended to move through the tree plantation to the line of trees and use it as cover to return to its bed in the bigger woods after full daylight.

At about forty yards, the hunter could see the deer plainly through his 4-power scope. It was a nice eight-point buck with neck swollen from the rut. Because of a slight upward slope to the land from where he stood to the deer, he never did see any of the animal below the middle of its ribs.

After he had observed it for five minutes or more, the buck brought its head up and turned slightly toward him. Its ears went up and pointed forward. Desperately the buck wanted a smell of the intruder it thought it saw among the old elm's twisted branches, but the winds were not cooperating. Now its tail stood straight up and bristled.

The hunter, whose arms now ached from holding his rifle at the ready, placed the crosshairs on the deer's neck. It was almost a frontal shot. The 140-grain .308 bullet missed the buck's neck, hitting instead high in the shoulder and angling back through the body cavity. Copper jacket separated from lead core, lodging against the deer's inside right shoulder. The shooter never did recover the lead core, which exited the lower right side.

By the time the hunter finished field-dressing the deer, it was 6:20 A.M. He walked back to the farmhouse to get his pickup truck, which he drove out to the tree plantation. Given the relatively warm day, he felt it necessary to skin and halve the critter quickly.

The presence of the gut pile in the Christmas tree plantation kept other deer from nibbling the seedlings. At the time of this writing, the hunter is eating deer, but the deer are not eating seedlings.

The hunter was successful because he hunted patiently and with a great deal of thought. He had killed a number of deer in his lifetime because he always studied the deer's habits in his immediate area. Along those lines, this hunt was tailored to fit "his" critters.

HUNT CHECKLIST

Weather
9 inches of new snow covering the ground. Temperatures of 29 to forecasted 33°F.

Terrain
Worn foothills, prelude to higher mountains.

Wind Direction
Steady out of west, 5 to 7 knots.

Conditions Previous Day
Front came through, bringing snow and colder weather.

How Hunters Moved
Drivers killed two deer at start of hunt, stander killed one, and a fourth was killed on a second drive by the drivers.

Clothes
Various military-issue wool and cotton pants, wool shirts, rubber boots, and rubber rain slickers.

Rifle Caliber and Scope
First deer shot with .30-06, second with .30-06 and .270, third with .338, fourth with .270. All had 4X or 6X scopes.

Sex of Deer
Two does and two spike bucks.

Time of Day
Hunt started at 7:00 A.M. and concluded at 11:00 A.M. Two deer shot at 7:20 A.M., one at about 8:15 A.M., and the fourth at 9:30 A.M.

Length of Hunt
About 3 1/2 hours until hunters were too cold and wet to continue.

Length of Shot
First and second deer shot at about 80 yards, third at about 230 yards, and fourth at about 60 yards, all in heavy cover.

How Deer Moved
Hunters caught two deer bedded down at the start of the hunt. One deer was up and eating when seen and shot across a valley. The fourth deer jumped up in front of driver.

Skill of Hunters
Four of the hunters were extremely skilled, having killed many deer in their lifetimes.

The whitetail deer country under study in this case is part of a group of foothills abutting more rugged mountains to the west. Because these rolling hills had been smoothed down a bit by Mother Nature, they cannot be characterized as rugged. The most extreme variation one would find in a day of hunting is about five hundred feet.

It snowed the night before the hunt, stopping as near as anyone could tell around 3:00 A.M. Five avid deer hunters agreed by phone the night before that they would be out by full light, or about 7:00 A.M., "no matter what the conditions." Their only concession to these firm plans was to agree to adjust where they hunted dependent on what they found in the morning.

Fully nine inches of new snow covered the ground, brush, and trees in their hunting territory, a north-south running valley that the hunters thought might contain deer. In some places the valley had fairly steep and at times open sides. Mostly it was flat ground choked with a tangle of brush and trees. The scrub understory was ten to twelve feet high. A slight five- to seven-knot wind blew from the west.

By 6:30 A.M., the hunters were on the county road at the north terminus of the valley. The valley rose up to the south an estimated 150 feet over a 700-yard distance. It was 29°F, with above-freezing temperatures promised by noon.

During a prehunt planning session, the five agreed that one of their number would hike up the eastern ridge to the top of the valley. Here he was to position himself in a spoon-shaped open area to watch for any deer jumped from below. One member of the party, an inexperienced out-of-stater who elected not to pay the relatively high fees for a nonresident license, agreed to act as a driver without rifle for the others. All but the out-of-stater were skilled whitetail hunters who had killed deer in the area on numerous occasions.

The valley was but 60 yards wide at the bottom, but in places it bulged out to a width of 250 to 300 yards. Two of the drivers intended to work each side, methodically pushing any deer they found uphill. Barley fields to the west and the ridge to the east delineated the country they intended to sweep. Four drivers seemed like a needlessly heavy density to move deer, but they all reckoned the critters to be holding tight.

The stander doubled-timed up the ridge, following a path that was mostly overgrown with small pines and firs. Although all had been through the area before, the stander knew the country better than the others. He was aware of the best place to wait and how to get into it without being seen or heard.

About one-quarter of his way up the ridge, the stander noticed three sets of fresh deer tracks crossing from his left (east) to his right (west) and into the targeted valley. Because of the heavy snow-covered brush, he could not see into the valley from his position on the path. He called two of the drivers on their walkie-talkies and suggested that they start their drive low and do an especially thorough job of looking for the deer he was sure were there and moving. He didn't want to chance not getting up and around the deer, so he kept going even as he talked on the radio. A plowed field marked the top of the valley, and he was doing his best to push on through the soft snow to get to the top before the deer all passed through.

All four drivers heard his transmissions and agreed to make an extra effort to catch the deer in the heavy ninebark and small, snow-covered pines low in the valley. Two headed out to the west side and two to the east. A radio went with each pair.

Perhaps four hundred yards up the hill, the not-yet-ready stander heard a single shot, followed a minute later by two very quick shots. All sounded like meat shots. The drivers carried two .30-06s and a .270. Although he was not sure, he thought he might have heard two .06 blasts and one from the .270. His educated guess proved to be correct.

At the start, the four drivers walked west within a few feet of the county road before taking their positions in preparation for the push. As the two on the east side worked into position, the lead driver spotted a doe sneaking through the brush on the other side of the valley. He fired once with his .30-06, catching the deer through the lungs on a slight forward angle. Range was no more than eighty yards. The doe looked quite large in the hunter's 4X scope, it was so close.

The doe jumped and ran perhaps ten yards up the valley before it stumbled and rolled headlong into the valley bottom. No additional shots were taken, as the shooter knew he connected and the second man was too deep in the brush to participate in the action. The two drivers on the west side saw nothing.

The lone shot spooked a second deer, a spike buck, also on the west slope of the valley. The second driver on the east side saw it first and fired with his .270. He hit it through the lungs, but the deer kept going until it was directly across from the first east-side driver, who shot straight across the valley, hitting it a bit lower in the chest cavity. It fell not two hundred feet behind the first deer.

Each driver took a deer and quickly field-dressed it. Meanwhile, driver three and the unlicensed driver kept bulldozing their way through heavy brush. After a bit, the weaponless driver, intent on pushing through the brush, got ahead of the others.

It was now 7:40 A.M. Even the limited mucking around in the snow-covered brush had soaked the men through. One hunter who wore cotton work clothes, including blue jeans and a cotton shirt and jacket, was especially miserable. Ironically, the unlicensed driver was the best dressed with wool coat and pants. He was now up the hill quite a ways ahead of the other three, who were anxious to get walking so they could warm up.

At the top of the draw, the stander was hot from the forced march. His trail was reasonably open, so he was not drenched by dumping snow off the brush. He heard on the radio that two deer were down but knew no details. After carefully and quietly working into his stand position, he turned the radio volume down lest the others started to rehash the kills and spook the deer.

The stander kept his position under a large pine tree, looking out from slightly above the valley terminus. After about twenty minutes, he saw the red plaid jacket of the unlicensed hunter. The guy had inadvertently crossed the valley and was heading uphill northeast of the stander rather than directly toward him.

The stander called him on the walkie-talkie and suggested that since they were far ahead of the other three gun-bearing drivers, they now should reverse the drive and head back toward the road. Using their single radio, the three below agreed to find a place to stand while the drive was reversed.

The upper pair moved back down the valley, the experienced deer hunter keeping the novice in line and moving slow and deliberate. Perhaps one hundred yards back down, stander (now a driver) spotted a deer on a green, grassy spot not completely covered by snow. It was a smallish, three-point buck looking uphill in the direction of the unarmed driver. Quickly, he called and told the other driver to stop for a couple of minutes till he worked out a plan for the buck.

The hunter tried valiantly to shorten the distance to the deer, which he estimated at about 230 yards, yet every time he moved even a few feet, a tree intervened, hiding the critter. Winds were steady out of the west across the draw, so the hunter suspected correctly that the buck was not winding any of the party, which now had it virtually surrounded.

The hunter guessed he had only a few more seconds in which to act before the deer was permanently spooked out of the valley. Moving around while trying to keep the deer in sight was treacherous, as footing on the valley hill was slippery due to the wet, greasy snow. Heavily cleated rubber pac boots made walking possible but not easy. Snow-covered branches laying downhill caused him to skip with almost every step, but the wind overhead and the fluffy snow masked his noise. The buck continued to look around or eat.

In desperation, he searched for a tree on which to brace his rifle for the long shot, yet nothing was at hand that he could get to and still see the deer. He determined that he was faced with a single, difficult, off-hand shot or none at all.

He braced the .338 Winchester Magnum against his shoulder, steadying the crosshairs of the 6X scope on the top of the deer's back. The deer now more or less faced the hunter, standing on a level spot about horizontally even with him. A four-foot opening through the trees was all he had. Carefully, he touched off a round.

Recoil from the shot jerked the scope off the deer. When the shooter was able to look again, all he saw were a number of tracks in the snow. He called on the radio, alerting the standers below and asking the other driver to come through to look for deer sign.

The shooter finally spotted the red plaid jacket fully one hundred yards behind the opening where the deer last stood. He vectored the driver over to the spot. Inexperienced as he was, the weaponless novice could not decipher the numerous tracks and blood he saw. The shooter asked him to stand dead still lest he obscure valuable sign while mucking around. The novice reported that he was not certain if there was any blood.

It took the shooter at least ten minutes to fight his way through the heavy brush across the valley and climb up the other hill. He would not have been certain of the location of the shot zone had he not had someone there as a marker. Meanwhile, the three men below were becoming very chilled as a result of their inactivity.

When the shooter finally reached the spot where the whitetail buck stood, it was obvious that he had been successful. Warm blood was splattered over the snow. It looked as though someone had thrown out gallons of it. The shooter reasoned that, because he had taken a virtual frontal shot, he had either a solid hit or a superficial scrape.

Up the hill about thirty feet, it looked even more like a slaughterhouse. Warm drops of blood melted through the snow in a circular pattern. Had the shooter not known what to look for, he would have missed it. The blood was obscured by its melting down into the fluffy snow, perhaps excusing the novice for not noticing it earlier.

It was relatively steep, tough hiking up the hill another hundred feet before the two found the dead deer. The bullet entered through the front of the left shoulder, piercing the brisket into the body cavity and exiting out the lower right side. Little meat was damaged as a result of the heavy bullet plowing through rather than shocking the critter.

Both men field-dressed the deer. It was the first in twenty years or more for the nonshooter. Together they pulled it up over the hill on the slick snow. Neither man wanted to leave the deer and come back through deep brush for it later.

All five hunters gathered at their trucks on the county road to the north of the draw. Two field-dressed deer still lay in the woods as a result of the drivers leaving them to run the hunt as planned.

Despite the fact that most of the men wore wool pants and jackets as well as rubber boot pacs, everyone was wet and cold. However, because conditions that morning were so ideal, they agreed to run one more hunt in a sister valley lying directly east of the valley that had just yielded three deer.

It was about 8:50 A.M. when three standers with rifles started hiking up the ridgeline trail, intent on spreading out at the top as blockers for the two coming up from below. Winds were still steady from the west. This time the drivers stayed out of the brushy valley long enough to allow the standers to get into place.

The three cold standers slipped into their predetermined places above. Winds crossing their position, unchecked by trees or landform, chilled them cruelly. A call on the walkie-talkies started the drive.

Below, one driver crossed the valley through extremely heavy brush while the other walked along the west edge. Walking about eighty yards apart, they drove about eighty yards till the lead driver on the right spotted a big doe sneaking through the tangled ninebark, busy watching the driver on the other side. He placed the crosshairs of his 4X scope on its chest cavity. The high brush limited visibility, but the round from his .270 found an opening. It punched through the backbone just ahead of the hindquarters, exiting through the chest cavity on a steep angle. Forty yards away the doe dropped in its tracks. It was now 9:30 A.M., with outside temperatures up to a cold, wet 32°F.

The crossing winds apparently had been

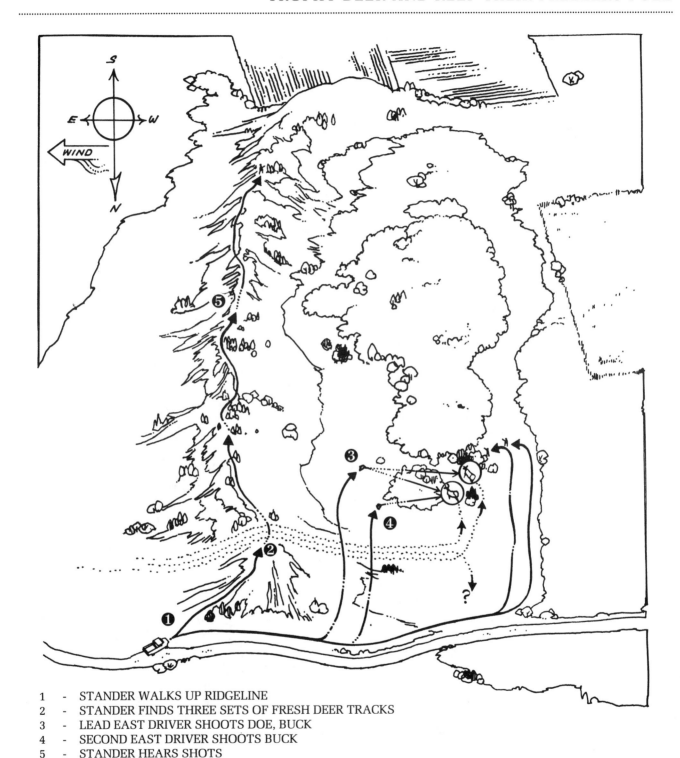

1 - STANDER WALKS UP RIDGELINE
2 - STANDER FINDS THREE SETS OF FRESH DEER TRACKS
3 - LEAD EAST DRIVER SHOOTS DOE, BUCK
4 - SECOND EAST DRIVER SHOOTS BUCK
5 - STANDER HEARS SHOTS

blowing over the doe, or she was far enough ahead so that she did not wind the shooter. In this case, he was the only one wearing cotton pants. Although wool would have been more silent, he was able to move through the woods fairly quietly. The breeze in the treetops masked

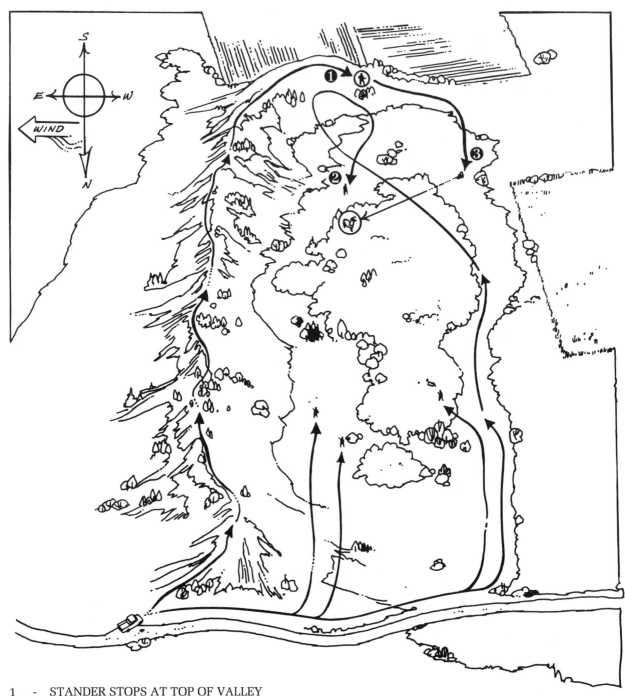

1 - STANDER STOPS AT TOP OF VALLEY
2 - UNARMED DRIVER COMES THROUGH AND IS TURNED AROUND FOR NORTHERLY DRIVE
3 - STANDER, NOW DRIVER, SHOOTS BUCK

his movement noise to some extent as well.

At the head of the valley, the standers waited till the deer was field-dressed and the drivers came through. It was about 10:20 A.M. when they decided to quit. Given the amount of work ahead, it was a wise decision.

They split the chore of dragging out the three deer remaining in the bush. Not one was more

OV - ORIGINAL VALLEY
1 - STANDERS TAKE UP POSITIONS
2 - DRIVER SHOOTS DOE

than two hundred yards from the vehicle. Other than the last deer shot, which the .270 slapped pretty hard, little of the meat was blood shot or mangled. It did, however, take till one in the af-ternoon to skin and halve the critters.

The hunters concluded that they had picked an ideal day in which to hunt. They were able to do so because they knew the country and how the deer reacted to different weather conditions. They hunted smart, adapting to conditions as they found them and altering the hunt when it was wise to do so. They also could spot game in the bush and then hit them, even firing off-hand over relatively long distances.

CHAPTER 3
SHORT DRIVE

HUNT CHECKLIST

Weather
10 inches of new, fluffy snow. Temperatures 28 to 30°F.

Terrain
Rolling hills to fairly steep cuts and draws.

Wind Direction
Steady out of east, 6 to 8 knots.

Conditions Previous Day
Snowing and blowing. Typical early winter conditions.

How Hunters Moved
Walked round to a brush-clogged valley. Split up, one man hunting each side.

Clothes
Shooter wore wool pants and shirt covered by slicker jacket. Driver wore cotton pants and sweatshirts. Both wore rubber boot pacs with vibram soles.

Rifle Caliber and Scope
Shooter used a .338 with 6X scope.

Sex of Deer
Old, barren doe.

Time of Day
Hunt started at 3:00 P.M.

Length of Hunt
About 2 hours start to finish.

Length of Shot
About 65 yards.

How Deer Moved
Out of brushy draw, up shallow drainage on large hill.

Skill of Hunters
Two hunters worked together often. They knew the country well and how the deer would move.

About ten inches of new, fluffy snow covered the area involved in this hunt. It had stopped about 5:00 A.M. after snowing most of the previous day and night. Winds were gentle but steady out of the east. Temperatures were 28 to 30°F.

The topography of the area over which the two hunters intended to operate was characterized by gentle, rolling hills covered by intermittent stands of fairly open timber, grassy meadows, and a few patches of dense ninebark. Except for the occasional stand of second-growth red fir and a few brushy draws, it was usually possible to see game out to two hundred yards or more. Leaves had fallen from the brush, creating a situation wherein deer were quite visible as opposed to even two weeks previous, when there was more cover. To some extent the deer did not realize they were no longer hidden.

Depending on one's perspective, the terrain where the hunt was planned could be considered as challenging to rugged. Sloping, soil-covered hills rose in some places 150 feet from the valleys below. There were no rock outcroppings or straight canyon walls—just steep, soil-covered hills. Old half-overgrown logging roads cut through the area, mostly contouring the hills.

By 3:00 P.M., when the hunters left their truck, temperatures were about 30°F. Walking could be done quite silently as a result of the fluffy snow, which had not yet started to crust. Full dark in that latitude in mid-November came about 4:45 P.M. The hunters assumed they would find deer moving just before dark.

They agreed to work out a single sloping hillside, having seen deer sign in the area on numerous occasions. Two years previous, the entire patch had been selectively logged, and the grass and new-growth brush were an attractive feed source for the deer.

Together they traversed a winding and somewhat hilly farm road until they reached its terminus at the hillside they intended to hunt. Winds were holding steady at six to eight knots out of the east and into their faces.

At the road's end the pair split up. One went sharply left into the timber, covering the top of the hill they were going to drive. He intended to cross four small draws that strung down the hill in a mostly easterly direction. His plan was to stay near the top, where walking would be easier and where he felt more likely to encounter bedded deer.

Hunter two headed down an old logging road to the right. This road followed along the western edge of a wooly, thick valley covered with brush and scrub trees that had not been logged or otherwise opened up. Visibility into the valley was nil; deer coming out of it would have had to cross the lane and then run uphill over fairly open country.

The hunter to the south wore all wool except for a short nylon rain slicker that covered his shoulders. The other wore blue cotton work pants, several layers of cammy sweatshirts, and a nylon cammy rain jacket. Going up the steep hills was only possible because of the heavy rubber boot pacs with cleated soles.

The first hunter walked partway down an open ridge at the edge of the draw. He went downhill only about fifty yards, stopped, and then contemplated walking through the four little draws. He hoped to jump whitetails by moving only a quarter of the way downhill, then shoot them while they ran up the opposite side hill or down into the draw. In the quiet snow, it was reasonably possible for him to top each ridge and head down into the next draw before the deer were jumped.

His first plan, however, was to walk along the first brushy valley in an attempt to ease a deer over to his partner. All of this was by prior agreement, as both men knew the country and the deer's habits from long experience hunting in that area.

A lack of tracks in the new snow covering the country road that the pair had walked in on suggested that there were either no deer in the area or that they were not moving yet. Because they knew that deer often crossed the brushy draws after snowstorms, they were optimistic despite the lack of sign so far. Few houses were located in the forest in that area, but they assumed that the local deer were accustomed to some human activity and not particularly spooked.

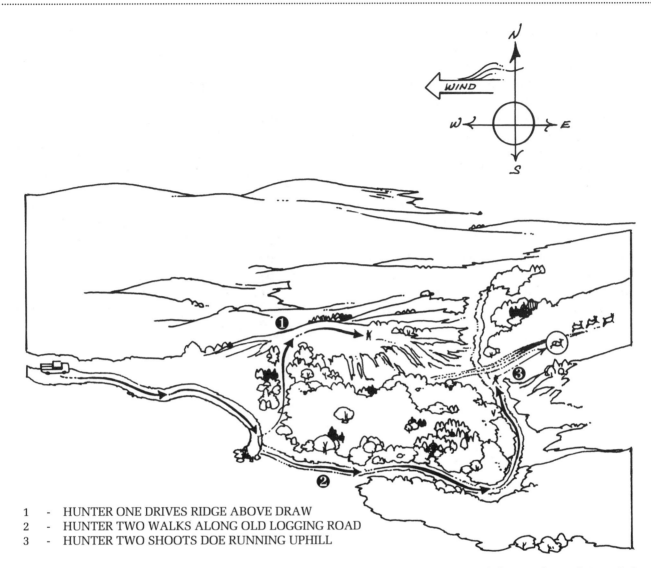

1 - HUNTER ONE DRIVES RIDGE ABOVE DRAW
2 - HUNTER TWO WALKS ALONG OLD LOGGING ROAD
3 - HUNTER TWO SHOOTS DOE RUNNING UPHILL

They were about one mile from their truck. The hunter to the north walked into the ridge he intended to descend, then stopped for two minutes to catch his breath. The hunter to the south moved down the little logging road. It dropped about eighty feet in two hundred yards, bordered on one side by a steep bank and the other by the valley. At the end of the slope, the logging road turned sharply left. It was a classic hillside hairpin turn.

One hundred yards past the turn, across the draw, the logging road straightened out into a mostly northerly path. Brush-covered hillside now bordered the path on the right. To the left it still followed the valley, only along the opposite side.

Later evaluation of the tracks indicated that four whitetails came up out of the brushy draw, no doubt jumped out of their beds by the first hunter/driver as he finished his pause and headed down the hill. Winds were still out of the east, forcing the deer to run into the wind.

The hunter on the logging road noticed tracks crossing his intended path, moving left to right out of the brushy valley. He jacked a round into his .338 Winchester Magnum and pulled the safety back. As he did so, he looked uphill in the direction of the tracks. About sixty-five yards up, a huge doe stood looking over her shoulder at him, her back mostly toward him. She jumped a couple of times up the fairly steep hill as he threw up his ri-

THE GREAT
AMERICAN DEER HUNT

fle. Two other deer came into view at that time.

He carefully placed the crosshairs of his 6X scope on the doe's chest and squeezed off a round, but she moved again at the moment of the shot. The round entered her bunghole dead center, continuing up through the body cavity along the backbone and exiting her flank at the place it attached to her ribs. It was an odd shot because of her position up the hill and her movement.

A fourth deer jumped up at the shot and, along with the other two, moved slowly uphill and out of the open draw, over a rise, and into a heavy patch of ninebark. Theoretically, the shooter had a chance for a second kill but elected not to take it.

It took less than five minutes to climb the hill to the dead deer. By the time he reached it, it was glassy-eyed dead. A huge pool of blood filled the body cavity.

At most the two hunters were four-hundred yards apart. On hearing the shot, the first hunter reversed his descent down the ridge, climbing back out to the place where the two parted company. He continued on down the logging road, intending to join his successful companion. It was about 3:45 P.M.

The successful hunter field-dressed the deer and dragged it down the open draw to the main logging road. He eventually was met by his friend, who helped him drag the body back to the county road. Later they found the deer weighed 125 pounds sans head, guts, and legs.

The hunters reckoned that they got their deer because they knew exactly how the critters—and each other—were likely to move. Also, they dropped everything when conditions were ideal for a short hunt.

CHAPTER 4
ALERT HUNTER

HUNT CHECKLIST

Weather
Dry, cool nights; warm, dry days. Temperature in low 40s.

Terrain
Deep mountain canyon with tree-covered side draws and grassy, relatively open hillsides.

Wind Direction
Out of west, 6 to 7 knots.

Conditions Previous Day
About steady as autumn approached.

How Hunters Moved
Four hunters planned to still-hunt through a giant wooded area bordered on two sides by a deep canyon. Successful hunter worked the canyon slope.

Clothes
Cotton work pants and flannel shirts.

Rifle Caliber and Scope
Successful hunter used a .300 Winchester Magnum with 6X scope.

Sex of Deer
5-point (western count) whitetail buck.

Time of Day
About 7:30 A.M.

Length of Hunt
Hunters worked country all day but killed only one deer shortly after sunup.

Length of Shot
About 8 feet.

How Deer Moved
Deer was bedded. When it got up, hunter shot it.

Skill of Hunters
All hunters were skilled and knew the country.

This whitetail hunt took place in a rugged mountain canyon in the western United States. The country had steep four-hundred-foot reliefs but was not rocky.

Four hunters drove an old power line road for about three miles as it twisted and turned through some reasonably heavy terrain. The road eventually dead-ended at a canyon too steep even for the road builders. Instead, the contractor had set two large steel towers near the crest of each canyon rim, simply spanning the hole in one giant three-hundred-yard leap. It was along and behind this deep canyon that the party intended to hunt.

The terrain abutting the canyon was gently rolling plateau covered with occasional dense stands of pine and fir. A few deep inner pockets contained thick cedar, much of which was windblown and tangled. Penetrating these deep thickets was considered to be virtually impossible.

On the canyon rim itself as well as the top three-quarters of the slope, the country became more open, with only scattered groups of trees in little finger drainages. These drainages carried some water during the spring thaw but were almost completely dry during hunting season. The main creek that had originally cut the canyon was full of white water and ran with a good measure of vigor and enthusiasm.

At the place where the road stopped and the hunters started, a sixty-yard-wide band of trees covered the hillside down to the creek. On the other side of the trees, brown grass and long-dead mountain daisies covered the hillside. Inside the hunting area delineated by the power line and the canyon, a number of well-used game trails wound through the heavy timber.

The four hunters planned to silently stalk the game trails. They hoped to jump resident whitetails from their beds or catch the few that might still be feeding at daybreak.

The total area of the hunting grounds was estimated to be about four hundred acres. Each hunter realized that ten minutes after he left the truck, he would be swallowed in country sufficiently vast that he might not see the others again the entire day.

As they always are in the mountains, winds were erratic. There was some movement of warmer lowland air up the canyon at sunrise. Speed was 6 to 7 knots at most and not always consistent. In the wooded area behind the canyon, winds were mostly out of the west into the faces of the hunters. Planning for the hunt assumed favorable air movement as they moved in from the east.

Weather in mid-October was crisp and cool at night, grading into warm to hot by midday. A protracted, dry Indian summer wilted the grass and turned the soil on the hillsides and forest floor to powdery dust. As they padded along the trails, the hunters could keep track of the winds by observing dust movement on the trail.

All four wore thick cotton work pants and either cotton flannel shirts or a thin wool shirt. Except for one hunter who wore tennis shoes, all wore surplus Vietnam jungle boots.

Rifles among the group were all scoped. Despite the fact that, in some places, the longest shot would be sixty yards, in other locations a two-hundred-yard shot might present itself. There were two .30-06s, one .270, and a .300 Winchester Magnum.

Ten minutes after leaving the truck, everyone was alone. They spread out in a manner that guaranteed that the entire area was covered and that a jumped deer might cross in front of two or more hunters. Meeting other hunters in this remote area was extremely unlikely.

One hunter walked about halfway down the dry, open canyon side. He knew he was low enough when he could hear the water flowing below him. His intent was to stalk through the finger drainages on a right angle, jumping deer out of the bottom as he walked across them. On the other side of each drainage he would sneak uphill to the top and repeat the process. It was an old, proven method of mountain hunting. Other than at the very bottom of each drainage, he had good visibility.

The next hunter up the hill planned to follow a game trail that skirted brushy, wooded clumps at the top of the drainages. His game trail contoured the ridge top, more or less maintaining the same elevation.

The third hunter followed a game trail into the wooded interior, where it intersected with a number of additional trails. Depending on conditions, he could take a trail closer to the canyon rim or further into the forest's interior.

Hunter four struck out across country, picking up a trail that kept to the right of hunter three. He was in heavy timber, with visibility often under eighty yards.

As per their understanding, the first hunter walked through the band of trees and out onto the grassy hillside. He turned downhill, walking till he heard water, then moved across the face of the hillside through the first finger drainage. He paused by a scraggly little pine, waiting for additional daylight. At that hour he shifted and shivered in the predawn cold. The others plodded along in the dark.

Ten minutes or more elapsed before the first hunter moved again. Being rested, he did not disturb the quiet with heavy breathing. At sunup he noticed a slight uphill component to the air movement. Breezes, such as they were, were either uphill or in his face.

He moved down into the next finger drainage. Starting up the rise and out of the drainage, he observed a small clump of brush about eight feet high. No more than six or eight stems plus some high brown grass made up the thicket. It was situated on the highest point between his location and the next finger drainage.

When he was less than ten feet from the brush, the hunter heard hooves pounding the earth, much like a steer disturbed from its bed. He saw a flash of brown through the limbs, brush, and high grass. He wasn't certain what he had ahead and slightly above him. There was even a kind of a snort.

Instinctively he threw his rifle to his shoulder, placing its 6X scope on the patch of brush. Immediately he saw one black eye, a horn jutting off on a crazy angle, and a patch of brown and white hair. Without hesitating, he swung the crosshairs back to the right about a foot and touched the trigger.

Upon discharge, a large-bodied, five-point whitetail buck leapt into the air, landing downhill on legs no longer capable of supporting it. With its nose in the ground, the buck rolled slowly toward the bottom. The shooter ran downhill to steady the deer lest it roll all the way down, creating a horrible packing job. Less than thirty seconds had elapsed.

He caught the deer and sat down to steady himself. After the situation was stabilized, the hunter used one horn as a handle to drag the carcass twenty to thirty feet uphill to a level spot. Draining the body cavity would be no problem on the steep hill.

The round from the .300 Winchester Magnum hit the buck solidly through the bone about two inches ahead of the spot where its neck attached to the body. No shoulder meat was ruined by the bullet, which the hunter viewed as most fortunate given the sight picture he had to work with and the fact that he did not know with certainty which part of the deer he was shooting when he fired. The heavy bullet punched through the grass and twigs, finding its mark perfectly. Had he paused a moment longer, the buck would certainly have popped over the rim and down into the next draw. The hunter may have gotten a running shot by double-timing up the hill, but it would have been tough.

After field-dressing it, he left the deer and continued on with the planned hunt. He saw a few additional tracks that may have belonged to the buck, but no other sign or game.

By noon it had warmed sufficiently that the successful hunter thought it best to go back for his deer. He dragged it on an angle uphill across the next finger drainage to the flat above. Dry, dusty conditions on the trail stirred a cloud, causing dirt to cling to the carcass, which concerned the hunter. At the truck he treated the carcass with pepper as a means of repelling flies.

None of the other hunters saw or heard game that day. Sign in the region was not plentiful. All four participants concluded that the buck was living by himself, waiting for rutting season, and that it was fortuitous that they found it lying in its bed overlooking the canyon.

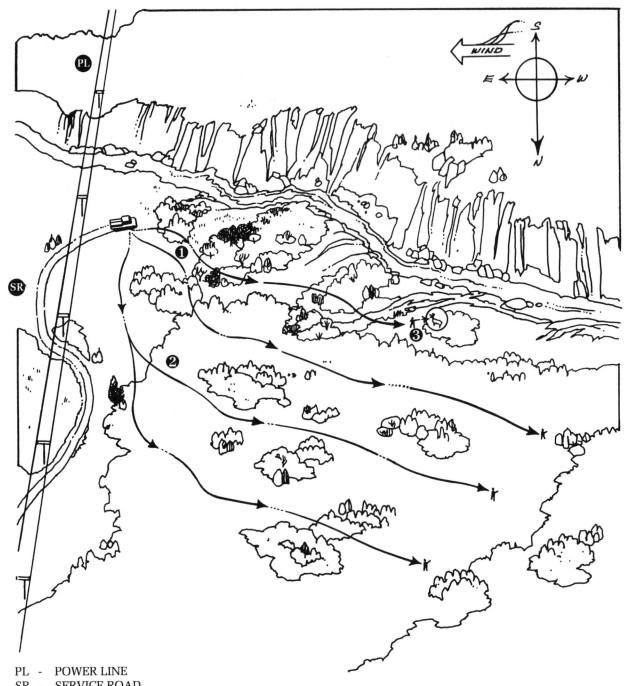

PL - POWER LINE
SR - SERVICE ROAD
1 - HUNTER ONE DRIVES THROUGH FINGER DRAINAGES
2 - OTHER HUNTERS STILL-HUNT ALONG GAME TRAILS
3 - BUCK SHOT AT CLOSE RANGE

CHAPTER 5

BEDDED WHITETAIL BUCK

HUNT CHECKLIST

Weather
Warm, wet early November snows dumped on area, creating wet, dripping conditions in the woods. Temperature was 30°F.

Terrain
Worn, rolling hills covered by pine, alder, poplar, and maple scrub.

Wind Direction
Out of east, 3 to 5 knots.

Conditions Previous Day
Wet snow fell day and night before.

How Hunters Moved
Hunted through a 60-acre wooded area.

Clothes
Heavy wool pants and shirts with nylon rain slickers.

Rifle Caliber and Scope
One hunter carried a .270, the other a .357 Magnum pistol.

Sex of Deer
4-point (western count) whitetail buck.

Time of Day
Hunt started at 8:30 A.M.

Length of Hunt
Hunters spent the entire day looking for deer at a time when conventional wisdom would suggest that the hunting should be excellent.

Length of Shot
Estimated at 135 yards.

How Deer Moved
Deer lay in bed in heavy brush. Hunter tried a shot with the .270, with no effect.

Skill of Hunters
Both had been hunting for several years and were considered to be accomplished deer getters.

Mature pine and thick alder covered sixty acres of prime whitetail habitat. On the north, the wooded area was bounded by a county road. When deer crossed the road occasionally, they did so with reluctance. Fairly open pasture land provided little place for them to hide; only the occasional pine, elderberry, or alder tree grew on the large, grassy field. Until snow obscured the grass, deer would come out of the dense woods and cross the road at night in an attempt to graze.

To the east, a private lane separated the wooded area from a larger wooded tract running east another mile or more. Deer crossed this lane with more impunity than the county road, but several recent gut piles placed along the lane kept them cautious. To the south, a large grass-covered field (probably the result of a government program) bordered the woods. All of this habitat was ideal for whitetails.

Early November snows covered the country the day prior to the hunt. Visibility was, to some extent, limited by the wet snow, which stuck to the trenches and limbs of the thick underbrush. Leaves that had obscured vision as recently as a week before were buried under the new snow. Conditions in the bush were dripping wet and slick.

It was 8:30 A.M. when the pair parked their truck at the corner of the woodlot and started the hunt. Both hunters wore relatively noiseless wool pants and jackets, and one covered his shoulders with a nylon slicker. Temperatures hung at the 30°F mark. Any tracks they saw were guaranteed to be fresh because the new snow had not finished falling at the time. It had been light since about 6:50 A.M.

Four ribbonlike, low marshy areas ran parallel across the woodlot. Water saturated the soil in these drainages, producing a lush growth of understory that was attractive to deer. The hunters planned to spread out about two hundred yards and push across these low spots one by one. In the past they had successfully jumped deer out of these covered marshy areas, which often circled back to one or the other of the drivers. Both wore waterproof boot pacs, allowing them to navigate the watery spots without discomfort.

Little wind moved through the area. At most a three- to five-knot breeze came in from the east, hitting the men in the face as they pushed into it. The four inches of new snow minimized walking noises.

They carried an odd combination of firearms. One hunter had a .270 rifle while the other carried nothing more than a .357 Magnum revolver. The hunter with the pistol wanted to collect a deer with the handgun, which would have been a first for their entire group of friends.

The first hunter nearest the county road waited an extra ten minutes until his companion could reach the southwest corner of the woodlot. When they both started still-hunting east, they were more or less lined up. The first hunter was about a hundred yards from the county road, while his buddy ended up about a hundred yards from the south edge of the woodlot. The second hunter could just make out the open field area to his right, but doubted if he could see a deer standing at field's edge. At most, it was possible to see or hear only sixty to eighty yards in ideal circumstances.

Numerous fresh deer tracks led through the area; by the first marshy crossing, each had passed over at least four different sets. Tracking a single deer would have been difficult due to the proliferation of sign. Neither felt they had moved deer, but it was impossible to be sure without seeing a critter.

Through the third drainage there still was no action. Hunter one—with the road to align him—was now at least eighty yards ahead of the man in the interior, who had more tangled brush to fight through.

Both hunters approached the fourth low area with extreme caution. They felt that the deer they knew must be in the area were bunched up in this last strip of heavy cover.

Hunter one topped a small rise and looked down into the last tangle of marshy brush. He saw a number of fallen trees littering the drainage. Crossing it in the wet, greasy snow would, he thought, be tiring and cold. It was about 10:00 A.M., with temperatures still hovering around 30°F.

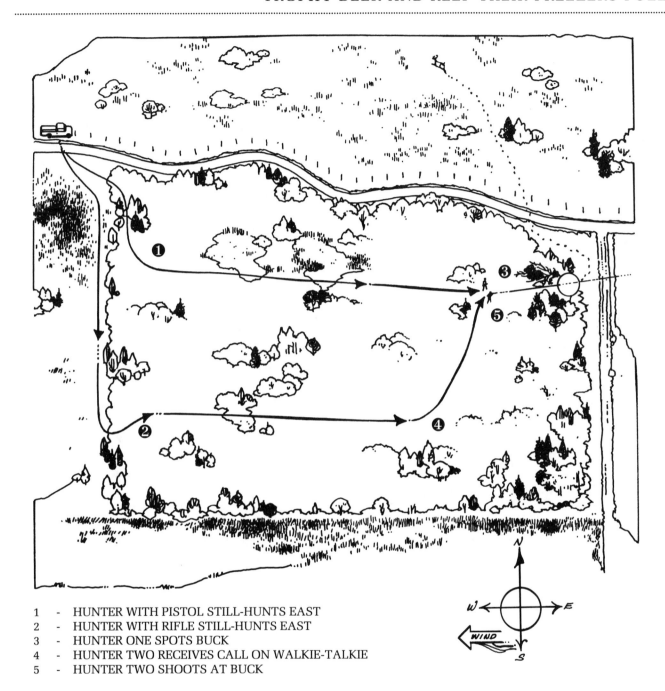

1 - HUNTER WITH PISTOL STILL-HUNTS EAST
2 - HUNTER WITH RIFLE STILL-HUNTS EAST
3 - HUNTER ONE SPOTS BUCK
4 - HUNTER TWO RECEIVES CALL ON WALKIE-TALKIE
5 - HUNTER TWO SHOOTS AT BUCK

He stopped dead still on the slight promi-nence for about five minutes, trying to locate a crossing through the marshy strip that he could maneuver without climbing over trees or sink-ing to his gonads in the mud.

During his patient wait, he thought he saw something move on the other side of the draw. At first he thought it was a bird, but when it moved again he was able to put his binoculars on the object. It was a single ear of a whitetail deer. After another three or four minutes of look-ing, a nice, mature four-point buck materialized about 135 yards away. It was lying under a spread pine tree with its back toward the spotter. Several layers of dense understory hid the buck, which still seemed undisturbed. Brush obscured the hunter at least to the waist, and the modest winds were still blowing from the deer to the hunter.

The hunter with the deer in view was the one with the .357 revolver. He wanted very badly to take the animal but reasoned that the long range and heavy brush made a good shot unlikely. Successfully stalking around to the buck also seemed unlikely due to the heavy brush and squishy marsh he'd have to cross. The hunter observed that once he left that exact spot, the critter became invisible—hopelessly obscured by the brush and limbs.

After perhaps ten minutes, the spotter called his companion on the walkie-talkie. It took the second man another twenty minutes to silently work his way to the spotter. An even greater time elapsed before he positively saw the bedded buck.

The hunter with the .270 cranked his scope up to 7 power. After additional hushed, animated discussion, both agreed that they should try the shot, as neither man believed he could improve his lie. A shot under the present circumstances was all they were going to get at that deer, they reasoned.

The rifle owner, an experienced and accomplished offhand shot, took a rock-hard stance, bracing the .270 on the shoulder of his companion. Upon firing, the buck instinctively flattened itself into its bed. After an instant it uncoiled like a spring, bounding straight up, then through the brush, down to the county road, and across into the open pasture.

Both hunters raced out to the road but were unable to see anything more than a large, white flag waving goodbye a hundred yards away.

Carefully and methodically they retreated back to their original spot, using it to orient themselves over to the deer's bed. The fresh snow made it reasonably certain that they would find any available blood sign, but there was nothing to see. Although they found the bed, they could not locate the bullet's point of impact. The rifleman thought that the thick brush might have deflected the round, but they could not find a piece of brush that obviously had been struck by a bullet. Where the round ultimately went or what it struck remains a mystery.

They hunted the remainder of the daylight hours without observing a single shootable critter. That night the topic of discussion centered around a hypothetical alternate strategy that might have been successful. The hunter with the rifle thought that he would have done better with his .300 Winchester Magnum with 180-grain bullets to buck the brush. The other man firmly believed that he should not have brought the pistol, or that he should have tried to sneak to the road, where he could have tried a shot when the buck crossed, even though there was no guarantee that the animal would cross the road after the shot.

It was the last time the man tried deer hunting with a pistol.

Using their skill and experience, the hunters were able to spot the deer in its bed. Having done so, however, there was no way for them to get close enough for a certain shot in the heavy cover.

Both hunters agreed that no foolproof solution to that deer puzzle existed. It was one of those times when luck was not with them, and no amount of skill could have compensated.

CHAPTER 6
CLASSIC DEER DRIVE

HUNT CHECKLIST

Weather
Unseasonably warm, dry autumn day. Low of 36°F at night, with daytime temperatures reaching 40°F.

Terrain
Slightly rolling farmland interspersed with patches of trees, brush, and weed fields.

Wind Direction
From the west, steady at 10 to 12 knots.

Conditions Previous Day
First frosts of autumn arrived several weeks earlier, but dry, warm Indian summer had prevailed over the region for a week.

How Hunters Moved
One hunter walked around an 80-acre wooded patch. Other two hunters drove the deer to her.

Clothes
Cotton pants and flannel shirts.

Rifle Caliber and Scope
.257 Roberts with 6X scope.

Sex of Deer
Large 6-point (western count) buck taken at start of rut.

Time of Day
Hunt started about 1:00 P.M.; shot taken at about 1:45 P.M.

Length of Hunt
Not over 1 1/2 hours, including dragging the deer out to the road.

Length of Shot
About 60 yards.

How Deer Moved
Buck and two does were jumped in wooded area by two drivers.

Skill of Hunters
Shooter had hunted some but not a great deal. Drivers were deer-hunting nuts.

This unseasonably warm autumn day found two avid deer hunters at home with time on their hands. A prolonged Indian summer at the start of their deer season altered conditions dramatically in favor of the whitetails. Both hunters wanted badly to hunt but, given current conditions, saw little chance of success. They reckoned that, with only two hunting, they had best stay home.

The wife of one of the men was not a hard-core deer chaser, but she could shoot well, was patient, and was able to interpret and follow hunting plans. Because the two men were so hard-core, she agreed to stand a drive or two for them, more to get them out of the house than to satisfy her own desire to hunt deer. She definitely did not want to spend the rest of the day dragging around mile after mile of country hunting with the two.

Their deer-hunting territory, in this instance, was reasonably flat, broken farmland. The country was dotted every three to four hundred yards with twenty-acre-or-larger patches of trees, brush, and weeds. Large numbers of whitetails called the region home—fed at the expense of the farmers and sheltered in the rough land too rocky or marshy to plow.

The small patches of cover consisted of aspen, pine, and hazel scrub. An understory of snowberry and ninebark cut internal visibility to forty yards or less at times, especially true early in the season before snow knocked the leaves down. The hunters had several patches in mind that they thought contained deer.

The scrub patch they selected to drive consisted of about 80 acres strung out on almost flat ground for about 800 yards. Width of the patch was but 150 yards, yet once inside, the drivers could not see each other or the harvested pea fields surrounding the scrub.

The wooded area was on a north-south line. A modest ten- to twelve-knot wind blew directly across it from the west. Temperatures at the start of the hunt (1:00 P.M.) were in the low forties, which was unusually warm.

Conditions in the woods themselves were crunchy/noisy, about like walking on cornflakes.

Still-hunting was virtually impossible. No major storm systems had rolled through to move the game about. By day, most deer were staying in the thick cover close to water; it was only at night that they wandered out in search of a stray pea in the harvested fields.

In keeping with the agreed-upon plan, the woman swung two hundred yards east (downwind) of the targeted patch so as not to disturb any deer bedded inside. The drivers gave her a full fifteen minutes to walk the thousand yards around to the south end of the patch before they left the truck to start the drive. Often they had found that, under present conditions, the deer would bolt out of the far end the moment they entered.

Stander, carrying her .257 Roberts rifle with 6X scope, circled out to and through a second parallel patch of scrub. Although she was not an experienced hunter, she heard enough kitchen tales to know that she had to sneak very quietly about fifty yards into the patch that was to be hunted. The drivers recommended this location because it covered all four of the possible exits a deer might use when exiting the patch. Any other stand covered two exits at most.

She took great precautions when entering the woodlot to avoid breaking branches, crackling leaves, or scratching brush on her clothes. To some extent the gentle wind in the treetops masked any noise she made. Her final position was against the trunk of the largest pine she could find in the proper location. She rechecked her rifle's safety and settled in for a long, quiet stand.

On the other end, the drivers moved in unison into the scrub about sixty yards apart. They were able to keep coordinated by the sounds of their crunching along the forest floor.

At one place, perhaps two hundred yards into the drive, the scrub patch bulged out into the pea field. The driver on the right bobbled out away from his companion until about one hundred yards separated them. As he did, he jumped two large does and a huge buck. All he glimpsed were a brief movement from the side and two seconds of tail wagging. Upon jumping the three deer, the driver gave a short, high-pitched "yip!" which was the prearranged signal to the other driver and stander that game was afoot. Driver two heard the signal and stopped dead still.

The driver who jumped the whitetails ran as hard as he could into the thicket in an attempt to keep the deer from circling back between him and the other driver. He ran so far into the thicket's center that he began to suspect that the deer might try to exit out the side rather than the end the stander guarded.

Moments later a single shot broke the silence. Both drivers agreed it sounded very much like a meat shot, although they were not familiar with the sound of a .257 Roberts. A long period of silence followed.

The stander had waited on duty about five or six minutes when she heard the "yip" from the other end of the scrub. She braced herself against the tree trunk and put her thumb on the rifle's safety.

Immediately she could hear the *crunch crunch* of a critter coming toward her. For a minute she could not see it, but she had a good general indication where to look. Suddenly, out from the brush a large, gray-to-brown buck trotted toward her position, moving on an angle that, if maintained, would carry it not ten feet away from her.

The buck was trying to wind behind and ahead of itself, but with little success. It obviously was skittish and agitated as it swung its ears front to back trying to pick up foreign sounds. Its peculiar cantering gait did not include the traditional waving of the tail. Range was now about eighty yards, and it continued forward in what seemed like a hesitant, stiff manner.

The stander made several attempts to locate the buck in her scope, but her infrequent hunting took its toll. Finally she found it—it looked as big as a cow. She swung on its neck, recalling long conversations regarding how neck shots wasted little meat and prevented long, drawn-out tracking jobs. It crossed her mind that her little quarter-inch rifle might not have sufficient poop to bring down such a large creature.

For the last time she centered the crosshairs on its neck and squeezed the trigger. When she recovered from the recoil, the buck was nowhere to be seen. Quietly and anxiously she looked around,

not wanting to move and give away her position on the outside chance the buck was still standing.

After a couple of minutes she spotted the critter lying about a hundred yards away. Its gray body hair blended nicely with the surrounding understory. It had turned back in the general direction of its approach, dropping about sixty yards from the spot where it was hit.

The drivers whistled and hollered but received no response from the stander, who was trying to maintain her composure while remaining alert for any other deer that might happen by. They eventually called to each other and then walked as rapidly as possible toward the stander. One driver preceded the other to the kill by about ninety seconds. Driver two found him standing over the buck muttering, "Will you look at this," over and over.

It was a beautiful six pointer.

They pulled the huge buck up onto a small rise and field-dressed it. Even though the country was reasonably flat, the animal was so large that it took them a full forty-five minutes to drag it out to the truck. At home, stripped of entrails and legs, it weighed 192 pounds. It was considered to be a very large-bodied and racked whitetail for that region.

Damage from the shot was not as the stander had supposed it would be. The round entered the buck's left side about two inches behind the front shoulder blade, angling back through the body cavity and out the right side through the lung. A small quantity of meat on the left side was bloodshot, but in general everything was in excellent condition.

By 3:00 P.M. the hunt was concluded, including skinning and splitting the carcass in half. The stander, who had only carried out the rifles, was ready to try again. The drivers, weary from dragging the huge buck, thought of urgent business elsewhere.

The shooter feels she was successful because she knew how to get into a stand carefully and quietly. The party had picked a good patch of timber to drive, but had she not been able to shoot as well as she did, the drive would not have been productive.

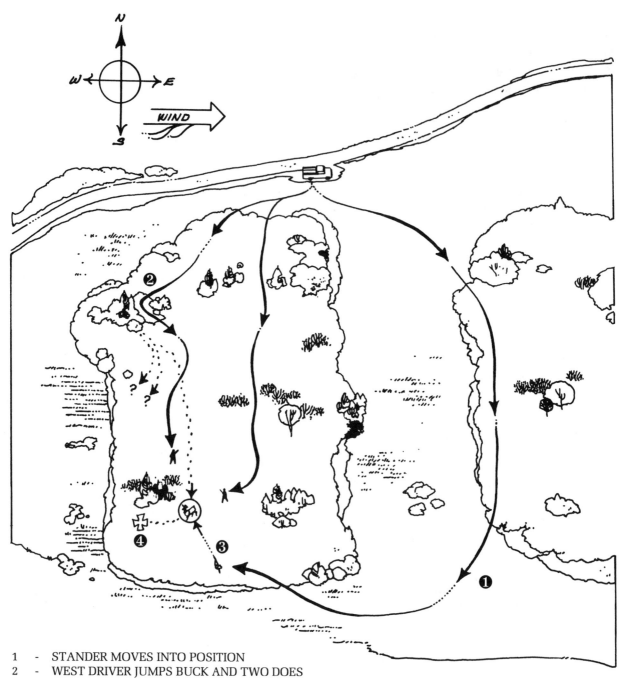

1 - STANDER MOVES INTO POSITION
2 - WEST DRIVER JUMPS BUCK AND TWO DOES
3 - STANDER SHOOTS BUCK
4 - BUCK FALLS

CHAPTER 7
CONFUSED BLACKTAILS

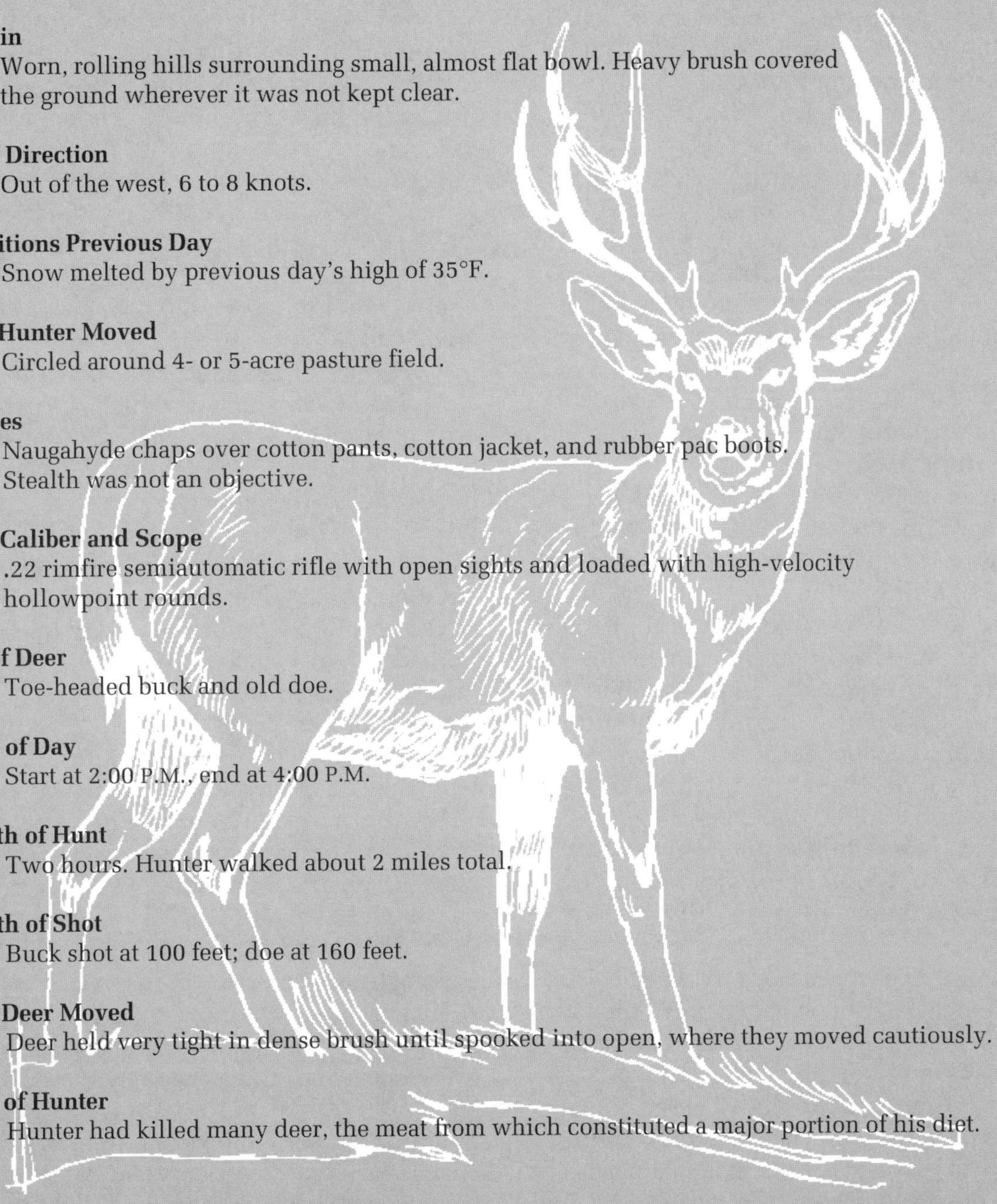

HUNT CHECKLIST

Weather
Cool and damp, 35°F.

Terrain
Worn, rolling hills surrounding small, almost flat bowl. Heavy brush covered the ground wherever it was not kept clear.

Wind Direction
Out of the west, 6 to 8 knots.

Conditions Previous Day
Snow melted by previous day's high of 35°F.

How Hunter Moved
Circled around 4- or 5-acre pasture field.

Clothes
Naugahyde chaps over cotton pants, cotton jacket, and rubber pac boots. Stealth was not an objective.

Rifle Caliber and Scope
.22 rimfire semiautomatic rifle with open sights and loaded with high-velocity hollowpoint rounds.

Sex of Deer
Toe-headed buck and old doe.

Time of Day
Start at 2:00 P.M., end at 4:00 P.M.

Length of Hunt
Two hours. Hunter walked about 2 miles total.

Length of Shot
Buck shot at 100 feet; doe at 160 feet.

How Deer Moved
Deer held very tight in dense brush until spooked into open, where they moved cautiously.

Skill of Hunter
Hunter had killed many deer, the meat from which constituted a major portion of his diet.

Some outdoor writers make a great to-do over the relative merits of hunting various subspecies of deer. It's an activity destined to produce several additional pages of copy when the story line is otherwise a bit thin. Like discussing the best rifle calibers for deer, analyzing relative smartness of species can always be counted on to bulk one's copy up to the 2,500-word minimum demanded by editors.

As an actual on-the-ground rule of thumb, real-life deer getters reckon mule deer to be the easiest (dumbest) to shoot, while whitetails are tough, and coastal blacktails are virtually impossible. Blacktails may not be particularly bright, but those who have taken all three agree that they are tough to shoot because it is a chore to make them break cover. Mule deer find cover only infrequently, using large distances as a defense. Whitetails use both space and cover. The little blacktail mainly hunkers down in whatever cover it finds itself.

The hunter in this case was a seasoned woodsman who spent his entire life in the bush hunting and trapping. As a result of his upbringing, he chose to lead a simple life that many city dwellers would judge to be hand-to-mouth. Established seasons and bag limits in his state still allowed him to thin out the large numbers of diminutive blacktail deer that infested his property in verminlike numbers.

He lived in a smallish three-room shack that, before siding was added, had been a log cabin. Gentle, rolling coastal hills surrounded the dwelling at a distance. Closer in the ground was reasonably level, dishing up to the hills out half a mile or more.

Virtually impregnable blackberry, salal, poison oak, and huckleberry brush surrounded the cabin up to the horse pasture, which lay in a seventy-yard radius out from the cabin and horse barn. Lush growth limited one's ability to see or even walk to places where the stock had eaten trails or kept the brush trimmed back. Still, numerous deer tracks in the November snow confirmed the hunter's suspicion that large numbers of deer were lying in the brushy tangle, coming out only at night to nibble the dark green meadow grass.

Temperatures were about 35°F during the day, dropping to 28°F at night. It snowed often but mainly at night, disappearing the following day. It did not snow the night previous to this hunt, which allowed the brush to dry out reasonably well.

It was 2:30 P.M. when the man decided conditions were such that he could hunt in reasonable comfort. Sundown that time of year was about 4:00 P.M. He had no time to scare up a hunting companion, nor did he feel he needed one in order to be successful. What he did need rather badly was a fresh deer hanging on the front porch, from which he could whittle fresh meat.

Winds came consistently off the ocean twenty miles west of the cabin. They blew steadily to vigorously throughout the day, never varying a great deal in intensity or direction.

The hunter wore rubber pac boots and cotton work pants over which he pulled Naugahyde logger's chaps as a deterrent against the remnants of moisture clinging to the heavy, thorny brush. It was a typically damp day that could make one miserable if one was so foolish as to allow his clothing to become soaked. Taken together, it was not an outfit conducive to slipping through the cover unheard by sharp-eared blacktails, but moving silently was definitely not part of this hunter's scheme.

His rifle was an old, battered .22-caliber rimfire Remington Nylon 66 semiauto charged with high-velocity hollowpoints. There was no scope, only the issue ramp front and notch rear sights.

He commenced the hunt by walking up his access lane about two hundred yards. At this place he hopped over the fence and moved into the thick underbrush. He literally plowed through, making little or no attempt to conceal his whereabouts or otherwise move quietly. He was looking for deer, but the initial purpose of the hunt was to move the critters out of the cover. Although the hunter carried a rifle, he was not prepared or planning to take a quick running shot.

He circled clockwise around the cabin, plowing through the brush. From his slight uphill position, he kept the buildings in view as a point of reference. Using a measured, unhurried pace, he kept on going round and round. It took perhaps fifteen minutes to make a full circuit around his compound.

At first the hunter took the path of least resistance through the brush wherever he could find one. His intention was to stay a consistent two hundred yards from the cabin. After two circuits he started to pinch in toward the field separating pasture from undergrowth. He saw nothing but numerous tracks in the mud.

During the third circuit he finally managed a fleeting glimpse of a chocolate-brown deer. It was the size of a large, thin dog, hunkered down trying to creep crosswise out of the hunter's path.

By the fifth time around, the hunter knew for certain that the deer were moving and that his plan might be successful. He attributed the promise of success to the fact that the little blacktails that customarily sat out human intrusion were becoming confused by the continual tramping through their area and the barrage of scent running through and across their beds.

At a slight break in the brush, hunter ran to the fence in time to catch a toe-headed buck in the act of jumping into the pasture. He was but one hundred feet from the little deer. The hunter stood at the ready till the deer came to a steady trot along the edge of the pasture.

He quickly pumped two rounds into the deer's chest cavity. It went down like someone hit it in the head with a double-bitted axe. Hunter correctly surmised that both rounds missed rib bones on the entrance side but bounced off bone on the exit side of the animal.

Without doing any more than confirming the fact that the deer was down, he ran back into the brush to the place where he crashed down to take the shots in the open and continued his march around the cabin. It wasn't more than another hundred yards round his route before he glimpsed a second deer sneaking through the heavy brush. It was but sixty feet ahead traveling to the hunter's right and headed toward the pasture field. At the most it looked to be eighteen inches high at the shoulders.

Hunter could not immediately find an easy path to the fence. Instead he vigorously busted brush till he came to a large boulder. He scram-

bled up on the rock just in time to see a doe running along the edge of the fence inside the pasture. It ran too close to the fence to jump it, so the hunter simply waited, .22 at the ready. Shadows from the disappearing winter sun were now growing quite long, and darkness near the pasture's edge hid the critter to some extent.

Perhaps because it thought it was hidden, the deer stopped dead still, looking over its shoulders and trying to focus on the cause of its disturbance. Apparently it did not realize it was, from the hunter's perspective, still out in the open.

Later, the hunter paced off the distance. It was about 160 feet, just about the maximum distance over which he was willing to shoot the little .22 rimfire.

Carefully, almost casually, he placed the front ramp blade in the rear notch. Nylon 66 rifles, he knew, were accurate enough, but the plastic trigger mechanism was disconcerting. He aimed high on the rib cage, almost out of the target zone, which was less than it would have been had the deer been standing sideways to him. As it was, the angle yielded a target about the size of a large grapefruit.

At the shot the deer stepped out of the dark and into the pasture, head pointed lackadaisically toward the ground. The hunter quickly fired again and then a third time. He could plainly hear the rounds slam into the animal's ribs.

Very slowly, as if in slow motion, the deer's head sunk ever lower and its back sagged like a worn, old horse. It stood for perhaps two minutes, then collapsed on all four feet simultaneously. It kicked futilely into the air and lay quiet.

Through it all, the hunter realized his rounds had connected. He did not wish to risk damaging any of the little hams so he simply waited patiently for the inevitable.

With the downing of the second deer, the hunter broke off the drive and climbed down to the pasture. He reckoned he had about thirty minutes in which to field-dress the two deer before it got dark. He removed the heads and legs, sliced through the neck skin of each, and used the holes as handholds to drag them to the cabin.

The deer weighed under ninety pounds combined. The hunter hung them on his front porch,

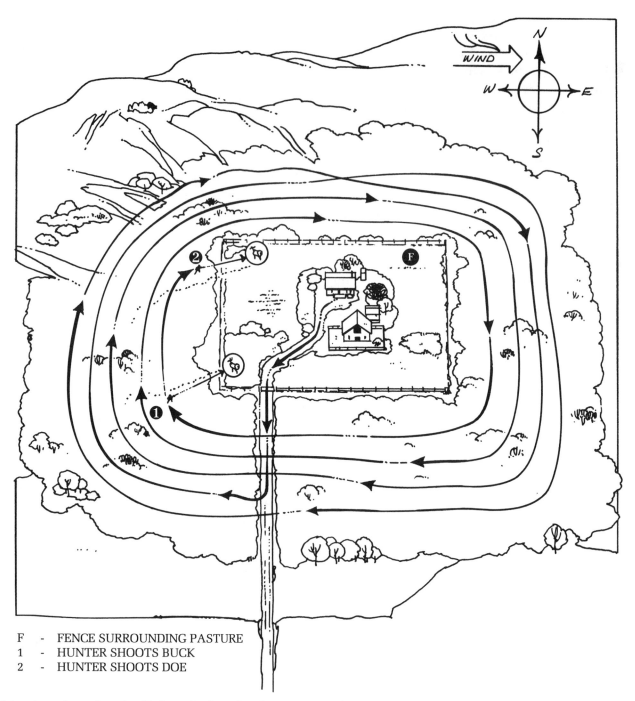

F - FENCE SURROUNDING PASTURE
1 - HUNTER SHOOTS BUCK
2 - HUNTER SHOOTS DOE

skinning them by the light of a hundred-watt bulb. Even though the blacktail doe was small compared to other deer species, it ate tough—like old wang leather.

The hunter reckoned he got the deer because they were lying in the heavy brush close to the grass, which he determined from the tracks in *the snow. He knew their habits and waited for a day when field conditions would allow him to persevere. He knew the country and was confident enough to stick with his original plan. Use of a relatively quiet .22 rimfire may also have been a factor with the little deer, as the shots did not scare them out of the area.*

HUNT CHECKLIST

Weather
Unseasonably warm, about 44°F at the start of the hunt. Barely reaching freezing two hours after dark.

Terrain
Hilly bordering on strenuously hilly. Hunters ran a drive in a fairly steep box canyon.

Wind Direction
From the west at about 5 knots across the canyon.

Conditions Previous Day
Brief afternoon shower the day before had wet the country down.

How Hunters Moved
Drove one in the middle and one on top around a box canyon. Deer was killed after the hunt outside the box canyon.

Clothes
Light wool pants and shirts, no jackets, and rubber pac boots with coarse cleats.

Rifle Caliber and Scope
.338 with 6X scope.

Sex of Deer
Coming 1-year-old whitetail doe.

Time of Day
Deer was killed just at dark, about 5:20 P.M.

Length of Hunt
Three hours, including walk in and pack out.

Length of Shot
236 yards.

How Deer Moved
Stayed in cover till end of hunt, when a doe and two fawns jumped out of small drainage ahead of driver.

Skill of Hunters
One hunter was an old hand. His companion had hunted deer only a year or two. The third hunter, who got into the hunt too late to participate, was very skilled.

This hunt involved a two-person crew. A third hunter planned to participate but was unable to leave work in time to join the departing duo until an hour after they left their truck.

Of the first two, one was an experienced deer driver, having hunted over the country they intended to run a minimum of twenty years. His companion was relatively new to the business but was at least peripherally familiar with the country as a result of two recent drives. The third hunter was also familiar with the country and an experienced deer shooter. He saw a number of deer that might have been shootable as he tried to catch up with the party but, without close coordination with his buddies, elected not to take the shots.

All agreed the weather that day was warm to unseasonably warm. A brief fall shower wet the hills down the previous day, but the day of the hunt it was clear and warm. At 2:30 P.M. when the hunters left the road it was 44°F. At night, temperatures dropped below freezing. Conditions were summarized as being a warm Indian summer day.

Most of the leaves on the ninebark and snowberry underbrush were a bright red or yellow. Except in isolated instances where the country opened up, the fact that the leaves remained attached cut visibility to fifty to one hundred yards. Blackberry brush and tall grass in sheltered draws had neither frozen nor dried out; cover in these places was still as succulent as midsummer. Because the ground cover was extensive, the hunters concluded that the only way to get a deer out was to "root" around in the brushy draws while a stander above watched possible escape routes.

The men wore light wool pants and thin wool shirts. Even though this apparel was a bit warm for conditions that day, the stander in particular wanted to slip into position as silently as possible. Each wore heavy cleated boot pacs necessary to negotiate the steep hills.

Darkness fell at that time of year at about 5:30 P.M. The pair faced a two-mile walk through the rolling hills till they arrived at the box canyon they intended to hunt.

Topography in this case was rolling to steep soil-covered hills. Too few rocks lay exposed to characterize the land as mountainous. The most extreme elevation top to bottom was four hundred feet, yet in places the terrain was sufficiently steep so that walking uphill took a great deal of effort. Contouring around the hills was also a chore, as slick grass and downed brush on the steepest slopes caused frequent falls. A single misstep could and often did result in one's rolling ten or twelve feet downhill before regaining his footing.

Large numbers of small valleys ran off the larger main hill. Often this lattice work of little side drainages held deer that bedded in the cool, green shade during the heat of the day. Top to bottom, these little valleys were no more than fifty feet in depth.

An old logging trail running out through the hills above the top of the grade provided an excellent view down into and ahead of the drainages. It provided easy opportunity for a stander to get ahead of the driver below as he pushed his way through the finger drainages. The stander had sufficient altitude to spot any deer that ran up the open hillsides into the next finger drainage. It was an ideal situation, though it called on the driver to display a great deal of skill and determination to get the deer moving.

Large numbers of deer were known to inhabit the larger hill and main valley making up the box canyon. However, the area had a reputation for swallowing up deer in a manner that virtually precluded their being driven. Often a driver was unable to move deer out of the miserably dense cover.

By 3:30 P.M. the two early departers completed their journey into the targeted drainage. The driver plunged downhill about three hundred yards into the heaviest cover. Winds came in from the west, blowing across the end of the box canyon and then uphill along the east side of the U-shaped landform. They were about five knots in intensity.

The driver intended to make two-thirds of a giant U, starting at the corner of the box end and driving across to the east leg, where he would turn left sharply and follow this leg on through to the north. He found walking difficult on the slopes, especially through the heavy brush. These conditions were not unexpected but onerous nonetheless.

The driver knew the limitations that terrain and cover were imposing on him. He wished the pair could have waited for their buddy to serve as a second driver, but—like tides—sundown waits for no man.

He walked slowly, stopping often to look and listen. When busting brush at the bottom of a finger drainage, he often cut uphill abruptly on a sharp angle, mashing through the heaviest cover. By doing so he hoped to alarm deer that had otherwise elected to hold tight in the thick bottom cover.

The stander at the top displayed a great deal of skill. As much as possible, he kept track of the driver, staying at least 150 yards ahead of him. When he moved, he kept uphill to the inside of the old road so that any curious critters were unlikely to see him move. When standing watch, he kept a low bush in front to screen his outline.

Stander carried an older, much used Mauser military rifle that had been rechambered for .308 cartridges. He used regular-issue open sights. The driver packed a custom-built Mauser in .338 Winchester Magnum with a 6X scope. Perhaps they should have exchanged rifles, but each was happy with the gun they had grown accustomed to.

In due course the driver pushed through the box end of the valley, turning north on the outward leg of the drive. He noticed quite a lot of fresh sign but did not see a deer until marking the turn. Toward the bottom of the hill, intermittent stands of dog-hair pine grew. These groves were characterized by thin, spindly trunks of trees, bare of branches up to about thirty feet. All grew in patches so thick that it would be difficult for any sizable mammal to squeeze through.

The driver briefly saw the flag from one whitetail waving as it ran between two groves of the thin dog hair pine. It was at least 200 yards downhill from his position. The stander did not see that deer, being at least 450 yards below and running in exactly the wrong direction. The driver observed the deer with his scope for a few seconds, comforting himself with the thought that he was moving at least some deer!

The stander walked to the end of the logging road, where it terminated irrationally. After pushing through some very rugged hills, it stopped at a place where the main hill became less rigorous and steep.

Several smaller finger drainages ran downhill from a ridgeline that was itself rapidly running downhill to open fields. Ahead five hundred yards the fields were mostly weed covered, probably the result of being in some sort of government program.

The driver pushed through the last two finger drainages till he was even with his companion above. Both had observed abundant sign but, other than the one downhill deer, had moved nothing visible.

Frustration and disappointment surfaced as they planned their next move. They had come through some excellent country in a very intelligent manner.

The stander above called the driver on his walkie-talkie. He explained that it was now about forty-five minutes till dark. They were a long, long way from their truck and headed in the wrong direction. The stander felt it was wise to break off the hunt and head to the vehicle. In addition, he dropped his jacket on the trail, making it necessary to return the long way back on the logging road rather than across country in a more direct line.

The driver agreed but said he intended to cross the two or three additional finger drainages ahead of him before heading back. No matter how they traveled, they acknowledged that it would be dark before they saw each other at the truck.

The stander immediately turned around, retracing his path in search of the errant jacket. The driver forged ahead across one additional drainage. He now looked out over land mostly covered with grass and short berry brush. Some elderberry and vine maple scrub covered the valley, but generally he could see out over a much greater distance.

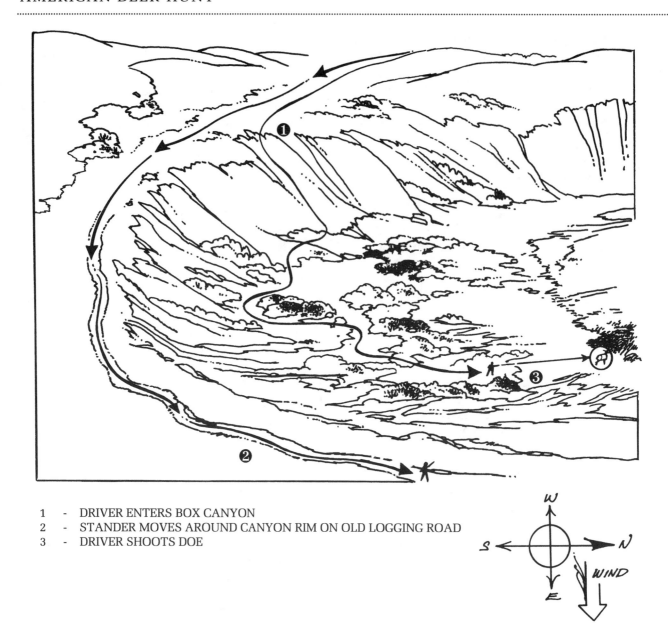

1 - DRIVER ENTERS BOX CANYON
2 - STANDER MOVES AROUND CANYON RIM ON OLD LOGGING ROAD
3 - DRIVER SHOOTS DOE

As the driver paused at the top of the next ridge, a doe and two coming one-year-old fawns bolted out of the scrub brush ahead. He threw up his rifle, thinking that it was a brutally long way to pack a deer to the truck. The hunter zeroed in on one of the smaller deer, reasoning that he would fire only once at the head. If he got it, fine; no meat would be wasted. It would also be possible to pack the smaller critter out.

He aimed ahead and left of the running deer. They moved about eighty yards; three more leaps and all would have been out of sight over the next ridge.

The bullet from the .338 caught the doe in the neck just at the base of the skull. It fell head over hoofs, never to move on its own again. It was out of sight on the ground, but the shooter felt it was a good shot. He paced off the distance to the hill. It was 236 yards. The range may have been slightly less in a straight line, but that was the number of long paces he took.

He field-dressed the deer, buttonholing the

legs so that he could pack it like a rucksack. His partner, now five hundred yards down the original trail, inquired over the radio about the shot. He accurately sensed that a deer was down as a result of the shot, which sounded as though it struck flesh.

It was now virtually dark. A miserable two-mile pack faced the shooter, who had to cross brushy, rolling hills strewn with fallen trees, logs, and rock. His anguish was assuaged a bit by the fact that the deer was small and that he could bundle it into a nice pack.

He slung the deer and the rifle and was able to make it to the truck about thirty minutes after full dark.

The hunter attributed his success to what was probably a very lucky shot, but one which was undoubtedly improved by his vast experience and the fact that he was cautiously reluctant to fire. They were in an excellent piece of country and were willing to push on till dark even when continuing seemed unreasonable.

CHAPTER 9

AFTER-DRIVE BUCK

HUNT CHECKLIST

Weather
Stable, with daytime temperatures at 25 to 27°F. Ground was barren, with no snow as yet.

Terrain
Gently rolling with no relief over 25 feet. Intermittent patches of timber covered rough country.

Wind Direction
Steady out of the west, 7 to 9 knots.

Conditions Previous Day
About the same. It was a crisp fall day with the promise of winter in the air.

How Hunters Moved
Two hunters drove a woodlot. Third hunter saw the deer as he walked along west edge of lot on his way back to the truck.

Clothes
Wool pants and jackets with cleated leather boots.

Rifle Caliber and Scope
.30-06 semiauto with 4X scope, .270 bolt with variable scope, and .338 with 6X scope.

Sex of Deer
Coming 2-year-old buck.

Time of Day
Deer was killed at about 4:35 P.M.

Length of Hunt
Less than 2 hours.

Length of Shot
227 yards, paced off by the hunter.

How Deer Moved
Deer held tight during drive but crept out to eat along edge of woods toward dark.

Skill of Hunters
Hunters had 8 or more years hunting together, and all knew the country extremely well.

Three deer hunters having eight years experience working together decided to organize a quick afternoon drive. Each knew the country over which they intended to hunt more thoroughly than their basement floors. To the man they had all killed nice deer over the past ten to twelve years. Each relied on their annual venison to feed their families.

Conditions the day prior to the hunt had been stable. It was late fall, with signs of an early winter. Cold winds blew out of the west at seven to nine knots, freezing most of the grass and knocking the leaves off the trees and underbrush. Like the previous day, temperatures hovered around 25 to 27°F.

If there was an unseasonable characteristic to the ground conditions, it was that there was only a dusting of snow despite the fact that it had been cold enough to freeze the ground four to six inches deep. At times the hunters could see some sign in the frostlike snow but never to the extent that they could determine direction of travel or location of the deer.

Insufficient snow along with the frozen ground made any tracking in the forest soil a difficult proposition. Because these hunters had hunted as a team over the same country for so long, they validly reckoned that they knew where the deer were lying this time of year and how they would move if disturbed. They felt confident that they could move the deer without further aid from surface sign.

The territory they intended to drive was gently rolling farm ground with intermittent patches of pine, scrub, maple, oak, and popple. Numerous thirty- to sixty-acre patches of timber intermixed with land used to raise oats, wheat, and barley provided excellent cover and feed for deer. One could safely assume that a few deer were lying in virtually every timbered patch. However, these deer were used to people; they seldom spooked or ran from them. Their common pattern was to sit tight till the people passed and then sneak away quietly.

Getting these deer out of cover where the hunters knew they lived was never as easy as one might suppose. Some of the patches were contiguous or closely so, allowing the deer to move several miles without really coming out in the open.

The trio agreed to drive a patch of ground lying about one mile from the county road. The woods ran north/south and consisted of about eighty acres of timber scrub surrounded on four sides by harvested grain fields. In years past they had killed several deer in the same woodlot, though it was the first time that year they had hunted this specific piece of ground.

The men wore heavy wool pants and jackets and leather boots with cleated soles. It probably was not quite cold enough for this type of gear but force of habit prevailed—they simply wore the clothes they usually did at that time of year.

One hunter carried a commercial .30-06 semi-auto, another a .270, and the third a .338 bolt-action. All of the rifles were equipped with either 4X, 6X, or variable scopes.

The hunter carrying the .270 agreed to be the stander and to walk around the patch of woods and approach it from the east. After waiting fifteen minutes for their friend to get into position, the two drivers started through the woodlot from the road. It was about 3:00 P.M.—full dark would arrive by 4:45 P.M.

Both drivers were considered to be extremely skilled. They walked as silently as possible given the crisp, frozen leaves underfoot, stopping often to listen and wait. They cut back and forth erratically, generally confusing the deer. As much as was possible, they attempted to keep track of each other. They were separated by about eighty to one hundred yards. The underbrush between them was thick enough that, even with two additional drivers, the deer could have held tight and allowed them to pass by. Neither driver had any firm indication that they were moving deer.

After about twenty-five minutes, both drivers passed through the wooded area without incident. They had noticed some sign but no live deer. They gathered up the stander at the end of the drive and debated what to do next out in the field of wheat stubble. Approximately forty-five minutes of daylight remained. They had been sufficiently confident of bagging a deer on the first drive that they had not made alternate plans.

One man elected to still-hunt through a wooded gully lying about three hundred yards to the south of the targeted woods. He left the group, intending to hunt till full dark before walking back to the truck by himself. Hunter two decided to walk east into another farm field. He wanted to wait till dark to see if a deer came out to eat. Later he admitted that the most he really hoped for was a chance shot at a coyote.

Hunter three was perhaps the most familiar with the country and also the most demoralized by the group's initial lack of success. He decided to strike out in the general direction of the truck, keeping an eye on the west edge of the woodlot the three had just run.

Winds from the west picked up a bit, blowing briskly from left to right. A deer as close as fifty yards ahead would have been extremely unlikely to wind him under those conditions. However, the hunter wore no camouflage and should have been fairly conspicuous walking forty yards from the woods' edge out in the open field.

He slowly walked north for about ten minutes, traversing perhaps 250 yards of country. He barely caught a glimpse of gray moving just over the edge of the horizon of the field. Through his 6X scope he was able to see the top two-thirds of a fork-horned buck standing in the open wheat field pawing for a few kernels of grain. It had moved straight out of the patch they drove not twenty minutes ago. Range was over 400 yards.

The hunter dropped to the ground so that the deer would be less likely to see him with its head down. He knew instantly that the wind direction gave him the edge. Crawling as fast as he could, he worked on shortening the distance to the buck.

Should the animal have decided to walk forward away from the woods, it would have disappeared completely into a fold in the gently rolling field. On the other hand, if alarmed, all it had to do was bound thirty yards back into the woodlot. The hunter realized that he had his work cut out for him as he attempted to convert standing deer into table venison.

He crawled along through the prickly stubble for almost 150 yards. Even through heavy gloves and thick pants his hands and knees were stabbed sore. Still, he was a long way from a certain offhand shot. He crouched down and then stood up with rifle at his shoulder, ready for action. If the buck bolted for the woods, he would try a shot no matter what the range.

The buck looked incredibly small and distant in the scope. The hunter considered dropping back down and crawling some more, but the deer stood up stock still, turning its ears toward him. Slowly the tail came up, indicated that if it didn't smell the hunter, it at least smelled a rat. It was now standing broadside to him but was so tiny even in the powerful scope that it really did not offer a good shot.

The hunter placed the crosshairs squarely in the middle of the critter's back. Summoning as much concentration as possible, he tried to take the best shot possible under the circumstances. It was, however, a standing offhand shot at a very long range. By the reaction of the deer, he knew he had one fleeting chance for a standing broadside shot and then the hunt was history.

He braced to take the shot. Holding his breath, he squeezed off a round from his .338 in the best, most-controlled manner possible. Recoil from the shot obscured his vision for an instant.

When he recovered, he thought he saw the deer running away from the woods, moving to his left. It was a split-second look, however. Now the critter was completely out of sight.

He kept his rifle ready as he quickly paced off the distance to the spot where he saw the deer. If nothing else, he intended to authenticate the range over which he missed. He was reasonably certain the buck had not returned to the woods, but he was not certain whether he had actually hit it. His hopes soared when he did not see a deer running out over the distant field. Wounding the critter seemed unlikely given the large-caliber rifle he used.

He did not see the downed deer till he was about sixty yards from it. The buck was hit high through both lungs. Before dying it jumped into a little depression, collapsing out of sight about 30 feet from where it was first standing. Given what proved to be a 227-yard shot, the shooter had not really known if he actually hit the spot at which he aimed.

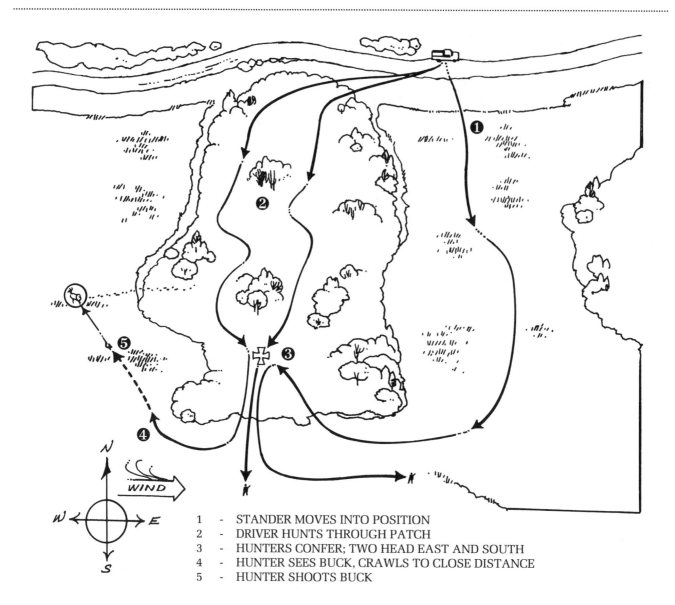

1 - STANDER MOVES INTO POSITION
2 - DRIVER HUNTS THROUGH PATCH
3 - HUNTERS CONFER; TWO HEAD EAST AND SOUTH
4 - HUNTER SEES BUCK, CRAWLS TO CLOSE DISTANCE
5 - HUNTER SHOOTS BUCK

Before starting to field-dress the critter, he called his two friends on their walkie-talkies. Both got over to the kill site in time to help the shooter drag out his buck.

It was just about five-hundred yards to their truck. Because the ground was frozen and a bit slick, they were able to drag the deer out with great dispatch. All three took their turns dragging.

Obviously the deer had come out of the woods the hunters had only recently run. Why it stood calmly eating in the field is still a mystery.

The greatest single factor to his success, according to the shooter, was his practice the summer before keeping blackbirds out of the neighbor's cherry trees. By being able to settle down and shoot with pinpoint accuracy from an offhand position, he increased his odds of connecting when the chips were really down. He also attributed his success to being alert enough to see movement out in the field and to knowing deer habits and movements through that country. He also felt his chances were increased by being able and willing to crawl 100 to 150 yards through some nasty stubble.

It may have been luck, but hunters like this one seem to be incredibly lucky year after year!

CHAPTER 10

BUCK CHAIR

HUNT CHECKLIST

Weather
Unseasonably warm with temperatures in the mid 40s. Ground was free of any frost or snow.

Terrain
Worn, rolling sand hills covered by scrub, pine, oak, and poplar.

Wind Direction
Gentle but steady out of north.

Conditions Previous Day
Heavy rain two days previous, otherwise unchanged.

How Hunters Moved
Two standers moved across wind onto stands about a half mile apart. Four still-hunted through area.

Clothes
Cotton flannel or wool shirts, wool pants, and smooth-soled leather work shoes. Some carried light jackets.

Rifle Caliber and Scope
Shooter had a .30-06 bolt with variable scope. Other five all had various bolt-actions with scopes.

Sex of Deer
10-point (eastern count) buck.

Time of Day
Buck was shot at about 8:20 A.M.

Length of Hunt
About 2 hours start to finish.

Length of Shot
Not more than 80 yards.

How Deer Moved
Deer came around hill through small depression after being pushed from its bed in thick cover.

Skill of Hunter
Hunter had killed a deer every year for the last twenty-four, but this was his best buck.

Virtually all of the deer hunters interviewed for these case studies maintain that luck has very little to do with success in the field. "It plays some small part," many said, "but that part is minimal at the very best." Conventional wisdom has it that those who simply wander through the woods hoping to win the lottery will be among those who average one deer killed every three years!

On the other hand, most expert deer hunters also agree that the only way to get a deer is to be out in the field looking. What they mean, of course, is that one must be out studying the country and the deer's habits. Those who wander around the woods with their brains in idle might as well stay home and talk to mother.

Now and then a case comes along that gives the impression that lightning does strike occasionally. Yet perhaps it only strikes those who are exposed, and in that regard the recipient of this hit was not actually lucky.

This case involves a deer hunter who, over the last twenty-four years, had shot at least one deer per year in a state where the kill ratio to licenses sold is well under 50 percent. Most of the deer were bucks, but some years he elected to shoot does, taking two or three if one included bow season.

The customary fall cold snap and accompanying snow did not arrive on schedule the year of this hunt. Instead of temperatures in the teens and twenties, the party went out on brown, open ground with daytime highs ranging from 40 to 45°F.

Heavy rains two days prior had knocked some of the leaves from the trees, but older, scrubby burr oak that held their leaves till early spring still obscured the woods in many places. Visibility was usually fair to about 80 yards and inconsistent to 120 yards.

Topography over which the group hunted consisted of worn, sand hills that rose no more than a hundred feet, with the occasional stone outcropping. Ground cover was scrub popple, oak, and pine. Remaining cover varied from popple at the fringes to red pine and jack pine mixed with ash and oak in the mature forest center. All was second- and third-growth timber. No vegetation stood over fifty feet high.

The hunters in this case had been combing the same area a minimum of eight years. Some of them had taken numerous deer there—okay-to-nice bucks, but nothing they would agree upon as a trophy.

Other hunters worked the area on occasion, but after opening day it was unusual to see anyone afield. Yet the hunting area was sufficiently "developed" to include a fixed stand referred to by group members as "the buck chair." Nontrophy whitetails had been killed from the artificial stand, but in deference to the few okay bucks taken from that location, it was "the buck chair." It consisted of a weathered two-by-four and two-by-six frame supporting an old nylon kitchen swivel chair. A short ladder provided access to the stand.

The stand was in an excellent location, both relative to the deer's observed movements from one thicket to another and their vulnerability as they came through. Three hunters were easily able to pick the rig up, moving it up to one hundred feet without stress. As a result, the exact position of the stand had been tweaked and refined through the years. Occupants of the chair were able to see the maximum number of deer in a spot so exact that the fewest number of pine and oak trees interfered with their line of sight.

Because of the high success ratio experienced from the chair, it was a popular stand, especially among the more portly of the hunters. Even though the topography of the area was fairly benign, heavier, older members of the group were inclined to pull rank to secure the spot. All was not harmony, however. Heavier, less agile hunters had a tendency to upset the chair's balance on their way up to its lofty heights nine feet above the forest floor.

The occupant of the chair was completely at the mercy of the other members of the group who acted as drivers. Someone had to muck around the country to get the deer moving. The stand was in a natural crossing area but not one the deer used unless disturbed.

A total of six hunters showed up for the push

the morning in question. All were unofficial members of a regular group that had hunted together for the last eight years or so. Enthusiasm for the morning's chase was dampened somewhat by the fact that it was already the fourth day of a relatively short season and the weather was unseasonably warm. All of them wore heavy cotton or wool flannel shirts, thin cotton jackets, wool pants, and common leather field boots. The warm weather had created some confusion, as they were reluctant to completely alter their customary field gear.

They did not form up on the road till approximately 7:00 A.M., a full hour after daylight at that time of year. While at the parking area, they divided up assignments, deciding who would go where. One hunter had previously passed up three spikes and forks so others in the party could get shots. He successfully used this fact as a bargaining chit to secure the coveted buck chair position.

The hunter hiked to the chair with some trepidation. Everyone in the party knew the country, but he knew how to drive it best. He was fully aware that without some smart, dedicated driving, his position in the stand would be worthless.

It was about three-quarters of a mile through the low hills to the stand. Winds were gentle and steady out of the north. The twigs and leaves were silent underfoot as a result of the previous day's soaking.

The hunter unloaded his .30-06 bolt and climbed to the top. Once in the chair, he chambered a round and set his 3-7X variable scope at 3. It was warm and comfortable in the chair. He had been up since 4:00 A.M. rousing members of the group and getting them out the door. Lines on the weariness graph crossed, and he relaxed too much, falling dead asleep. It was 8:00 A.M.

Another member of the group walked in about half a mile to a second stand about half a mile away. The stander two took a position overlooking a deep, dry stream bed. At times in early spring, water ran through the channel but seldom in fall or early winter. The scrub-covered channel connected two dense sections of woods that the drivers knew would be used by deer trying to move from one section to another.

The men at the road waited fifteen minutes for the standers to sneak into position. They then walked to the north along the county road for about three hundred yards and cut left (west) on an old, partly overgrown pulp wood trail.

The wooded area they intended to cover was at least one mile square, connected in some parts by other similarly large, wooded areas. A few farmed fields intruded into the woods here and there. It was the drivers' intent to walk out specific, predetermined sections of the woods. They trusted that their knowledge of the area would put either themselves or one of the standers in view of a deer. In years past they had often taken deer in this manner.

Under these circumstances, the four men were both still-hunters and drivers, adapting to the country as they went. As such, they started together from the pulp road, but within twenty minutes they were all walking in zigzag patterns, running in and out of each other's sight. They were driving south, 150 yards apart. It was an excellent strategy, calculated to confuse the deer, but one that did not guarantee that the whitetails would not either sit tight or sneak back around the drivers.

The four drivers hunted for about an hour while the man in the buck chair slept soundly and the fellow by the dry creek fought to stay alert. Standers were downwind of the drivers, in excellent position should anything have been jumped.

Abundant sign was evident in the loose sand comprising the forest floor. Except in the most general sense, its very nature made aging the tracks impossible. Not one of the drivers saw a single deer, but all agreed that there had to be a great many in the immediate area.

The stander in the chair woke from his slumber at about 9:00 A.M. He vividly recalled looking at his watch in astonishment over the length of time and the soundness with which he slept. He slumped in the chair in a daze for another minute or two.

Over to his left he noticed movement in the slight trough through which deer often moved. Quickly he focused on the dark gray-brown shape

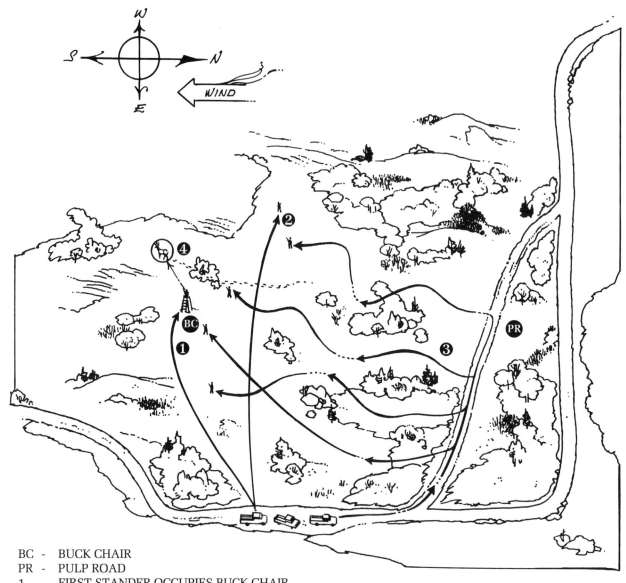

BC - BUCK CHAIR
PR - PULP ROAD
1 - FIRST STANDER OCCUPIES BUCK CHAIR
2 - SECOND STANDER OCCUPIES SECOND STAND
3 - DRIVERS HUNT SOUTH, PUSHING DEER AHEAD
4 - BUCK EMERGES FROM BRUSH AND IS SHOT BY STANDER

of what appeared to be a buck with "a dozen blond, fingerlike posts streaming from its head."

He brought his rifle up, placing the crosshairs ahead in an opening in the tree trunks and waiting till he saw hair in the right edge of the scope. When he did he jerked the trigger. The recoil took his eyes off the buck for an instant.

The deer kept running on what was probably its predetermined path. The shooter could see no immediate difference in how the deer acted. Intuitively he believed it was a good shot, but he did not really remember hearing a meat shot. Range was about eighty yards. The buck ran on for another hundred yards. The shooter did not even consider taking another shot but rather swiveled around in the chair to watch as it ran.

He did not actually see the buck fall, but he didn't see it leave the immediate area either. Carefully he crawled down off the stand, walking over toward the deer's location.

He found a beautiful, mature, ten-point buck shot high through the top of the heart and lower rear of the lungs. The bullet penetrated side to side very nicely. Its neck was large and swollen from the rut.

The shooter was not at the buck more than two minutes when one of his party walked over the hill to him. The driver had not seen a deer ahead but strongly suspected that he had one going.

The driver knew the country and knew how deer would come through if, in fact, they were there. The stander had no idea if any other deer had come through prior to the big buck. The driver distinctly heard a meat shot and was confident, knowing it came from the direction of the buck chair, that a kill had been made.

Together they field-dressed the deer, taking care to protect the cape. The shooter rationalized that since this was his best buck, he was going to have a head mount made.

By 10:00 A.M. they were able to drag the deer to their truck. By then word had spread through the group. They met at the vehicles and decided to call it a day.

The shooter attributed his success to the fact that he was disciplined enough to pass up earlier opportunities on lesser deer during previous hunts. Therefore, on this hunt he was able to take the best stand served by an excellent, knowledgeable driver who understood the country. He also felt it was important to know how to successfully shoot through heavily covered country.

The shooter steadfastly maintains that there was only the slightest element of luck involved in the kill, although it was his best after a lifetime of deer hunting, taken in ninety seconds from sound sleep to shooting.

CHAPTER 11

DEEP VALLEY WHITETAIL

HUNT CHECKLIST

Weather
About 38°F with gentle winds and warming sun.

Terrain
High mountain meadows and valleys, about 5,000 feet elevation.

Wind Direction
Out of west, steady and gentle.

Conditions Previous Day
One of the first hard freezes deposited dusty frost on the ground.

How Hunters Moved
They worked slowly uphill through draws, valleys, and brush patches. Hunter saw deer while he was cutting through a draw from one meadow to another.

Clothes
Hunters wore cotton pants and shirts and nylon rain slickers. Shoes were common leather field boots.

Rifle Caliber and Scope
Shooter had a .338 with 6X scope.

Sex of Deer
Fork-horn buck.

Time of Day
Buck was killed at about 3:30 P.M. as it came out to feed.

Length of Hunt
Hunt started at dawn and lasted till they brought the buck down at sundown.

Length of Shot
About 241 yards downhill.

How Deer Moved
Deer came out of a brushy draw to nibble some new grass shortly before sundown.

Skill of Hunters
Both hunters were very experienced, having hunted and killed many deer in the general area.

This case took place in territory sufficiently steep and varied to be classified as mountainous. As with all mountainous terrain, there were enough flat areas on little buttes and plateaus that anyone looking at only a small portion of the country might call it high, rolling hills.

It seemed curious that whitetail deer rather than muleys were resident in this country, but the hunter, who had taken numerous of both, reported the hill was, in fact, a whitetail area.

Fresh, green grass grew on the flats and in the high meadows, invigorated by early fall rains. Deer were attracted to the fresh grass. Perhaps it was Mother Nature's way of adding a few extra pounds before the rigors of winter drove them to lower elevations, where the pickin's were not as numerous or fresh.

The meadows were located at about 5,000 feet. Peaks surrounding the meadows rose much higher but were never good places to find deer. Poplar and aspen mixed with pine and fir grew in the draws and in random clumps on the mountain.

Fresh, green leaves still held to the bushy undergrowth, obscuring one's view into the draws and brush patches where deer were most likely to hide. Leaves on this brush would shortly turn red and brown, falling to the ground with the first snow.

Temperatures, influenced both by the elevation and the fall season, were virtually impossible to predict. In a general sense, one could expect a chilly 38°F on the exposed flats and draws, while in the long canyons it was often much colder during the day and warmer at night.

The day before this hunt, a hard freeze turned the grass and brush white. This was high mountain wire grass, however—it continued to thrive despite the cold snap, happy for the moisture from whatever source.

Two deer hunters left their car at first light, about 6:20 A.M. They walked steadily for thirty minutes, mostly up a steep mountain trail. Their path took them due south on an incline so steep that even the light nylon windbreakers they wore caused them to overheat. They also wore cotton work pants, flannel shirts, and common leather field boots.

One man carried a .300 Winchester Magnum with a variable scope. The other had a .338 with 6X scope. Their trail took them 1,200 yards virtually straight up the side of the mountain through reasonably thick wooded areas. They observed quite a bit of sign on the trail but saw no deer.

They made a great number of side drives and hunts through the deep valleys and patches of aspen on either side of the trail. One might drive through an aspen thicket while the other watched uphill, or they both pushed through larger patches. Although both expected to jump numerous deer, they saw not one animal.

Close to noontime they topped out onto the high plateau that had been their original goal. Almost six hours had elapsed since they left the road, only half a mile away. Although winds in the mountains are always variable as well as unpredictable, a constant six-knot breeze out of the west hit them on their right side all morning.

They had come a long way, but the actual top of the mountain lay ahead at least another 1,200 yards. Such as it was, their trail petered out at the meadow. Toward the west the meadow fell off to the lowlands, providing an incredibly beautiful vista. Both agreed it was invigorating hunting this type of country, but it would have been even better if they had seen an occasional deer.

The hunters sat down at the large meadow and ate a leisurely lunch. After lunch, one hunter cut sharply east into a second meadow. He hunted the fringes, looking out over patches of pine and juniper. Thin mountain air blew past him, carrying his scent ahead into the cover. The other hunter stayed in the first meadow intending to hunt its fringes as well.

Nothing was moving that time of day. Their alternatives were to hike back downhill to the vehicle and motor to a new spot, or to stay where they were till dark, hoping their luck would change. From extensive experience they knew that large numbers of deer inhabited the area this time of year. Because of weather, migration patterns, food availability, and hunting pressure, mountain hunting is always a chance proposition, they reasoned. They elected to continue on where they were.

By about 2:00 P.M., the hunter in the first

meadow slowly moved off into the western wind. He walked along a heavily wooded thicket all the way down to the end of the plateau. Trees and brush now blocked his way. His only chance was to see something moving in the thickets, an unlikely event, he reasoned, until evening was closer at hand.

The hunter walked about a mile on this plan until he was in heavy cover and working his way downhill. He did not want to fight brush nor the steep mountain terrain so he turned around, heading back the way he came.

The hunters were out of communication, so they did not realize they basically were working the same plan. Their most significant difference was the fact that the east hunter was moving with the wind while the west hunter had the wind mostly in his face.

The east hunter worked through an area of fresh green grass that he thought would be a major attraction for any deer in the area. He saw only a few tracks, leading him to believe that most of the deer had already moved downhill. This condition puzzled him; since the weather was still relatively warm, there was no snow, and feed on which deer thrived seemed to abound. Both hunters looked forward to discussing this seeming paradox.

The west hunter hiked back up the mountain, essentially retracing his steps of an hour earlier. After awhile he came to a deep, brush-covered gully south of and parallel to the large meadow in which he had spent most of the afternoon.

An ancient, gnarled wild apple tree grew in the gully at its downhill terminus. It stood where the gully emptied into a much larger brush and timber patch. The hunter wanted to check for sign below the apple tree but hesitated. It was at least two hundred feet down into the draw. After he sacrificed his elevation to look at the base of the tree, he realized he would have to climb back out again. It was impossible to see more than fifty feet in the draw, and thin air and steep climbs were taking their toll on his resolve.

Since he had seen little sign on his side of the ridge, however, he decided in favor of the trek down to the apple tree. He worked his way from side to side downhill so as not to stumble on the steep incline. Once at the tree, he found that the apple crop had been abundant that year and that the deer were eating the apples as well as the high grass growing under the tree.

Trails crisscrossed the little twenty-square-yard patch around the tree. At first it looked as though cattle grazed through the area, but only deer tracks were evident in the loose soil. Their age was a mystery—it was simply too dry to tell if they were from last week or the last hour.

As he was on his way down to the bottom of the draw, the hunter had looked through the thicket to the other side and noticed a second high meadow to the south of the gully. It was not possible to see all the way through, but he did note a tiny game trail leading through the tangle. He decided to cross on the trail and then chug up the opposite hill into the meadow above. It was "six of one/half dozen of another" if he retraced his steps or if he climbed up the south side of the draw to the other meadow. Both meadows provided an overview of the same basic country, and climbing to the second meadow would give him some new country to cross.

Up in the south meadow, a thoroughly winded hunter found he had a long hike up a very steep hill. He pinched to his left so as to walk at the edge of the brushy draw.

The draw itself was no wider than forty feet, but the brush was so thick and tangled that the hunter knew that even though it appeared he could see through it, he really could not. It could have contained deer.

Another well-used game trail ran uphill along the side of the brush. He hadn't noticed it before but reckoned that its presence and position were logical. Occasional tall trees standing out of the draw as well as scattered pines in the meadow obscured the track. On he went, climbing up as fast as he could.

He managed about 250 yards before he turned around and started walking backward. This was an old trick learned from a relative, allowing him to survey the country over which he had recently passed. He gave no thought to the location of his companion.

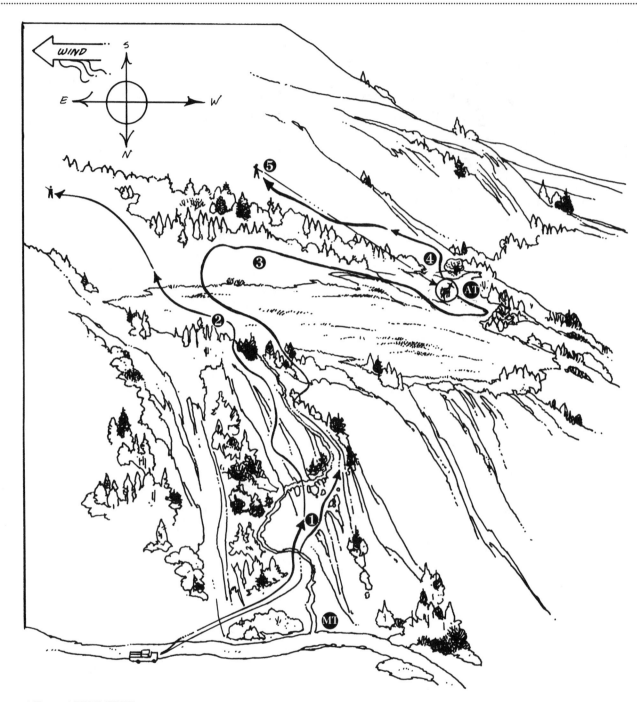

AT - APPLE TREE
MT - MOUNTAIN TRAIL
1 - HUNTERS DO SIDE DRIVES UP MOUNTAINSIDE
2 - HUNTERS EAT LUNCH AT FIRST MEADOW
3 - HUNTER MOVES ALONG THICKET
4 - HUNTER ENTERS SECOND MEADOW
5 - WHILE WALKING BACKWARD, HUNTER SPOTS AND SHOOTS BUCK

As he backwalked, the hunter noticed a flash of dark gray-brown on the gully's edge near the apple tree. Through his 6X scope it looked very much as though a fork-horn buck was working its way out from the apple tree and uphill toward the north meadow. It was concentrating on eating, its head on the ground.

The hunter had come through that exact spot just fifteen minutes earlier, a fact that did not seem to concern the buck in the least. He continued nibbling on the fresh grass. The angle of the draw was such that the winds were almost straight from the buck uphill to the hunter.

The hunter tried moving downhill slowly. He was out in plain sight on a ridgeline with nothing but sky behind him and absolutely no cover available. When the deer looked up, he knew it would see him.

After moving less than ten feet, he realized that closing the distance was not likely to succeed. Not only was there an excellent chance that the buck would see him, but the farther downhill he went the more the buck was obscured by trees and brush between them.

The hunter cautiously moved sideways out into the open a few feet till the deer was plainly in view. He sat down on the steep hill, tucking his knees under his chin. Once seated, the deer would never detect him unless the winds somehow shifted. He sifted dirt and dust into the air to keep track of the wind.

He studied the deer for five minutes or more. Range, he guessed, was about 250 yards—not an insurmountable distance from a good rest, but far enough. His braced sitting position was a plus, as was the fact that the winds were gentle and steady.

The hunter placed the crosshairs on the top of the deer's back. It was facing downhill about half turned away from him. At the shot, the deer simply collapsed. The hunter was able to get his eyes back on the target in time to see the round strike the deer.

Over the ridge in the east meadow, his companion plainly heard the round hit flesh. He turned back and headed toward the sound of the shot.

The shooter watched for signs of life through his scope. The animal was hit solidly, as he would later discover, about four inches down in the middle of the back, high through the lungs. Its backbone was severely damaged, precluding any movement, but the shooter did not know this at the time so he waited, anticipating a second shot.

His companion trotted over the ridge into the first meadow as quickly as he could. It was now about 3:30 P.M.; it would be dark no later than 4:30 P.M. The shooter waved his companion down to the deer. They both arrived at the kill simultaneously. The shooter paced off 241 yards.

Working quickly, they field-dressed the deer, buttonholing it for the long, miserable pack out. The shooter carried it up out of the draw and across the open meadow to the downhill path. The second hunter took over, packing it down the risky, steep trail. They arrived at the truck at dusk. It was the only deer either had seen the entire day.

The shooter attributed his success to staying "right" with the wind, taking the tough alternatives, and not giving up. One must also conclude that he was either fortunate or skilled when making his stalk and for being able to pull off a 240-yard shot. He did not feel the shot was a major consideration. The most important factors, he said, were knowing when to sit down and take the shot and having enough rifle to do the job.

HUNT CHECKLIST

Weather
Warm days and cool nights. Highs of 50°F during the day and lows of 35°F at night.

Terrain
Extremely steep, rugged, often rocky canyons. Very few developed roads.

Wind Direction
Steady all day out of west at about 10 knots.

Conditions Previous Day
Rain earlier in week but warm and dry the previous day.

How Hunters Moved
Hunted the edge of a huge, flat plateau in opposite directions, then did one drive on either side in an attempt to push deer through a saddle.

Clothes
Cotton jeans, flannel shirts, and Vietnam jungle boots.

Rifle Caliber and Scope
Doe was shot with .308 with 6X scope, buck with .300 Winchester Magnum with 3-7X variable scope.

Sex of Deer
One big doe and a moderately large spike buck.

Time of Day
Late morning. Kills were made about 11:00 A.M.

Length of Hunt
Hunters were on the ground about daybreak. Even with the incredible pack, they were done by 2:00 P.M.

Length of Shot
125 yards to doe, about 150 yards to buck.

How Deer Moved
Doe was driven out of brush through saddle. Buck was jumped out of bed but stood looking back at hunter.

Skill of Hunters
Hunters were all experienced but had only been over this country once before.

In this case study, the hunter was a rural woman whose deer-hunting-addicted husband put her name into a lottery drawing for a mule deer tag in a reputed trophy area. On drawing one of the coveted tags, they found that not everything worked as planned, as the tag she drew was for a doe, not the trophy buck he had originally envisioned. In addition, she determined to fill the tag herself—securing, as she said, their year's supply of hamburger.

The country for which the tag was valid was notorious for its limited network of roads, extremely deep canyons, severe rocky bluffs, and large population of sizable mule deer. The only real trick was driving in close enough to be able to walk in and then pack the critter out once it was on the grass.

The few roads over the area were seldom improved to the extent that they were graveled or graded. Most were either ancient logging, cattle, or mining roads. All were subject to syrupy, axle-deep mud with the onset of the slightest precipitation. Upon season's opening, it often was possible to drive no closer than four or five miles to the hunting area. If one waited too long, heavy snows were likely to cover the area, making access even more unlikely.

It was mildly crisp, cool, and dry when the woman and her two hunting companions drove in to the hunt. Temperatures were 35°F at night, rising to 50°F by noon. The roads and trails were bone dry, leading to problems with dust rather than mud. Grass on the canyon's top rim was also dry, but it grew brightly down in the many side draws and canyons where it could water on subterranean moisture.

The party wore cotton jean-type pants, flannel shirts, and Vietnam jungle boots. Each carried binoculars with which to scan the vast country ahead, and they had a set of powerful walkie-talkies to coordinate their hunt over the large, difficult area. The female hunter carried a .308 with 6X scope, one man had a .338, and the other a .300 Winchester Magnum. They also packed a large lunch, planning to stay in the region all day.

Despite the relatively dry conditions, they were able to get their four-wheel-drive truck only to within two miles of the hunting ground. They started their walk in at first light at about 7:00 A.M. It got dark in that region at that time of year around 4:30 P.M.

Besides the doe tag, one of the male hunters drew a buck tag. He headed out east from the parking area, walking around a large, deep canyon. Winds were steady out of the west at about ten knots. Other than a bit of southerly component to his hunt, he was moving mostly with the wind. Winds down in the deep, sheltered canyons, however, were often not a factor.

He skirted the rough, rocky canyon, moving out onto a relatively level plateau. Second- and third-generation lodgepole and ponderosa pine mostly covered the plateau, interspersed occasionally with open rock-strewn meadows. Heavy ninebark and sumac brush clogged many of the side drainages, providing abundant cover for deer.

The female hunter and her companion headed almost due east from the truck. They crossed the deep canyon, climbing down five hundred feet or more and then up again onto the same high plateau. It was not country for the faint of heart.

The three had hunted the same piece of real estate several weeks earlier. At that time one hunter had spotted four deer grazing quietly on the side of a canyon. They were too far away to stalk and shoot as well as being much too far to pack out. The other two had seen a couple of deer jump over a ridge much too quickly to get off an aimed shot.

At that time, they reckoned that was an exercise in learning the country and the deer's movements. They expected a somewhat easier hunt this day as a result of their previous scouting.

The hunters working together contoured around the canyon and down into its bowels about two hundred feet below its crest at the plateau. Every hundred yards or so they crossed through a line of waist-high sagebrush behind which a deer could easily lie hiding.

After walking about two miles around the steep canyon rim, they came to an unusually large side canyon. They cut down into it by first walking out onto a jutting peninsula, then hiking down into the draw three hundred or more feet.

Hundreds of fresh deer tracks covered the muddy canyon floor. Without stopping, they started the long arduous climb out of the canyon. About two-thirds of the way up the hill, they sat down a moment to catch their breath. While sitting there looking out over the steep valley through which they had just come, a nice mule deer buck with an excellent rack followed by a big fat doe ran out of cover. The deer contoured around toward the peninsula from which the hunters had just come. They studied the deer through their rifle scopes and binoculars. Range was about 175 to 200 yards to the buck and about 500 yards down to the doe, which had chosen to cut downhill at a faster rate than the buck.

Raising their companion with the buck permit on their radios was not a viable option. It was a very large buck and would have been a horrible pack up to the plateau. Similarly, it would have been possible to get the doe out only by quartering her and making four hour-long packs. By mutual agreement they let both deer go. These muleys were shootable, they agreed, but everything after that was impossible. Many deer inhabited the area; some must be in easier places, they reckoned.

After the two earned the top of the canyon again, they were able to reach their companion. He said he was sitting on a long hogback ridge overlooking a modestly steep bowl. He suggested that the two join him for a drive down through the bowl, where packing a deer to the plateau would be more reasonable.

It took about an hour for all three to physically hook up again. By then it was almost 11:00 A.M., a time when they agreed most deer bedded down for the day. Common wisdom suggested that the muleys would hunker down till evening and that the last chance of seeing one was just before full dark.

Nonetheless, they agreed to one more coordinated effort before sitting down to eat lunch. The woman volunteered to walk down the hogback ridge extending almost due south to a place where she could see down on either side. Although she had never hunted in that exact place before, from where they were it looked as though a game trail crossed the saddle ahead. If she found abundant tracks suggesting a crossing, it would be an ideal place to stand.

Both men backtracked up the ridge about three hundred yards, dropping off into the side canyon. As they walked, they met two other men hunting the high plateaus. They agreed that the additional people in the area were not a factor.

After splitting up and dropping down two hundred yards, they started to contour around each side of the ridge toward the saddle and the stander. Little clumps of ponderosa pine and hawthorn brush dotted the slope. They tried to push through these as much as possible without working too far downhill, moving any bedded deer ahead of them.

They were little more than halfway round to the stander when they thought they detected the muffled thump of a shot. It was not possible to confirm by radio, but both men thought they had heard a faint noise.

A second shot twenty seconds later was much more audible, perhaps not taken pointing so far down into the canyon, they reasoned. In about ten minutes, the stander came on the radio. She had shot twice at a doe but could no longer see it, so she was not sure if it was down or not. Range was about 125 yards to her right, she said, at a very steep place on the hill.

The drivers continued their push through to the stander at the saddle. It was about a six-hundred-yard drive. The driver on the right side of the ridge called on his radio, reporting that he could see a buck for which he was adequately tagged. He said that the animal was well above a steppe palisade and that a pack or drag would be reasonable on the relatively gentle grade two hundred yards from the top.

Both the driver to the left and the stander heard the shot. However, the shooter called immediately in anguish, saying he apparently had gut shot the deer and that it had jumped off the steep rock bluff. Five minutes later he reported being able to see it lying dead, but at least five hundred yards below the plateau rim. He was on his way down to it, but reckoned it would take him two full hours to drag it uphill.

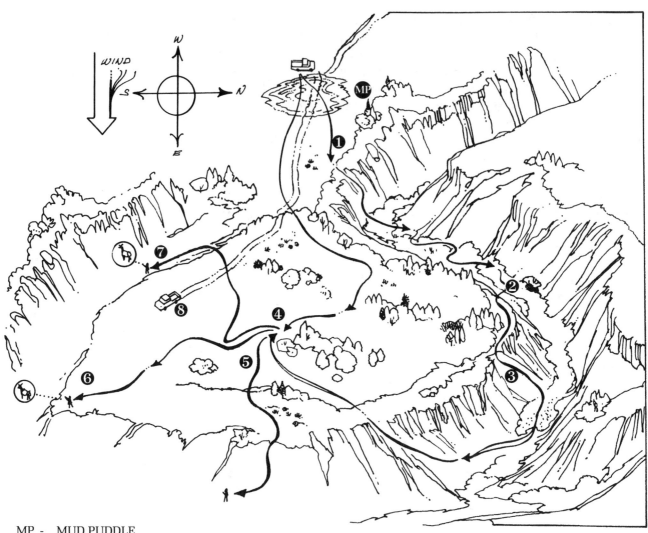

MP - MUD PUDDLE
1 - TWO HUNTERS ENTER DEEP CANYON
2 - HUNTERS EMERGE FROM CANYON, WALK ALONG RIM
3 - HUNTERS RE-ENTER CANYON VIA LARGE SIDE CANYON; FIND MANY TRACKS AT BOTTOM
4 - THREE HUNTERS CONFER
5 - ONE HUNTER DRIVES AROUND EAST SPUR OF FINGER SADDLE
6 - STANDER SHOOTS DOE FROM FINGER SADDLE
7 - SECOND HUNTER SHOOTS BUCK IN CANYON
8 - TRUCK DRIVEN CLOSER TO HAUL OUT DEER

Almost simultaneously the woman reported a nice mature doe down at 125 yards, shot through both lungs. It had fallen behind some sagebrush but was in a good position for field-dressing on an otherwise steep grade.

The remaining deerless driver cut sharply to his right, struggling uphill to the plateau. He did not even want to think about seeing another deer,

much less shooting one. After a somewhat worried conference on the radios, the unencumbered driver agreed to hurry back to the truck to see if he could somehow get it closer to the kills.

He arrived at the truck at 12:45 P.M. It took him thirty minutes of very intense, very experienced work to winch the truck up over a mud hill, through a deep puddle, and out onto the relatively flat, dry, but rock-strewn plateau. After another twenty minutes of hunting and pecking and lots of log and rock rolling, he was able to make his way along a cow trail to within three hundred yards of the downed doe.

He climbed down into the saddle and, with the type of effort that was in common supply that day, was able to shoulder the deer and get it up to the truck. The female hunter had field-dressed and buttonholed it for him. He was so exhausted after the two-hundred-pound pack that he couldn't even talk on the radio.

The woman raised the second packer, finding that he was about four hundred yards from the rig pulling along a rather modest-sized spike buck. It was not as big a trophy as he wished, but it was enough to pack under the circumstances.

The first packer recovered his strength sufficiently so that he was able to climb down into the canyon and help drag out the buck. The woman hunter moved the truck a bit closer. It was 2:00 P.M. when they had both critters safely on board the truck. All three were so exhausted

that it was difficult for anyone to drive, yet thirty additional minutes of heavy-duty winching was required to get the truck back across the muddy barrier onto something resembling a trail. Back home they worked well into the night skinning and cleaning the two deer in preparation for cutting and packing.

The first hunter attributed her success to being able to recognize an active game trail, having the wind in her favor, and hunting with drivers willing to go into some fairly steep, difficult country to root out a deer.

Part of the success of this story involved the truck driver, who was able to winch the vehicle over one hill where all four wheels were off the ground simultaneously, thus making it possible to get to the kill sites and get the deer out. He attributed his success to learning how to run a winch as a kid on the farm.

The last hunter believed the fork-horn buck actually got him. He believes the only thing he did correctly that day was to get low enough in the canyon to see a deer and drive it to the stander.

CHAPTER 13
SNOWSTORM WHITETAIL

HUNT CHECKLIST

Weather
20°F with high winds and heavy, blowing snow. Accumulations of 5 inches of snow in sheltered areas.

Terrain
Rolling hills, quite steep in places, and open farmland with few rough spots covered with low brush.

Wind Direction
Gusting out of the west to 25 knots or more.

Conditions Previous Day
Clear and cold, but no factor the day of the hunt.

How Hunter Moved
Hunter parked his jeep on a county road and walked about 1 1/2 miles in to a brush patch he suspected might contain deer.

Clothes
Heavy wool pants, thermal boot pacs, two wool shirts, heavy wool jacket, and nylon windbreaker.

Rifle Caliber and Scope
.338 bolt with 6X scope.

Sex of Deer
Large fork-horn buck.

Time of Day
Hunter left vehicle at 8:00 A.M., an hour after sunrise. He shot the buck about 9:15 A.M. and had it in the vehicle by about 10:30 A.M.

Length of Hunt
About 2 hours, start to finish.

Length of Shot
About 120 yards.

How Deer Moved
Deer was waiting out a snowstorm in a sheltered brush patch far from civilization. When disturbed, it ran out into an open field, where hunter shot it.

Skill of Hunter
Hunter had killed deer annually for his family for 20 years and knew the country as well as anyone around.

It seems probable that experienced, motivated hunters who have hunted over their home range for years and years can take advantage of the most adverse weather to bag deer. Conventional wisdom has it that deer will bed down during a storm and cannot be hunted successfully. Certainly this is true, yet skilled hunters who know where the deer are likely to bed often are able to walk right up to them during a storm. Under these circumstances, these hunters know that the deer are extremely reluctant to move, making them easier to shoot.

The day in question was one of the most vile and miserable of the season. At daybreak when the hunter got up, there already was a total of five inches of fine new snow covering the ground. Winds were howling out of the west, gusting to twenty-five knots or more. Radio advisories suggested staying off the highway, as blowing snow was expected for at least six hours. In places on country roads, drifts were trapping cars and trucks.

The temperature was around 20°F, but the high winds and fine snow created miserable conditions, much more severe than the temperature suggested. The hunter wore heavy wool pants, two wool shirts, and a heavy wool jacket covered with a nylon slicker. Boots were insulated leather with rubber boots over the top. He wore the wool to stay warm rather than to slip silently through the bush.

He motored his four-wheel-drive jeep through drifts to the hunting area, parking on a county road at about 8:00 A.M. It was a full hour after sunup, yet the day was gray and dreary as the storm howled on. He could park his vehicle only in this one spot, which entailed about a 1 1/3-mile walk to the brush patch that he had in mind. During normal weather it would have been a relatively short march, but on this day it was a contest to go even a hundred yards.

The hunter thought that the specific patch of ground he was interested in might contain a deer, and he was well aware of the fact that no deer would move with such a storm in progress unless he virtually walked on their backs. There was little chance of seeing so much as a mouse out in the field that morning.

It had been at least ten years since he had looked at this particular brush patch. The last time he had been there, he did not run anything out of it. Nevertheless, while there he concluded that it was an ideal location for a lone buck; he just never had gotten back that way to look again until the day of the storm.

He left the jeep and walked out over an open farm field, heading a bit north but mostly west into the wind. He moved in a northerly direction almost subconsciously, as it was a means of not having to face the wind head-on. The hunter had to stop and rest at a 750-gallon fiberglass fertilizer tank. He had come about three-quarters of a mile.

The hunter hiked up to another county road. The targeted area lay back behind another four hundred yards. He stood at the road for a minute or two, debating whether it was smart to expend all that energy checking out an absolutely unknown situation. His adventuresome instincts got the best of him, however, so he trudged across the road, through a little valley in the giant, windswept field, and then up a steep hill toward the brush patch.

The area he was walking toward contained about fifteen acres of four- to six-foot ninebark, elderberry, and maple scrub. From the top rim about fifty feet above, the property spread out before him in a giant bowl. The lateness of the season as well as the violent weather took care of what few leaves might have clung to the bushes. He could see down into the entire area perfectly. It might have been possible for a bedding deer to lie still and avoid detection, but this seemed doubtful against the fresh white snow.

Another road lay ahead of the brush patch four hundred yards to the west. He reasoned that the deer would not want to try escaping west into the wind and across the road, and he didn't want it to go that direction. A shot on a deer running back east would be much easier to accomplish.

The hunter glanced out over the brush field and immediately backed away from the rim lest he be seen. He continued west another forty feet, placing himself more near the center overlooking the brush.

When he returned to the rim, he carried four

eight-inch clods of frozen dirt taken from the plowed field behind. His rifle, slung over one shoulder, was not within immediate reach.

The hunter launched one of the clods out over the rim. It cracked into the frozen brush about two-thirds of the way across to the other side and about fifty feet in from the east end. He stepped off another ten or so yards and launched a second chunk of clod into the brush. He was in mid-step for the next toss when the deer appeared.

He first heard it thumping the ground and cracking the brush. Immediately he saw it running out from the bushes below, moving back in the direction from which he had just come.

In retrospect, the hunter believed that the second clod either hit the deer or splashed pieces onto its back. Yet the deer did not seem to know from what quarter the disturbance had come. Thirty feet above, the hunter was in a position where the deer could not see, hear, or smell him.

He placed the crosshairs of his scope on the critter. Through its six powers, the deer looked very large. It was, in fact, a large whitetail buck but, alas, one with very common forked horns. It stopped momentarily as if thinking, "Do I really want to get out in this miserable weather?"

The hunter estimated the range to be one hundred yards and calmly moved the crosshairs to the middle of the buck's back. He tapped the trigger of the battered, ancient .338 bolt-action rifle, probably one of the first Winchesters ever sold in that caliber. The round caught the critter high in the back, penetrating its right side near the kidney and exiting out through the left lung. It ran a foot or two before collapsing in the snow.

The hunter watched it thrash around for a moment or two before it gave up and lay still. He was confident that he had a kill so he did not replace the round in the rifle chamber.

He paced off the distance on his way to the deer, thinking that this critter might now have *him* rather than the other way around. In a matter of minutes he had the animal field-dressed. It was so bitter cold that he had to work quickly. Because the rack was small and the pack distance great, the hunter decided to leave the head in the field.

He was now faced with a six-hundred-yard cross-country pack over two eighty-foot hills and slippery fields with a 175-pound animal before arriving at a farm road over which he could bring his vehicle. He tried for about ten minutes to either get the big buck up on his shoulders or buttonhole the legs so that he could carry it as a pack. Even placing the deer on a steep hillside under which he could stand did not work. The beast was simply too big.

After several unsuccessful attempts, the hunter cut a hole in the neck skin to use as a hold as he dragged it over the snowy fields. Given its large size and the steep hills, the buck skidded along fairly well. It took about thirty minutes to pull the deer into a side ditch along the farm road connecting to the county road.

Having stashed the deer, the hunter set out for his vehicle parked about a mile away. If the weather changed at all, the storm had grown in intensity. To save time and energy, he walked uphill across country rather than following the road. He estimated that he saved five hundred yards of walking by doing so.

His plan was to reverse his walk of an hour earlier. He marched mostly east and a little south, but every time he turned south, wind-driven snow bit his face. As a result, he failed to walk sufficiently south to intersect the road on which his vehicle was parked. Visibility was under two hundred yards.

The hunter understood the country over which he walked reasonably well, but when he came to a grassy pasture he realized he was disoriented. By dropping down into a little sheltered valley, he was able to find his direction, walk to the road, and ultimately get to his vehicle. It was after 10:30 A.M. when he drove back out to the stashed buck.

The hunter concluded that it was one of the most unique deer hunts in which he had ever participated. In retrospect, he believed he was successful because he was persistent and perhaps obstinate. Normal people usually do not go out deer hunting in snowstorms, he recollected, especially over country with which they are not familiar. He bagged the deer because

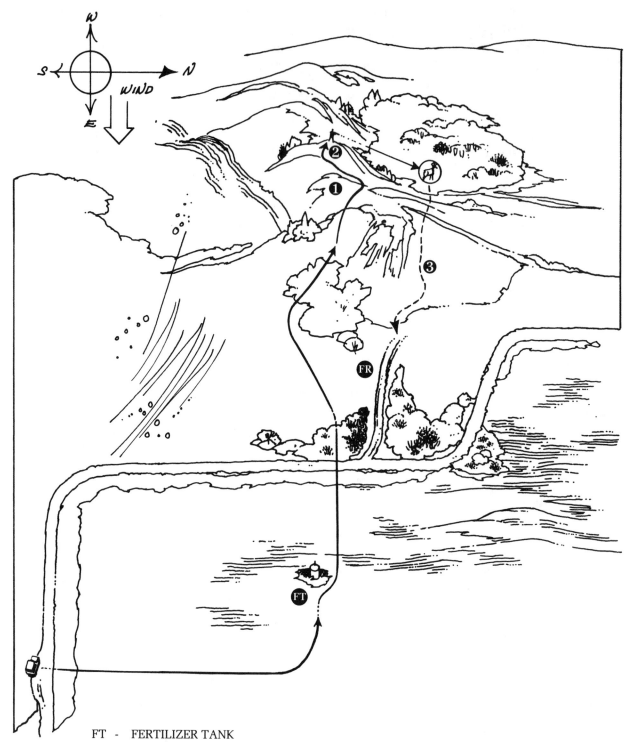

FT - FERTILIZER TANK
FR - FARM ROAD
1 - HUNTER THROWS DIRT CLOD INTO BRUSH
2 - HUNTER THROWS SECOND CLOD; SPOTS AND SHOOTS BUCK
3 - HUNTER DRAGS DEER TO FARM ROAD

he was willing to tough out a rough situation, operating on the hunch that the brush patch might harbor a deer. He was also experienced enough to know how to get the critter to jump under his terms and conditions.

Occasionally one encounters a situation in which external forces are more rigorous than the hunt itself. Obviously this was one of those.

CHAPTER 14

LONG DRIVE

HUNT CHECKLIST

Weather
28 to 33°F. Snow covered part of the ground. Gray, overcast, dreary skies.

Terrain
Very gently rolling with enough dips and swales to hide deer and hunters moving from one patch of woods to another.

Wind Direction
Out of the west, light but consistent.

Conditions Previous Day
Snow earlier in the week, which had melted everywhere except in sheltered draws and wooded areas.

How Hunters Moved
Hunter one walked to west of brush patch, another jumped deer from the east. Deer were jumped again by first hunter, who ran them southeast to hunter three.

Clothes
Heavy wool clothes with rubber boot pacs. Because they alternated standing and driving, hunters overdressed to some extent.

Rifle Caliber and Scope
.308 Mauser, .308 mountain rifle with 6X scope, .300 Winchester Magnum with variable scope.

Sex of Deer
Three does.

Time of Day
Hunt started at 7:00 A.M., one-half hour after daybreak, and ended at full dark.

Length of Hunt
Entire day. They covered 6 or 7 miles.

Length of Shot
Various from 40 to 450 yards.

How Deer Moved
Deer bounced back and forth between three hunters, all of whom took multiple shots.

Skill of Hunters
Experienced deer getters who had killed numerous deer in this country.

Supersuccessful old-timer deer getters virtually always maintain that it is essential that hunters not only know the country thoroughly but that they be able to anticipate the movements and reactions of their compatriots. In modern times, this regimen is negated a bit by the use of two-way radios. This case nibbles on the fringes of the psychology of knowing intuitively how fellow hunters will react but is mitigated by their use of radios.

Three conditioned, able, experienced deer hunters set out just after daybreak at 7:00 A.M. to "run" a number of little wooded areas in their hunting territory. In years past, each had killed numerous deer in the same general area as the ones they planned to drive that day. They started the hunt not with nervous anticipation but with the snug realization that the deer were around and they would certainly get some of them.

The country over which they hunted was rough wooded land interspersed with farm ground planted with a variety of crops, including peas, alfalfa, wheat, oats, and barley. By hunting season, all of these crops were harvested. Intermittent stands of poplar, pine, oak, and scrub maple comprised the larger trees growing in twenty- to fifty-acre patches mixed in with the ag land. In some places, dense ninebark and blackberry bush covered the ground under the larger trees.

It was gently rolling but not quite hilly country. Worn soil covered the hills. There were few rock outcrops. Deer or hunters could easily move undiscovered through any one of hundreds of little dips and swales. From afar it looked as though the land was nearly level, but when one actually went out on the ground, the situation was far different.

Approximately four inches of snow covered the land earlier in the week. Temperatures up into the mid thirties as well as a persistent west wind dissipated the snow, except in sheltered draws and protected hillsides. Some of the brush patches caught and held enough snow so that limited tracking in them was possible; out in the fields only an occasional patch of tracking snow

aided the hunters. Temperatures the day of the hunt were from 28 to 33°F.

Because the hunters intended to switch duties driving, standing, and still-hunting, they all wore complete wool hunting outfits, including insulated rubber boot pacs with cleated soles.

Little snow remained up on the trees and brush, so wetting above the waist was not a consideration. They did not wear or carry rain slickers. Though chilling out while on stand was a problem, the three wore more clothes than would have been necessary had they planned to do only one task or another.

Rifles used on the hunt included a .308 Mauser with issue sights, a .308 mountain rifle with 6X scope, and a .300 Winchester Magnum bolt with 3-7X variable scope. They expected some shooting over long range across flat, open country, so in that regard the rifles they carried were probably not ideal. Like deer hunters everywhere, though, they took the rifles they had and were accustomed to.

The three missed their chance to watch the sun come up out in the field by at least thirty minutes. It was full light before they started "running out" various brushy draws, isolated woodlots, and grassy overgrown farm fields. They walked five miles each through various patches they knew from past experience should contain deer, but by noon they had not jumped the first deer.

The hunt did not degenerate into a disorganized tangle, however. Their knowledge of the country and of each other's habits, as well as their walkie-talkies, assisted them mightily. Without a thorough knowledge of the land over which one is operating, use of radios is not helpful. It does no good, for instance, to broadcast the fact that one is on the south edge of the elephant-shaped woodlot or at the big rock where Farmer Bohen broke his plow unless all know exactly what and where that is. It also is imperative that all the partners know how the deer had come through on prior hunts and how the calling hunter will react to situations that may unfold in his sector.

Using their radios and knowledge of the country, the three were able to cover what amounted to a tremendous amount of territory. In spite of these efficiencies, however, noon passed without so much as their seeing one critter. Because of snow conditions afield, tracking was fraught with difficulties; they were uncertain about location and numbers of deer.

By 3:30 P.M. they were worn out, bewildered, and discouraged. It definitely was time for the Last Drive of the Day.

What followed on that last drive was extremely confusing, chaotic, and disjointed. Because much of the action overlapped, the account that follows—garnered from three independent witnesses—often does not flow smoothly. It is distilled into a somewhat stylized unfolding of events.

At the time of the last drive, the three team members were strung out in a four-mile line running roughly east to west. A six- to eight-knot breeze blew over the country from the west.

Over the radios they agreed that the most westerly hunter should walk about one mile north across some open farm ground to a forty-acre patch of heavy ninebark brush. He was to stand the patch at the southwest corner in hopes that the center man could get over there from the east and run a deer out. Winds were not perfect for this plan, but the group hoped to move some deer by some device. The brush patch lay in as deep a draw as was found in that country, leading the hunters to conclude that winds might just blow over the top of the draw harmlessly. In times past when they had run that patch, the deer always came out across the open fields in a manner that gave a west stander a reasonable shot. Wind direction did not seem to matter in those cases. If winds were getting into the draw, the deer might pick up the west hunter's scent and run out to the north where no one stood.

The middle hunter walked parallel to the west stander perhaps a mile east of him. Both moved almost straight north. He intended to walk along the brush in an attempt to run out any deer present. His spacing put him comfortably to the east of the brush.

Hunter three to the far east was farther south of the east/west line formed by the first two than he should have been. He was mired down in an extremely thick patch of ninebark. When the three laid their plans for the final drive, he started bulldozing through as quickly as possible in hopes that he could catch up. Because he knew the country, he pretty well knew where the other two were as well as how they had to move to pull off the drive. Hunter three was reasonably certain he was too far away to participate in any significant fashion.

Ten minutes later, the middle hunter suggested that hunter three walk rapidly through the wooded area to a thin line of trees and brush lying to the northwest of his current position. Deer from the main drive might circle back there, the fellow explained on the radio. Hunter three could see little logic in that maneuver but agreed anyway.

It was at least half a mile through the brushy peninsula to the draw the first two intended to drive. It seemed doubtful that hunter three could get through from his present position in time to participate, unless it was to pack a critter out.

Fifteen to twenty minutes elapsed before the far-west man reported by radio that he was on stand one hundred yards from the south end of the targeted draw. The driver reported that he was crossing a fence near the drive area and would be ready to start throwing rocks and clods in just a minute or two.

He walked to the head of the drive area and, much to his dismay, found the adjoining farm field planted in tall canary grass. He reported over the radio that he was going to muck around in the grass field first, lest there be a deer lying there.

Perhaps three minutes elapsed before the driver got up three big whitetails bedded in the tall grass. He took a single quick shot before they ran out of sight into the far south end of the big brush patch.

The stander across the other side saw the deer jump up and run to the edge of the cover. They stopped ten feet inside the brush, perhaps wary of the his scent blowing in from the west. He estimated the range to the deer at 250 yards.

The driver assumed that he missed his shot at the runaway deer. He urged hunter three to hurry through to the end of the peninsula of trees. Hunter three, who had hunted that area on numerous occasions, had no experience with deer lying in canary grass or with their escaping through the little peninsula through which he now ran.

The stander reported he could make out the outline of one of the deer in the brush through his binoculars, but he could not see it using the open sights on his military rifle. He fired into the brush at a place where he thought the deer stood but could detect no immediate effect from the shot.

Both of his friends urged over their radios that he fire again. A wounded deer could be tracked and killed, they argued, but a healthy deer would run forever. Being a conservative old deer hunter, the stander elected not to waste ammo on something he could not see with certainty. As he told it later, he could remember when, as a kid, the family bought ammo one round at a time with which to hunt deer. He could never be enticed into shooting up the country promiscuously.

The driver worked his way down toward the deer's location as reported by the stander. Stander ran down three hundred yards or more toward the south end in an attempt to close off the deer's escape route.

Pursued by the two converging hunters, the three deer broke out of the brush patch, running at top speed toward the peninsula through which hunter three was running.

Both the stander and driver fired once each at the running deer. They were four- to five-hundred-yard shots, not of the kind likely to have much effect. Although hunter three in the wooded peninsula was not yet to its terminus, he could make out the running deer coming across the field toward him.

The driver reported by radio that he knew the exact spot where the deer entered the peninsula. Hunter three fast-walked out in the open field along the other side, hoping to get a shot at one of the critters. Because of the great distance, neither of the first two hunters could see their friend charging along the edge of the peninsula.

Hunter three finally spotted a doe standing chest deep in brush. Quickly she jumped out into the open field, moving to the hunter's left. A slight dip in the field hid her from the knees

down. Hunter three hurriedly placed the crosshairs of his scope on the deer's chest and jerked off a round from his .308.

As he fired, the deer jumped to his left, disappearing immediately over a little rise. As far as he knows, the shooter never saw that deer again. Enough snow covered the ground at that place to confirm where she stood as well as her leaving the area. At most, the shot was a seventy-yard attempt. He tracked her as best he could in the intermittent snow, covering at least three hundred yards, but no sign of blood turned up. As he followed the track, another shot rang out.

The driver from the first run had walked to the woody peninsula, jumping a second deer that took refuge there. He had a straightaway, running shot over about 150 yards. It also was a clean miss. Hunter three on the spoor did not see the second deer, which came in his general direction and disappeared into a large wooded area to the south before he could catch a glimpse of it.

The third deer ran east through the peninsula over to a large wooded area. It disappeared without offering the hunters any kind of plausible shot.

All the hunters fired at game. Two of them had reasonably easy shots that they should have made. They were not novices given to shooting up the countryside or even to missing very many deer, but on that day there was to be no meat for the table.

After several weeks of hashing and rehashing the hunt, the participants settled on several observations.

The man with the .308 Mauser who had to spot the deer through his binoculars might have done better with a modern scoped rifle. The old-timer had used that same gun to kill numerous deer in years past, however, and was not inclined to change to a newfangled weapon less likely to withstand the beating to which he normally subjected his rifles.

The driver who ran the deer out in the high grass could have been more prepared. Yet he did not expect grassy cover in that place, much less deer bedded there.

It was reasonable to expect the deer to run toward the west stander. Yet they didn't go that

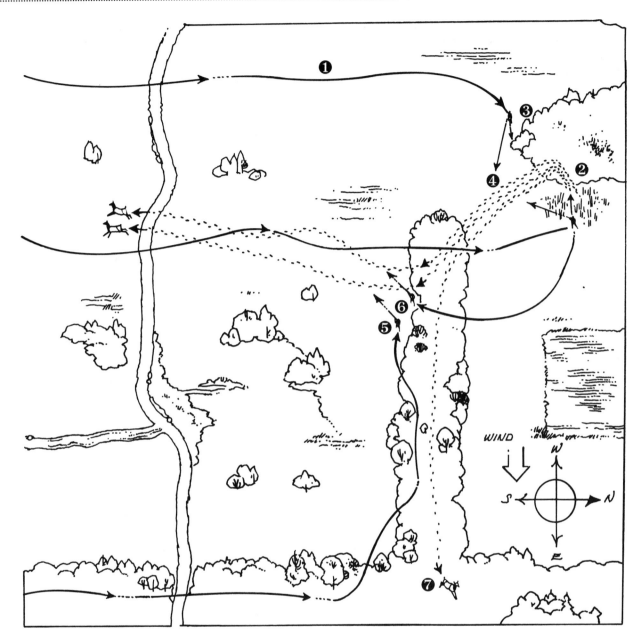

1 - STANDER MOVES INTO PENINSULA
2 - DRIVER JUMPS THREE DEER IN TALL GRASS; TAKES A SHOT
3 - STANDER TAKES SHOT INTO WOODED PATCH
4 - THREE DEER BREAK COVER; STANDER AND DRIVER SHOOT AND MISS
5 - HUNTER THREE EMERGES FROM PENINSULA; SHOOTS AND MISSES
6 - DRIVER JUMPS SECOND DEER; SHOOTS AND MISSES
7 - THIRD DEER ESCAPES THROUGH PENINSULA

way. Nobody had gotten a decent shot after the critters left the cover of the draw.

The hunter back at the peninsula had the best shot. He originally had little confidence in the drive, but even if he had, it was virtually impossible for him to come from such a far distance to a better position in the time allotted. He simply should have made the seventy-yard broadside shot.

The next day, that hunter took two boxes of ammo out to a walkaround range, where he practiced random offhand shots. Apparently the practice helped—he, and the others, eventually finished the season with deer.

HUNT CHECKLIST

Weather
Gray 30°F day with highs expected in the mid-30s.

Terrain
Single, large 1,250-acre hill with many small rills and drainages running down its sides.

Wind Direction
Out of east at a consistent 5 to 7 knots.

Conditions Previous Day
Snow that had melted on the southern exposures. Some snow remained in the protected drainages.

How Hunters Moved
Hunted uphill to the east, contouring around the large hill. After an hour, hunter sat by a small finger drainage till deer showed themselves.

Clothes
Cotton shirts and pants. She wore hunter's wool. Both wore regular leather hiking boots.

Rifle Caliber and Scope
.308 bolt-action with open sights.

Sex of Deer
Large doe and huge 5-point (western count) buck.

Time of Day
10:15 A.M.

Length of Hunt
About 4 hours start to finish. Both deer were shot in a matter of a few seconds.

Length of Shot
About 40 yards for doe, 70 yards for buck.

How Deer Moved
The doe came from brush patch below. The buck was working down a relatively open draw and was scared out by the first shot. Buck may have been following doe.

Skill of Hunters
Both hunted the area often, having taken many deer in the region.

The hunter in this case lived two hundred yards off a county road on a large red clay hill. The hill was fully two square miles, or not less than 1,250 acres. It rose up out of the countryside to a total rise of about 450 feet. The hunter's home lay about a third of the way up the hill at the edge of some dense trees and brush.

Scattered jack pine grew on the hill from place to place and in the many little rills and draws that ran like gnarled fingers from the domelike cap at the summit. These trees covered ground interspersed with wire grass that covered probably 65 percent of the remainder of the country.

To the northeast the hill interconnected with terrain that would definitely be considered as mountainous. Lines of pine and fir provided cover wherein the many deer in the area could live, eat, and breed. They ventured out from the dense mountain cover as their adventurous natures dictated.

Only a few rough jeep trails cut around the hill, due in large measure to a lack of anything of value to which the trails might run. Numerous rock outcrops and the slick mud made road building a formidable task.

The man often hiked over the hill from his home on its southwest slope. He knew every draw and rill, especially those that had sheltered deer in the past. It was his experience that significant numbers of whitetails inhabited the area.

Most of the meat used by the man and his family came off the hill in the form of venison taken by himself, his wife, and their two children. Few outside hunters bothered to look over the hill. Access across smallholder private property was difficult, and the man and his family kept the deer reasonably well cropped out. Other hunters did not have the ability or inclination to learn the lay of the land as well as this fellow who resided there.

It was mid-season before the hunter had a chance to look at his hill seriously for a killable deer. A week prior he had hiked several miles up to its summit in an attempt to determine if the deer had moved in, as well as how they were moving. He did not pack a rifle during his scouting mission. Since that hike, four inches of snow

had covered the region. Warm afternoon suns had melted any snow on southern exposures as well as some of it in the many cuts and rills.

Over dinner the night before, the man and his wife decided to hunt "their" hill for a few hours at least. Sunrise came at 6:45 A.M. but they were not able to leave the house till 8:00 A.M.

Temperatures stood at 30°F when they left for the hunt. Forecasts indicated a rise to 35 to 38°F by noon. They wore cotton work pants and cammy cotton sweatshirts. His more cold-blooded wife wore several layers of wool. Both used regular waterproof leather hiking boots.

They carried .308 rifles with open sights. She was often in the woods when deer were bagged but had not, as yet, killed one on her own. He had killed numerous deer and was considered one of the better hunters in the region, principally because of his willingness to be extremely patient.

It was muddy and slippery due to the melting snow until they reached the portion of the hill where dead wire grass both stabilized the soil and dried the ground out a bit. Hunting about two hundred yards apart, they set out very slowly to contour around the hill in a counterclockwise rotation. About an hour out, perhaps a mile from the starting place, he spotted a nice buck running with three or four does at least four hundred yards ahead.

Winds were mostly steady out of the east into the hunter's face, but they also blew downhill to a lesser extent. He knew that in this area the winds could be extremely fickle. He tried to work with them in times past but was often thwarted by sudden, unexpected shifts.

The band of deer galloped off for another 150 yards until they disappeared from sight over a little rise. Apparently they moved out of one of the little tree- and brush-choked draws. The man concluded from their leisurely, less-than-urgent pace that they had heard either him or his wife rather than smelled them. At that moment she was above and probably ahead of him, as best as he could determine.

The hunter moved up to the next draw into which he thought the deer disappeared. As draws in the area went, this one was fairly open, covered with grass and the occasional pine here and there. A well-used game trail ran up the hill from the bottom of the little valley.

It was about twenty-five feet down from the face of the hill to the bottom of the draw. From rim to rim across the top was about sixty feet, he estimated. His wife originally agreed that she would walk for about an hour, then sit down for an hour or so of watching. He was not certain where she was or where she would choose to sit down and watch. He hoped she would intersect the draw above him, getting a shot at or driving the deer back down to him. He thought that it would be very unlikely for the deer to come back down to him.

He crossed through the little depression and walked up on the opposite rim to a position where he could again see out 150 yards or more around the hill. Winds still blew into his face or slightly downhill.

The hunter walked along the last rim for another fifty yards or so. He would not have been surprised to see his wife, but he did not. After finding a relatively soft, comfortable grassy spot on a little prominence, he sat down. It was a place where he could see ahead on the hill as well as forty or fifty yards into the draw.

He sat patiently in that place for at least an hour. Sight distances were as good as one could expect. Low wire grass covered the hill, with the occasional pine standing in the distance. Grass in the draw was probably more succulent, perhaps because of additional moisture.

Significantly, the draw ran down behind the man into a wider woody patch of undergrowth. The area was nearly covered with small trees, limiting his view in that direction.

The hunter was something of a pariah among his peers in that he not only enjoyed hunting alone but was also enamored with devices they considered to be quirky. He, for instance, was the only one who used scent tubes fastened to his boots. He also attempted to rattle up deer but has been unsuccessful with the device as of this writing. And, while sitting patiently overlooking the countryside, he gave a single long call on his silver "buck whistle" every ten minutes. He continued

this procedure faithfully for what he later estimated were seven or eight cycles.

His wife had walked to the top of the same draw but had seen no game. She then sat for an hour, watching patiently over the countryside as well. She could not hear the buck whistle nor see her husband, but she knew from past hunts what the general pattern would be.

Even in the relatively warm weather, the man started to chill a bit. As he stood to stretch his legs, a large four-year-old whitetail doe broke cover from below, running up out of the draw he had crossed an hour before. It ran on an angle uphill, around and out of the draw.

Without thinking, the hunter turned back, flipped his safety off, and fired. The deer kept on running with no observable impact or change in its pace. Although there was no apparent result, he felt in his bones that it had been a "good shot." From where he stood, it was a mostly broadside shot taken at about forty yards.

He bolted another round into his rifle's chamber. No sooner had he completed the reload than a huge five-point buck broke cover from above. It raced on a contour out of the side valley, down the draw, and up over the slight rise in the general direction of the doe. The hunter was high enough on the opposite rim to be able to get off two quick shots.

He fired by complete reflex. Not more than five seconds had elapsed between the doe's appearance and the buck's crossing. The buck was about level with the shooter at about seventy yards when he fired the first shot. It was about two-thirds broadside to him, moving steadily. There was no visual impact. His second shot was also taken mostly broadside but at a more severe angle. He fired just as the buck topped the draw, turning directly away from him.

At this point the hunter did not really know what he had. He reloaded his magazine and walked across the draw to the place where he had last seen the buck. Up on the opposite side at the place at which he touched off his last shot, he could see a large gray-brown lump with a butterscotch patch lying sixty yards ahead.

As he approached, the buck swiveled around,

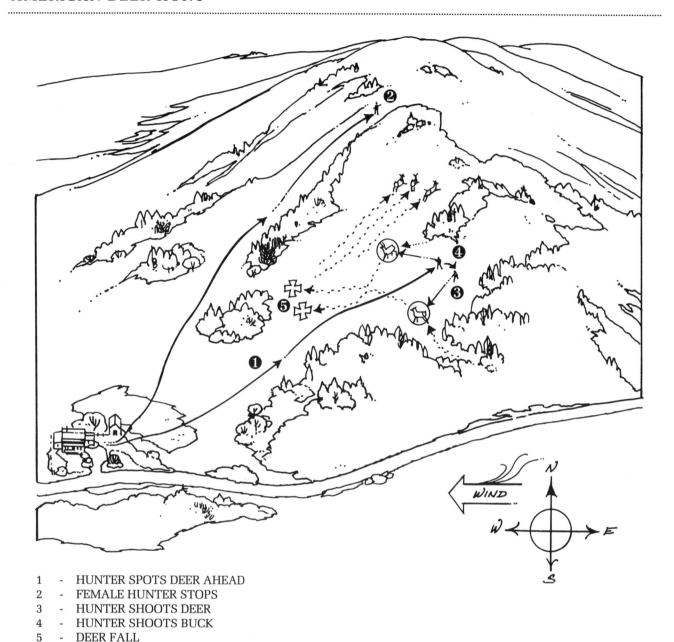

1 - HUNTER SPOTS DEER AHEAD
2 - FEMALE HUNTER STOPS
3 - HUNTER SHOOTS DEER
4 - HUNTER SHOOTS BUCK
5 - DEER FALL

swinging its head defiantly. The man watched a few moments until the animal lay still. It was a magnificent five-year-old buck with a large swollen neck, heavy, perfectly balanced horns, and huge muscle structure. It was shot twice through the chest cavity. One round went through the heart, left to right, and exited the critter. A second round raked forward through the intestines and legs, exiting just behind the right shoulder.

Thoughts regarding the whereabouts of the doe did not immediately enter the hunter's mind, but as soon as the buck was dead, he walked ahead on the game trail. He almost hoped he had not been successful. Both deer had traveled in the same basic direction out of the little drainage. "Perhaps," he thought, "I didn't really hit it." About forty feet past the buck, however, he encountered large clumps of blood.

Another twenty feet ahead, lying behind some

small Christmas trees over a little rise, he found the doe. The .308 round punctured its heart, blowing out the critter's left side. For a whitetail doe, it was quite large.

He hollered to his wife, who was already on her way downhill to help. She thought she had heard a meat shot but was unsure because she was too close to the shots. He field-dressed the doe while she walked down to their house three-quarters of a mile away. It was 11:30 A.M. when she headed back uphill pushing a wheelbarrow.

With tremendous joint effort they were able to wheel the field-dressed doe down half a mile to the county road, where they stashed it in a side ditch. Wheeling the huge buck was even more difficult than the doe. Its large, ungainly head, which they had left intact on the carcass, tipped the wheelbarrow on the uneven hillsides. Even getting up a small rise so they could start down was extremely excruciating.

It was fully 2:30 P.M. when they got the second deer to the road, loaded it in their truck, and drove to their garage. Skinning and caping the deer lasted well into the night.

The hunter attributed his success to knowing the country, being extremely patient, and to the large amount of target practice he undertook with this hunting rifle. He hit two-for-two that day. In retrospect, he does not know what to make of his deer scent and whistle, but reckons they did no harm.

CHAPTER 16

MOUNTAINTOP DEER

HUNT CHECKLIST

Weather
Warm, dry, early fall day in mid-40s.

Terrain
Very steep to rocky hills falling off four hundred feet or more; brushy draws running from a hogback.

Wind Direction
Squirrelly, with gentle 4- to 6-knot winds, mostly out of the northwest.

Conditions Previous Day
Warm and dry.

How Hunters Moved
Driver moved out on saddle ridge, down steep side hill, through brushy draws, and into large timbered section. Stander moved along ridgeline above driver.

Clothes
Flannel shirts, blue jeans, and jungle boots.

Rifle Caliber and Scope
.308 with 6X scope.

Sex of Deer
Old whitetail doe.

Time of Day
Left their truck at about 2:00 P.M. Deer was first shot about 3:30 P.M.

Length of Hunt
About 4 hours, including dragging the deer out.

Length of Shot
About 40 yards.

How Deer Moved
Deer was spooked out of heavy timber, crossed a saddle, and was wounded by stander at the ridgeline of the saddle. It ran into the brush, requiring a long tracking job.

Skill of Hunters
Stander shot second deer of his life. Driver was an old-timer who knew the country well.

Large buttes, hills, or—if they are sufficiently rocky—mountaintops, generally are not places where one would expect to encounter deer. Exceptions occur only early in the season or when the deer are caught trying to cross from one side of a ridge to the other.

The weather the day of this hunt could best be described as traditional, warm, early fall. Leaves still clung tenaciously to the maple, alder, and ash understory growing in the region. Perhaps half the overstory cover was pine and fir, which stood bright and green as a result of their recently completed season of growth. Heavy stands of ninebark and hazel limited visibility to ninety yards or less in the woods. In other grassy openings, it was often possible to see deer two hundred yards out.

Temperatures that day hung in the mid forties, more the type of weather when hunters worried about flies ruining their meat rather than freezing toes or leaky boots. Winds on top of the mountain were variable to absolutely squirrelly. Before starting, the two men tried to determine if, as was common, they were mostly out of the northwest. On top of the hill they found them to be swirling around out of virtually any direction.

Two hunters were really not enough to adequately handle the country they intended to run that afternoon. Neither hunter had pressing duties that day. It wasn't an ideal situation—whitetail fever simply overwhelmed them.

One man was extremely experienced, having killed scores of deer in his lifetime of hunting. He had hunted this specific area on numerous prior occasions. He reckoned that he might be able to still-hunt the spot adequately enough that he could overcome the lack of numbers. He also counted on directing his partner's hunt via their walkie-talkies.

The second hunter was younger, a student. He was full of energy and enthusiasm but had killed his first deer only the previous year. Although he was inexperienced, the seasoned hunter hoped to capitalize on the younger man's boundless energy.

Both wore cotton jeans, flannel shirts, and army surplus jungle boots. Other than camouflage slouch hats, no attempt at wearing hunting clothes was made past grabbing some old stuff out of the closet. Virtually no other hunters worked that area. If another party would have shown up, the hunters would have been very surprised.

They left their truck on the county road at about 2:00 P.M. Sundown in that area that time of year was expected at about 5:00 P.M. No attempt was made to plan the hunt to coincide with the evening feed. The pair had time on their hands, figuring that enough daylight remained to squeeze in a hunt. They intended to push through some excellent brushy draws running from the mountaintop on down—places where the old-timer knew deer often bedded down.

Warm weather, the seasoned hunter knew, would push the deer uphill into cooler grass-covered draws. Those draws containing even a small trickle of water would almost certainly shelter deer. In this particular case, an in-depth knowledge of the country vis-à-vis the deer's habits strongly motivated the hunters. They were inappropriately confident of success.

Climbing steadily, they were able to follow a path uphill to the mountain's summit, arriving there about 3:00 P.M. It was a long, arduous hike—discouraging, in part, because the specific area they intended to hunt lay over on the other side and downhill again.

As they suspected, winds at the summit were blowing harder and with more irregularity than they would have wished for. It was impossible to determine from which direction they would blow down on the south side past the crest.

Together they walked out on a long hogback ridge leading southwest away from the summit to the end of the trees and underbrush. Back behind, a number of tree- and brush-choked draws, some with active springs, comprised the targeted area.

The old-timer placed the youngster back on the ridgetop with instructions to keep track of him below as best as possible and stay fifty to one hundred yards ahead. When jumped, these deer liked to run uphill to the top of the ridge. It was a steep mountain; by the time the critters reached the top, they generally were winded. In that regard, their actions were much like humans—they often were easy targets as they paused to rest at the top of the hill. The old-timer hoped to surprise a deer or two himself, allowing the "kid" on the top to handle whatever happened his way.

This plan did have its flaws, however. The older driver sometimes could not see the jumped deer running uphill because they were hidden in one of the shallow draws. The youngster did not know from previous experience when the deer would likely move and when he should best move to keep watch.

The first of the six brushy draws was widely separated from the second. Under these circumstances, the driver hoped the jumped deer would run out across the hundred yards of open grass-covered hillside. He wanted to get a shot from below but realized the stander above was more likely to see the deer in the open.

The driver dropped off the ridge at least 350 yards, stopping when the side hill was not quite so steep at a place where an ancient cattle trail contoured along the hillside. He turned sharply left (east) and started working his way very slowly through the area. After no more than ten minutes, stander lost sight of the driver below.

Using their walkie-talkies, they were able—to a small extent—to mitigate their separation and lack of numbers. Yet the young hunter did not know the country well enough to adequately explain where he was standing.

The driver pushed through the five draws without incident. Ahead lay a large sixty-acre patch of fairly large timber. It was an excellent piece of ground from which to drive a deer but, once in the dense patch, he would not be able to direct the efforts of his stander. Thus he simply allowed the young man to operate on his own devices.

The driver called the stander, letting him know he was entering the timber and that at least a few deer would come over the top. He suggested that the stander take up the best position he could find, looking out over as much country as possible. The driver explained what the stand above should look like, hoping the novice could find a place that looked reasonably similar. They were now about five hundred yards apart, with a

steep sudden grade between them.

The driver plowed through heavy, tangled brush down into a small blackberry-choked draw. Even in the damp soil in the draw he saw little fresh sign. He began to have second thoughts regarding the quality of the area and was about to turn uphill when he heard a single shot.

The stander carried a .308 bolt-action with 6X scope. The driver could not tell if it was that rifle he heard or if someone else was hunting the area. He also did not know if it was a meat shot. He called on his radio, but it was at least five minutes before he got a response.

"A deer came out of the heavy brush above at the very top," the stander told him. "I shot at it but have no idea if I hit it."

"Where did you aim?" the driver inquired.

"At the deer," came the reply.

"What sex was it?" driver persisted.

"I think it was probably a doe," the stander answered.

The driver instructed the stander to go over to the exact spot from where he shot at the deer and place his hat on the ground there. Then he was to look around for blood and tracks. If he didn't find any sign, he was not to mush around on the ground, obliterating what precious little there might have been.

The young man took another four or five minutes before reporting that he could see nothing on the ground. No blood, no tracks, no nothing. The old-timer started the long, heavy grind up the steep hill to his companion. He was worn to a frazzle by the time he reached the top. Had it been possible, he would have reversed duties with his spry, youthful partner.

The driver located the spot duly marked with the stander's hat. He noted several tracks and a few scattered drops of blood sprayed onto green leaves ten feet away. His tracking job was somewhat more difficult due to the bright red color of the fall leaves.

The stander pointed out the trail he thought the deer used to leave the scene of the shooting. It was difficult to determine if the tracks they found were fresh or from earlier that morning. About eighty yards on, the trail turned almost

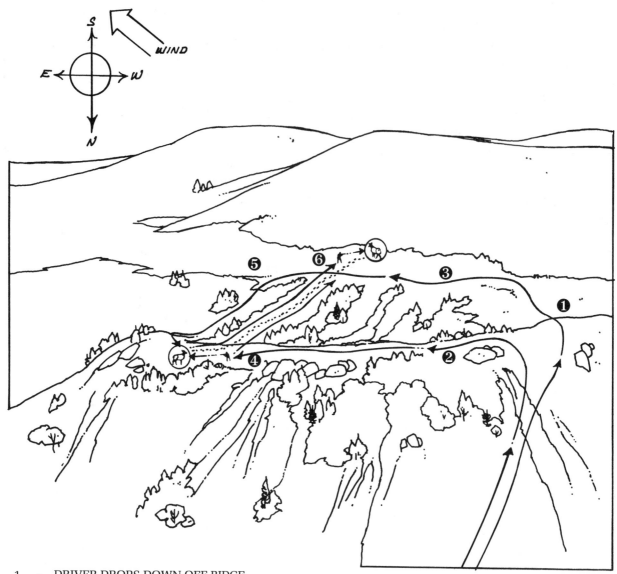

1 - DRIVER DROPS DOWN OFF RIDGE
2 - STANDER MOVES ALONG RIDGELINE
3 - DRIVER PUSHES THROUGH DRAWS
4 - STANDER FIRES, WOUNDS DEER
5 - DRIVER CLIMBS HILL TO HELP FIND DEER
6 - DRIVER AND STANDER TRACK DEER DOWNHILL AND KILL IT

straight down into a wooly patch of ground. There the driver found a teaspoon-size spot of blood. He had the stander wait at the sign while he circled through the brush.

As he circled, the deer jumped up and ran about a hundred feet before disappearing in the heavy brush again. Both men fired without visual effect.

The young hunter moved up to the spot where they were certain they had last seen the deer. The driver found the bed from which it had jumped. Approximately two coffee cups of dark red blood mixed with small bits of suet lay on the green wire grass. The driver was certain the deer would die, but perhaps not before they found it.

They were now about 150 yards below the

summit where the animal had been wounded. The driver walked down a little trail, again leaving stander as a marker. He did not see more blood, but a number of tracks were obvious in the dry powdery ground.

As he slowly walked along with the stander moving fifty yards to his rear, he saw a doe's head looking up from behind a fallen log. Without waiting even a second, he pulled his rifle up and shot the deer through the head. Range was no more than sixty yards. He did not want to chance the critter's running off again.

It was a huge doe, hit from left to right high in the right lung and out through the left kidney. Had the rifle been a bit more powerful, the first shot would have put the deer down at the summit. As it was, they were 350 yards down on the wrong side. An ancient logging road ran down the summit on which they might be able to bring in a truck.

The hunter sent his young companion back to the road for their truck. He field-dressed the deer and, with great effort, pulled it up the hill. His method was to walk two steps, stop, pull two feet, and walk again. The terrain was simply too steep and the deer too large to drag on a continuous basis.

The young hunter was able to get the truck back in on the logging road far enough that together they were able to drag the deer over the hill and down to the vehicle. Deer and hunters were in the truck ten minutes before dark at 5:30 P.M.

The old driver believed the hunt was successful because he knew the country, was able to get the deer out of hiding, and could, in general, direct the novice hunter into taking a stand in an almost correct position. Good tracking skills and techniques prevented the deer from being lost in the brush.

HUNT CHECKLIST

Weather
About 38°F with gray skies.

Terrain
Rolling to steeply rolling hills with elevation difference of 350 feet at times. Hills were covered with loblolly pine, poplar, scrub oak, and tulip. Greenbrier and honeysuckle covered the ground.

Wind Direction
Out of the northeast, steady at 4 to 6 knots.

Conditions Previous Day
Gentle, misty rain with afternoon temperatures of about 40°F.

How Hunter Moved
Down an old, gently twisting, mostly level logging road.

Clothes
Cotton work pants, flannel shirt, and lucky hunting vest. Rubber boot pacs.

Rifle Caliber and Scope
.243 bolt with 3-9X variable scope.

Sex of Deer
8-point (eastern count) buck.

Time of Day
Hunt started about 3:00 P.M. Buck was shot at about 4:30 P.M.

Length of Hunt
About 3 miles, spanning not more than 3 hours start to finish.

Length of Shot
About 38 paces.

How Deer Moved
Buck was making its round of scrapes spaced out along an old logging road. It ran on an angle behind hunter.

Skill of Hunter
Through the years, hunter had shot a great number of deer in various sections of the United States.

This case involves an experienced deer hunter who, having hunted over much of the United States, took the time to properly figure out some new country in which he found himself. It was only four months before the start of the deer season when he and his wife moved to the location in which he now wished to bag a deer.

Heavy, pasty, obnoxious red clay made up all but the top inch or two of the hills. In the wooded areas, an overlay of decomposed organic material and other recently deposited sticks, leaves, and trash made walking on the slick ground possible. The red, muddy ground was stacked up so steeply in places that removal of even a few trees caused immediate mud slumps in the valley below. Reliefs in the rolling to steeply rolling country varied from 200 to as much as 350 feet. There were a few internal valleys where the land smoothed into broad fertile flats of 20 to 80 acres.

Few real roads cut through the region. Those that did avoided the steeper hills, sticking in serpentlike fashion to the valley floors. Because these roads also concentrated water, those that were not paved were often impassable during the wet fall hunting season.

The hunter lived out in the remote country but worked in a nearby city. His employer allowed flexibility wherein he sometimes could slip away for scouting/hunting expeditions.

Several weeks prior to this hunt, the man had started the slow, methodical process of exploring the area around his house. He was an addicted deer hunter who could not have missed deer season even had he wanted to. He found the area to be covered with second- and third-growth mixed pine and hardwood. Virtually all of the pine was loblolly; hardwoods consisted of scrub oak, tulip, poplar, and some sweet gum. In places where hardwood groves dominated and the understory was thin, it was possible to see through the tangle up to one hundred yards in places. Greenbrier and honeysuckle comprised most of the underbrush. Leaves from the deciduous trees had mostly fallen to the forest floor. Only the perpetual dampness, which had turned the fallen leaves into a soggy, cushioned mat, made it possible to walk quietly in the woods.

Winds in the area generally blew gently out of the east to northeast, influenced by the high hills. As in any hilly terrain, easterly winds can be blowing out of the west ten minutes later. The hunter always tried to hunt into the winds, but he was often foiled by their squirrelly nature in the mountains.

During the hunter's scout, he found several recently "visited" deer scrapes in the area. It appeared to him as though a buck moved along an old, virtually overgrown logging road, stopping every two hundred yards or so to paw and snort. Tracks were abundant, suggesting that the critter worked back and forth on a regular basis. Its trail did not follow the old road with slavish consistency; rather, it weaved from side to side.

A gentle, steady, almost mistlike rain fell over the country the previous day. This was damp, wet country; light rains could be expected at least two or three days a week. Winds that day held steady out of the northeast at a relatively benign four to five knots. Having considered all of the factors, the hunter correctly concluded that conditions were ideal for a lone stalk. He planned accordingly, working through lunch and then leaving his desk at about 1:30 P.M.

At home, he jumped into an old pair of cotton work pants, an old flannel shirt, his lucky cotton hunting vest, and rubber pacs with cleated soles. Temperatures were almost up in the forties, with continued gray, overcast skies. There was no sign of an immediate return of the drizzle.

He took his .243 bolt-action rifle with 3-9X variable scope. His vest contained a length of rope, matches, a compass, and the remainder of a box of ammo. Inadvertently, he left without a knife of any kind.

The hunter double-timed down the four hundred yards of blacktop to a place where a graveled county road took off at a thirty-degree angle. Continuing on with his brisk pace, he marched another five hundred yards down the gravel. By the time he got to the obscure, almost overgrown logging road, it was about 3:00 P.M. Full dark, he reckoned, would arrive about 6:00 P.M.

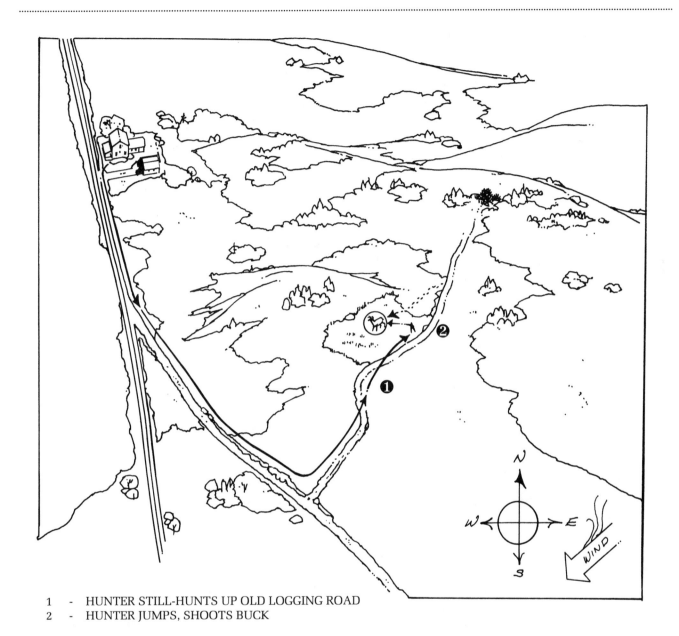

1 - HUNTER STILL-HUNTS UP OLD LOGGING ROAD
2 - HUNTER JUMPS, SHOOTS BUCK

At the old logging road, the hunter dropped his pace back considerably. After being sure the winds were basically in his face, he moved up the grass- and leaf-covered path with extreme caution. Overhanging trees and brush sometimes blocked his way but, swiveling at the hips, he was able to glide around these obstacles.

He maintained a hundred-yard sight distance. At times the barren brush obscured his view, but in general he was satisfied with the scope of things. An abundance of recent sign encouraged him. He noted with satisfaction that most of the scrapes had been worked recently.

He continued on, moving slowly and cautiously for about an hour, traveling half a mile or so. His path twisted and turned, avoiding high hills. Soon he passed into a semiopen area inhabited by a stand of eight- to ten-inch timber with tall, brushy tops and barren, postlike trunks. Pine trees, understory, and other visual impediments were minimal. New, green wire grass grew in abundance in a low, swampy area to the left of the path.

Cautiously, the hunter stalked a few feet at a time. Suddenly he heard a snort and then the muscular pounding of hooves against the dense, wet ground. To his left he caught a brief glimpse of a big-bodied whitetail running through the trees. Apparently it had been feeding on the new grass when the hunter came up on it. After looking for an instant, the hunter realized it was a large buck with an excellent rack.

He threw up his rifle, starting the process of locating a clear area through the woods wherein he could get a good shot. By reflex, he tracked the buck through his scope as it ran, mostly parallel to him but quartering away slightly. The deer was running with the wind. Had the buck continued, it would have run behind the hunter and into the deep woods.

As soon as the crosshairs passed the buck's head, the hunter concluded that he had an opening. He touched off a round reflexively, reinforced by his many years of bird hunting.

The buck threw its massive head to the right, then went down, pitching end over end into a heap on the ground. It was hit with the .243 round at the extreme base of the neck where it connected to the skull. A huge, ugly tear marked the spot where the round struck. There was no exit hole; the bullet broke up on the critter's heavy neck bone. Range from hunter to buck stepped off at thirty-eight paces.

The buck's neck, swollen from the rut, was now badly bloodshot. By the time the hunter walked the few feet in from the path to the critter, it was glassy-eyed. The hunter realized that he could not make soup from the neck bones as he usually did because of the shock damage.

He now had a beautiful, large, eight-point buck on the ground, but no knife with which to field-dress it. The time was now about 4:30 P.M. The successful hunter contemplated his situation for only a few moments. After pulling the deer forty yards to the old logging road, he took off at a speedy, measured pace for his house.

At his house he found his wife recently returned from work. She threw on an old set of coveralls and rubber boots and came with him to help with the kill. He grabbed a common kitchen knife and stone with which to dress the critter. They drove to within three hundred yards of the downed buck before fallen logs, deep puddles, and brushy undergrowth stopped their four-wheel-drive truck.

Later, they weighed the deer with entrails gone but head remaining. It was a hefty 170 pounds, which would have required an excruciating pack had the relatively flat logging road not been there. By 5:30 P.M. they were able to hang the buck in their garage.

The pair finished skinning and caping the critter by full dark. The hunter was uncertain if this was the only buck using the many scrapes he observed, but it probably was, as he saw no other deer that day.

Success, the hunter believes, was due almost entirely to his taking the time to scout the country thoroughly. He was willing to drop everything when field conditions were ideal and to hunt slowly and meticulously. When the time came, abundant practice with a shotgun made it possible for him to hit a deer moving under adverse circumstances. Leaving his knife at home may have been, his wife believes, a subconscious ploy on his part to enlist her aid in getting a large, cumbersome critter out of the woods.

HUNT CHECKLIST

Weather

Very cold to bitter. Temperature of 18°F.

Terrain

Single high mountain covered by Douglas fir and ponderosa pine, with an understory of huckleberry, snowberry, and ninebark.

Wind Direction

Dead calm.

Conditions Previous Day

Snowy and cold with 8 inches or more of accumulated snow. Temperatures were falling.

How Hunters Moved

Took skid roads contouring around the mountain, spreading out about 200 yards apart.

Clothes

Wool pants, shirts, and jackets, not so much for quiet as for warmth.

Rifle Caliber and Scope

.270 with 4X scope, .300 Winchester Magnum with 4X scope. The deer was killed with a .338 with a 6X scope.

Sex of Deer

Huge 5-point (western count) forest mule deer.

Time of Day

Deer was killed about 7:45 A.M.

Length of Hunt

About 3 hours, including the pack out.

Length of Shot

About 150 yards, perhaps more.

How Deer Moved

Deer was pushed out of heavy cover by hunter farthest down in the drive, coming into view of the center man, who got it sneaking through the trees.

Skill of Hunters

Three young hunters who had killed numerous deer and were aided by large amounts of energy and enthusiasm.

Hunters living in parts of the intermountain west claim that a subspecies of mammoth forest mule deer exists in the remote mountains. Most wildlife management biologists question the existence of such animals despite persistent reports from hunters and packers who claim to have brought them out. The mule deer, these people say, are dark brown to almost black and are characterized by relatively lighter horns and truly incredible size. Packers claim that they have to cut even the does in half before a horse can pack them.

This case involves three experienced men who, although in their early thirties, had killed twenty or more deer each. In addition to their skill, they were assisted immeasurably by youthful energy and enthusiasm.

The hunting ground, in this instance, was about forty miles from their home. It was comprised of a series of single but sometimes interlocking, relatively high mountains. Reliefs in the area definitely suggested mountains. Differences in elevation often reached eight hundred to a thousand feet top to bottom.

Thick stands of second- and third-growth ponderosa pine, Douglas fir, and larch covered most of the mountain. Only a few grassy open spots existed on the well-lit portions of the slopes. Deep north-facing draws running finger-like off the top were choked with dog-hair cedar. Neither man nor beast larger than a coyote could squeeze through these wilderness deserts. Dense stands of snow brush, ninebark, and huckleberry made up the understory.

Ongoing logging operations on the mountain were harvesting second- and third-growth saw logs. As a result, game proliferated on the fringe areas, grass grew on the roads, and hunters had access into areas they could not otherwise reach. Removing the larger trees made it possible for hunters to see game out to two hundred yards or more in some cases.

Weather in the mountains had been snowy and cold throughout the previous week. When the hunters left their homes, it was 18°F, which was, accurately, predicted as the high for the mountains. About eight inches of crunchy, older snow covered the ground except under bushy pines. There were no leaves remaining on the few broadleaf trees and bushes.

A few poorly maintained dirt roads led into the mountain area. Snow was plowed from them only when logging companies wanted to move their cut. These roads often were churned up until they were syrupy, axle-deep mud. Hard frosts sometimes improved the roads slightly so that it was possible to get a common four-wheel-drive vehicle through to the hunting territory.

Sunup that time of year came about 6:30 A.M. The three hunters departed their homes at 5:00 A.M. for the hour drive into the mountains. At the pulloff into the hunting area, they found that it was sufficiently cold for crunching snow to be a serious impediment. Deer, they reasoned, could hear them walking for a hundred yards.

All wore heavy wool pants, jackets, and shirts. Their boots were insulated rubber and leather pacs. Upon leaving home, they had no good idea how the winds would be moving in the mountains, but they found winds at Sand Mountain, their hunting site, to be at a dead, cold calm. Frozen puffs of breath hung in midair like filmy curtains.

Their road made a sharp left-hand turn at the pulloff area. It was as close to Sand Mountain as they were going to get by vehicle.

After parking the truck, they exercised their rifle bolts in the cold, making sure they were functional. They carried a .300 Winchester Magnum, a .270, and a .338, all with either 4X or 6X scopes.

The trio found that they were favored by the lack of wind movement. They were able to hunt in any direction that seemed best. On the other hand, the crunching snow suggested that they would have to see and shoot any deer at a distance before their walking noises spooked the critters.

The three men walked single file through a fifty-yard band of standing timber along the road. They climbed sharply uphill into areas that had been intermittently logged and passed by the previous fall. Numerous pine boughs, treetops, and other leavings "swamped" off the saw logs littered the ground.

It was extremely helpful that a great number of small skid roads paralleled the side of the steep mountain. The three men spread out about two hundred yards apart and walked on the roads. They could see each other briefly at times, but as rapidly as they identified their partners' positions they came to a patch of standing timber and disappeared therein. At the edge of some clear-cuts, vine maple grew in such profusion that the gray mass of branches also hid the hunters from each other.

Their general plan was to keep moving clockwise around the mountain, hunting till dark at 4:30 P.M. if necessary. Had they hunted the entire day, they might have run out of territory. However, Sand Mountain stood another five hundred feet above them. They could have circled completely round and then moved uphill for another circuit, but it was big country, pretty much incapable of being hunted out by three men in one day. A few other hunters worked the general area, but the men would have been surprised to encounter them on that specific mountain that day.

Part of the reason they picked this mountain was that the chances of seeing another group of hunters in such a remote place was slim to non-existent midpoint in the season, when weather in the area was generally so severe and unforgiving. Hunters in these mountains sometimes found their vehicles snowed in to the extent that they were forced to wait till early spring four months later to get them out.

As they contoured along the skid roads, hunter two in the middle saw three deer running along a trail above his position. One other skid road lay between him and the deer road. Because the snow was so noisy, he decided to move up two roads in hopes of seeing the whitetails from above, as it would be much easier for him to see down into the bare timber from higher on the mountain. He did not know for sure where his friend above would be coming through, but he suspected that the man was much higher on the mountain, and that his move would not be a problem.

Because the country was very steep, it took the middle hunter several minutes to fight his way uphill over fallen, rotten logs and tangled treetops. Upon reaching the second skid road, he walked till he located three sets of fresh deer tracks. Later on, he puzzled over the fact that they were whitetail tracks rather than muleys.

The hunter followed the tracks along the road, keeping far to the outside and trying to be alert ahead as well as downhill. He saw no movement ahead, but below he caught a glimpse of something dark and large moving through the bare tree trunks. By reflex he puffed into the still air, looking for any change in wind movement. Through his 6X scope he could make out a huge buck with an equally large rack that seemed much lighter in color than the critter itself. Its horns lay resting comfortably on its back as it skillfully squirmed through the heavy brush and timber at the edge of the cut.

The hunter searched around frantically for something on which to rest his rifle for a shot. He found two eight-inch ponderosa pines down off the skid trail about fifteen feet. Initially he was reluctant to climb down due to the possible noise and because he might have dropped down out of sight distance of the buck, but he went ahead anyway, making his way to the tree destined to be his rifle rest. Fortunately he did not slip on the snow, crack a stick, or otherwise give his presence away.

At the tree he found a clear area through the timber and past the path along which the buck was moving rapidly. The hunter estimated that it was about 150 yards to the target.

He placed the crosshairs on the opening. The instant he saw hair on the right side of the scope, he pulled the trigger. Recoil from the .338 destroyed his sight picture for a moment.

On steadying his rifle, he thought he could see a large dark mound on the white forest floor. He clambered downhill with as much dispatch as the slippery snow-covered logs would allow. At the bottom he found a huge mule deer buck lying with a shot through its heart and lungs and a fist-sized chunk blown out the right side. It fell behind an ancient root clump that hid the critter to some extent.

The hunter attempted to pull the deer round

1   -   HUNTERS CONTOUR AROUND MOUNTAIN ALONG SKID ROADS
2   -   MIDDLE HUNTER CLIMBS TWO ROADS
3   -   HUNTER SHOOTS BUCK

so that its head was uphill, but it was so large that he was not really able to move it. In a few moments, his friend came down from above. They were able to slide the animal around so that it could be field-dressed. They estimated its weight, based on the many whitetails they had shot, at between 340 and 360 pounds. It had a massive swollen neck and a fine five-point rack.

They hollered occasionally as they gutted the deer till the third man came through. Being the lower guy, he reckoned he moved the deer out of its bed along the side of the mountain to the place where the middle hunter got his shot. The going was tough for him because of the thick, tangled brush.

By pulling together, they were able to get the somewhat lightened field-dressed buck up onto a skid road two hundred feet away. Fortunately the road was both snow-covered and sloping downhill toward the truck. In spite of these advantages, it took two men pulling on the horns together about thirty minutes to get the deer back to the main road. They took turns, two pulling while one carried the rifles.

It was about 8:40 A.M. when they loaded the deer into the truck. As best as they could calculate, the shot was made at 7:45 A.M. The buck weighed right at three hundred pounds on their perhaps inaccurate spring scales at home. The bitter cold plus the strenuous physical work had completely snapped their strength.

The hunters attributed their success to the wind and snow conditions being proper, a hunting plan that was appropriate under the conditions they faced, and the fact that the man with the big rifle knew how to get a round through heavy timber in an effective manner, killing a deer that probably figured it was sneaking away safely.

HUNT CHECKLIST

Weather
Warm and dry, about 45°F during the day, dropping to 35°F at night.

Terrain
Single, large 1,200-acre tree-covered hill with ancient apple orchard on one side. Rolling farmland surrounded hill.

Wind Direction
Out of the northwest, 8 to 10 knots.

Conditions Previous Day
Warm and dry, early fall weather. Little change.

How Hunters Moved
They took a long, circuitous route over the hill to be able to hunt into the prevailing wind. At the orchard they spread out about 50 yards, still-hunting the area.

Clothes
Light cotton pants, shirts, and jackets. Vietnam jungle boots.

Rifle Caliber and Scope
She carried a .308 backpack rifle with 6X scope. He carried an old .25-20 lever-action with open sights.

Sex of Deer
3-year-old doe.

Time of Day
Hunters started walking at about 2:00 P.M. Deer was shot at about 4:30 P.M.

Length of Hunt
About 3 1/2 hours, including a long pack to the pickup.

Length of Shot
Short range, estimated at about 30 yards.

How Deer Moved
Two deer were jumped above and to the side of uphill hunter. They ran ahead and circled back with the wind into lower hunter.

Skill of Hunters
He hunted over this country often and had killed numerous deer in the past. She hunted some, bagging deer by herself and with others.

At times, deer hunters go to great extremes to make current conditions, with which they must contend, work for them. In the process, they may expend huge amounts of energy, but they also usually get their deer.

Of the adverse conditions that can be mitigated by vast amounts of intelligently applied energy, wind direction must top the list—that is, it isn't possible to change the wind, but it is almost always possible to change the direction from which one hunts the wind. In this case, two hunters climbed over a high hill that was virtually a mountain so that they could hunt into the wind.

This situation involves an extremely able, experienced deer hunter who took his nineteen-year-old daughter out in some excellent whitetail territory with the intention of showing her some shootable deer. She had already killed several deer in the past, both hunting with her father and still-hunting alone. She was far from a novice deer hunter.

Their targeted territory was an extremely high domelike hill set back from the nearest country road about three miles. The sometimes craggy hill was covered with thin volcanic soil over at least two-thirds of its area. It rose up 800 feet from the gently rolling agricultural land surrounding it, comprising some 1,200 acres or more.

The only agricultural purpose for the hill was to produce timber. Up until the early 1950s, cattle had been grazed on the land, but even that activity had been curtailed. Most of the more level land surrounding the hill was farmed for wheat, barley, peas, or oats.

Cover on the hill was mostly ponderosa pine, red fir, and poplar. The understory was tall grass, snowberry, and ninebark as well as some heavy stands of blackberry. Excellent, lush stands of wild prairie grass grew on the relatively open west side of the hill and in the clearings wherever the evergreens and ninebark did not dominate.

Early settlers in the region had speculated that apple trees might grow and produce well there. As a result they planted scores of trees in widely spaced rows on the hillside. The original planters were now gone, but their trees lived on in a wild, unruly manner. Many were gnarled and thick,

growing in tangles of live and dead branches. Some of the trees no longer kept their original boundaries. Volunteers had sprung up by the hundreds, spawned no doubt from the randomly dropped fruit.

To an extent the wild grass and the wild apple trees coexisted in the same place. As a result, sight distances were often one hundred yards or more. In other areas of heavy timber, visibility was usually thirty yards or less.

Because of the cover, grass, and apples, large numbers of whitetail deer inhabited the region, though not many actually lived in the orchard. During the day they bedded in the heavy cover, and toward evening or in the early morning they were drawn to the grass and apples. Deer trails cut through the orchard region as if an engineer laid them out to provide maximum coverage.

Early in the season, the father had walked the three miles back into the wild orchard to determine if a crop of apples had been produced and if the deer were coming in to eat them. It was a valid and necessary scouting expedition—Mother Nature produced apples in these wild, unkempt trees only every third or fourth year.

As it turned out, the long hike in was well worth the time and effort—he found signs both of abundant apples and deer. Because it was relatively early in the season, few apples had fallen from the trees. Deer by the dozens came in under the trees, trying to reach the almost ripe fruit. Later, when hard frosts knocked them off and the grass got old and dry, deer would be in the area by the score. Now it seemed as if they came only in representative numbers to keep track of the orchard.

It was an absolutely delightful 45°F when the two finally coordinated their schedules for a hunt. Fleecy, scattered white clouds dotted the sky. It had been similarly warm and pleasant the entire previous week. As a result, they wore light cotton jackets and shirts. Their boots were the Vietnam jungle variety, ideal for hiking through relatively dry, steep country.

They parked their pickup on a gravel road at about two in the afternoon. They expected sundown at about 5:30 P.M. The best hunting, the father concluded, would start at about 4:00 P.M. or later. Because of the relatively long days, he believed that thirsty, hungry deer often came out before dark to eat and drink.

She carried a cut-down backpack .308 bolt-action with 6X scope. He used an ancient lever-action .25-20 that had been in the family for years. The rifle had been used to kill numerous deer.

After parking their truck, the pair discovered that winds were coming into the targeted hunting area from the northwest at eight to ten knots. Their most direct route into the apple orchard would have put them mostly upwind of the deer, blowing their scent directly into the heavy cover from which they hoped to push a deer. As a result, they concluded that since the wind was wrong, their only alternative was to bite the bullet and hike up over the top of the hill, coming in from the south and into the wind. They were faced with a minimum 3 1/2-mile hike up over about eight hundred feet of relief from the road.

Even on a relatively warm, pleasant fall afternoon, hiking over a high hill can be a chore. The pair got to the top about 3:30 P.M. They sat and rested for a while, discussing hunting strategies in subdued tones as the sun sunk slowly. By the time they started again, temperatures were dropping and the lengthening shadows provided some cover.

About two-thirds of the way back downhill, they turned sharply right, moving directly into the freshening, cool breeze. They passed through some tall pines and then a difficult patch of blackberry bushes. Distance between the two was little more than fifty yards. Their strategy was to stay within sight of one another, still-hunting the orchard. Occasionally they lost sight of each other as the bushy apple trees and the random pine obscured their vision. Wild grass in the area hid the hunters from the waist down.

They slowly moved through the orchard for twenty minutes or so. Without warning, the daughter—who was uphill—jumped two large does. She remembers that the brush and grass made a swishing noise as they ran and that their pounding hooves sounded much like horses.

The deer came from thirty-five to fifty yards

to her right, starting at the edge of the orchard. They ran ahead sixty to eighty yards and then started to circle back on a path that would take them right back to her father below. She heard them long after they disappeared from view.

She snapped her fingers twice as a signal to her father, who saw or heard nothing but her signal. He froze dead still, trying to determine what it was that caused her alarm. At that time he could not see her.

As he stood absolutely still in the lengthening shadows, he detected "something" chocolate brown moving ahead. It came round an apple tree toward and a little below him to his left at a range of about eighty yards. In one fluid motion he tilted his hat, the crown of which carried a few old, dried pine needles. They fell off the hat, blowing back behind him. Winds were still perfect. Again he saw some slow, cautious movement ahead of him, this time close enough that he was sure it was a deer. At that time, he was not aware that she had jumped them.

The hunter inched forward slowly and methodically. After ten feet both hunter and deer stopped moving. He still could not see his partner. He wanted her to get the shot, but he brought his rifle up slowly and carefully, cocking the hammer as it came. The deer acted as though it did not hear the soft metallic click. If it showed any reaction, it was curiousity toward either the man or the clicking sound. Slowly and deliberately, it stepped between two apple trees, put its head up in the air, and swiveled its ears forward.

Obviously it was trying to hear or smell whatever was ahead. The deer may also have been trying to locate the hunter that had jumped it from above. It was trying to circle the first hunter but probably had no idea there were two people in the orchard.

As soon as the deer jumped, the daughter stopped dead still, waiting to see where they ran. They were quickly out of her sight, but she heard them crashing brush and grass a moment longer. It was silent, then the noise returned. She knew whitetails often circle and figured they were now trying that strategy. Far ahead, perhaps one hundred yards, she saw the top half of a deer looking about.

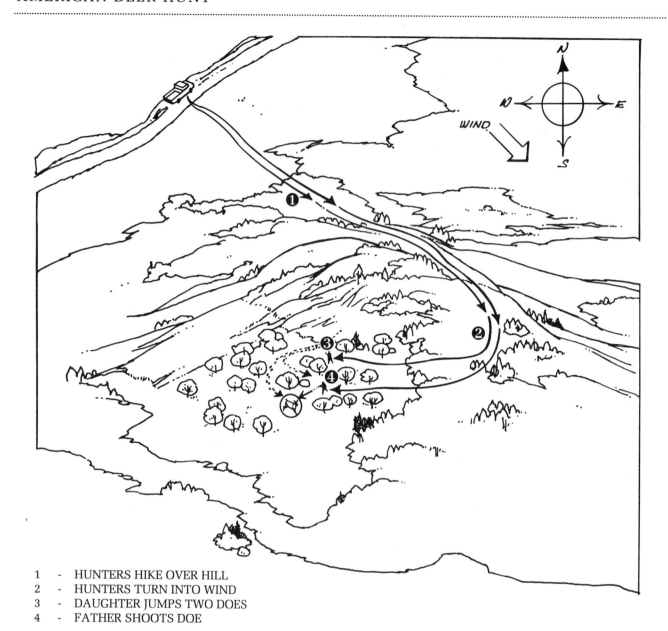

1 - HUNTERS HIKE OVER HILL
2 - HUNTERS TURN INTO WIND
3 - DAUGHTER JUMPS TWO DOES
4 - FATHER SHOOTS DOE

Below, her father watched his deer intently, unaware that she also had one in sight. His deer stepped ahead again, shortening the range to thirty yards or less. He placed the front bead about two inches above the top of the deer's head and waited till the weight of the long-barrelled rifle began to take its toll. Carefully, he steadied and squeezed.

At the shot, the deer in front of his daughter bolted uphill. His deer fell in its tracks.

He quickly ran over to the downed deer. It had taken a hit in the center of its skull just above the eyes. He pulled out his hunting knife as he jumped on the deer. It was already showing signs of reviving from the shock, but the hunter quickly sliced the animal's throat and rolled off to let it thrash around.

His daughter, thinking he had shot at and missed the deer she had sighted, trotted down the hill to determine the source of all the commotion. He whistled softly several times to direct her in to the kill. They were done hunting, but they did not want to call attention to their situation in front of other hunters that may have been in the area.

It was dark by the time they got organized and had field-dressed the critter. Shadows at the base of the hill, even in the short brush and scrub, were long and converging. He buttonholed the deer, hoisting it to his shoulders for the long pack out. Both agreed it was fortuitous that they did not both shoot deer and that they did not have to cross over the top of the giant hill on their way back to the truck.

It was well after dark when they reached the road. At home they weighed the field-dressed deer. On the pack out his estimate was 140 pounds, but sans head, feet, and entrails it weighed just 97 pounds.

They attributed their success to good scouting, knowledge of the country, and their willingness to do the tough hunt by climbing over the hill and swinging around so the wind was in their faces. It helped that they still-hunted very carefully and that she knew when to stop and how the deer might try to escape. He believes he could never have taken the deer with his small rifle had he not let the doe get as close as it did. His quick reaction when it was knocked down allowed him to keep it down.

HUNT CHECKLIST

Weather
Temperatures in the low 20s with a foot or more of fluffy new snow on the ground.

Terrain
Rolling hills and large fields intermixed with wooded patches. Low, swampy areas mixed in with woods. Hunted woods was 1,500 acres with a mile-long, 200-yard-wide strip attached.

Wind Direction
Brisk and cold winds out of the west at 10 to 12 knots.

Conditions Previous Day
Cold and snowy.

How Hunters Moved
Four hunters pushed through 3-mile-long woods and saw nothing. Put out a stander in the wooded peninsula and redrove in a hook pattern into the strip.

Clothes
Wool everything plus heavy insulated boot pacs.

Rifle Caliber and Scope
Successful hunter used a .308 bolt-action with 4X scope.

Sex of Deer
4-point (western count) whitetail buck.

Time of Day
Hunt started at daybreak, or about 6:45 A.M. It was about 9:15 A.M. when whitetail was shot.

Length of Hunt
About 3 hours start to finish. They did two drives and then several unsuccessful drives later.

Length of Shot
40 yards.

How Deer Moved
Came from south, crossing toward stander. When it turned straight toward him, it was too late for the buck to change directions again.

Skill of Hunters
All were skilled and experienced. Stander knew the country well and was a good shot.

several skilled, experienced hunters often got together for a number of late-season whitetail drives. Through the years these large drives had become something of a rite of winter for members of the group. There were up to fourteen men who hunted together, but because of jobs, duties, and general scheduling problems, they seldom could all make it for every hunt. They would announce the time for the next hunt and adjust their plans according to who showed up that morning.

Every man in the group had killed numerous deer. Each knew the country well, could walk all day, and could—without compromise or excuse—hold up their end of virtually any plan. They hunted every Saturday during the season and at least one day during the week.

Their rule was that each hunter kept what he shot unless that hunter had already used his tag. If a problem existed with their system, it related to the fact that it took a minimum number of bodies to run the grand drives they planned. If too few showed up, they were unable to handle some wooded areas they knew would be productive.

The gently rolling country over which they hunted was farmed and open, but large patches of fairly dense woods also dotted the region. Any roads in the area followed the major drainages, avoiding the higher hills. The sparse population kept the number of roads to a minimum. Often, two- to three-hundred-acre lots of woods were accessible only after a hike of a mile or two from the road.

Timber in the region was composed of mixed pine and fir with occasional stands of poplar and maple. Where creeks and gullies cut through the land, dense stands of cedar grew. Low, swampy, poorly drained areas were soft and slushy under the snow. These were not navigable by hunters or hunted—deer seldom ran through the swamps even when pushed by skilled drivers.

About a foot of puffy, new snow covered the region they intended to hunt. Winds blew steadily out of the west at a chilly ten to twelve knots. Temperatures hovered in the low twenties but were intensified by the incessant winds. It was a day when experienced hunters wanted to drive rather than stand. Wind-driven snow quickly

filled new tracks. Those with any age at all were obscured, creating a situation where everyone was an excellent tracker—if they spotted a track, it had to be fresh!

Farmed fields surrounded the woodlot that they had selected to drive that day. It was a fairly compact piece of country—about two miles long and a mile wide—but, because of the heavy understory, twelve drivers working against four standers would not have been too many. As the participants recalled, the major deterrent to the hunt, other than the large area that each driver was responsible for, was a long, thin neck of woods extending west toward other woodlots nearby. This section of woods was more a large fencerow about a mile long and perhaps two hundred yards wide at its greatest. It was separated from the targeted woods by a low, marshy area about thirty yards wide.

The six hunters who showed up were enough to make a credible drive through the country they had selected. Four men started out immediately from their truck. They had to walk approximately three-quarters of a mile till they reached the targeted woodlot. They hurried as much as possible so as not to find the standers frozen stiff when they finally came through.

Two standers drove their trucks around three miles to the opposite side of the patch. They had more than a mile to walk in off the road to their agreed-upon positions.

After waiting about fifteen minutes for the standers to get into position, the four drivers plunged from the fields of wheat stubble into the woods. Winds continued out of the west. They spread out as evenly as possible in the sometimes dense cover. Visibility ranged from forty to two hundred yards. In times past when they had taken inexperienced hunters on this drive, they became so thoroughly disoriented that they turned around and came out where they started.

Each driver knew he had to line out his direction, stop often, walk backward, and generally work out the brushy areas in a most professional manner. During past drives they had bounced deer from one to another before the critters were sufficiently spooked to run to the standers at the far end. The drivers often were shooters as well, so constant alertness was necessary.

On the far end, the standers knew from past experience that their best alternative was to get well into the cover and take up a position on an old logging road, natural opening, or grassy hillside. In all cases they were one hundred yards or more from the edge of the field to their stands.

The now shivering standers were in their positions well before full light. Drivers were at the edge of the woods at first light. Full daylight came at 6:45 A.M.

It took the drivers about 1 1/2 hours to get through the three miles of woods. This push surely tested the resolution of the standers. Although everyone wore heavy wool pants, shirts, and jackets and insulated rubber boot pacs, it was difficult to keep warm without some movement.

No one saw a deer on the first drive, but all agreed that fresh sign in the snow suggested that there were a great number of deer around. In some places, deep paths were cut through the snow, indicating that numerous critters were using the same trails time after time. In other places, snow was raked from the top of the grass and clover growing in sheltered areas in the woods. The deer were there—they had simply failed to get them out.

The six discussed their situation and concluded that four drivers were insufficient to get deer out of heavy cover on such a vile, raw day. Their first alternate plan was to send two warm drivers through to the south side and simply turn the drive around, rerunning it in the other direction. This idea earned instant scorn in the ranks. They needed to find some smaller patches, the troops suggested. "We can't ask standers to wait almost two hours for drivers to come through these large woods," they said.

The compromise they crafted involved sending one stander around to the long strip of woods leading west to the road. The rest intended to drive in a hook through the woods leading into the peninsula. Then they would send two men to the road and drive the piece again to its end.

One of the hunters was aware of a small, open, meadowlike spot in the strip just to the west of the swampy area. He thought a deer might cross the swamp into the strip, coming into the opening where he could get a shot.

Winds were wrong for the drive, but the men decided to try it anyway. Their feeling was that if the hunt didn't work, they could continue on through the strip to some smaller wooded areas across the road to the west.

The drivers again stamped snow for fifteen minutes while the stander walked about a mile across an open pasture to his position in the peninsula.

Driving in this instance was extremely complex. The men were to make a giant J through the woods, wrapping around to the west strip where it joined the main patch. Each person had to navigate from his own experience. They could never see far enough ahead to know their exact route.

The drivers on the far east had the farthest to walk. Their route probably comprised a mile and a half or more. The three inner men had less distance to travel, but they had to do it correctly or they would all be crossed up. Each man reasoned that they could bounce a deer back and forth between them if they did it right.

They held out little real hope for the lone stander, who was going to be in the wrong place under the wrong conditions. This was a drive that only the well-seasoned hunter could understand, much less participate in.

The stander reached his position in the strip well before the drive started again. It was now about 9:00 A.M. As planned, he took up his spot uphill from the little opening. He was pleased to note that several beat-down trails crossed the opening in front of him. Much to his consternation, however, the cold winds were absolutely wrong, blowing from his back and into the clearing.

The stander positioned himself close in, almost under an old yellow ponderosa pine. Snow fallen from the boughs had piled up in front in fortlike fashion. He was completely hidden from the thighs on down, and mostly hidden by branches from there on up. He waited quietly for about twenty minutes until he plainly saw a dark gray deer streaking toward him up the hill from below. It came angling from the south and evi-

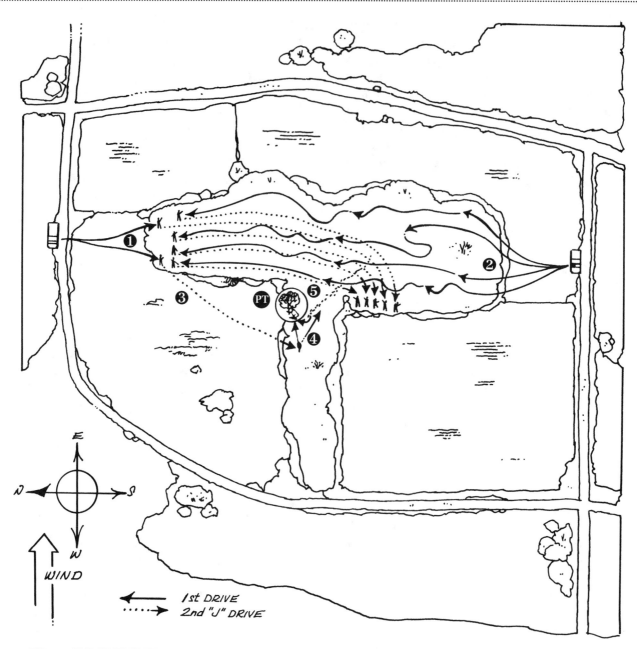

PT - OLD PINE TREE
1 - STANDERS TAKE UP POSITION
2 - DRIVERS START FIRST DRIVE
3 - AFTER FIRST DRIVE, ONE MAN GOES ON STAND IN
     WOODED STRIP WHILE OTHERS PERFORM "J" DRIVE
4 - STANDER TAKES TWO SHOTS AT RUNNING BUCK
5 - BUCK RUNS INTO PINE TREE

dently had not yet winded him. He brought his .308 bolt with 4X scope to his shoulder.

As he did, the four-point whitetail buck came bounding up the little rise. It continued across the clearing in the direction of a large fallen pine. At the pine the buck bounded into the air. The hunter tracked it through his scope. It was not a terribly difficult shot because the deer was coming almost straight toward him. It was, however, classic because of the deer's great leap over the fallen tree.

Instinctively the hunter fired at the deer in midair. Perhaps it was the shot, or maybe the buck finally winded the man, because on coming back to earth, it immediately switched directions, running almost directly away from him. He bolted another round and fired a second time.

It appeared that this second shot had no more effect that the first. The buck continued running briskly until it collided headlong with a huge, old pine. The shooter initially believed his shots confused the deer, causing it to run into the tree.

After a bit he spotted a large red mark on the snow where he had first fired. Upon detailed examination, the stander was amazed to discover that very little had gone the way he initially thought it had. Round one, fired in mid-jump at about forty yards, hit the buck squarely in the brisket. The round passed up almost the entire length of the deer, lodging against its rear ham. It took off the top of the heart, puncturing the diaphragm and stomach on its passage through the critter. It was a dead deer at that point, but the critter didn't know it yet.

The second round fired from behind at the running deer scraped along its left flank, cutting a furrow in the skin to the bulging shoulder muscle, where it deflected, taking out a thumb-sized chunk of muscle. Running into the tree stopped the deer cold, but it was not the ultimate cause of its demise.

It was only a few minutes before all of the drivers had assembled to admire the deer. Four of them had been within three hundred yards of the animal when the shooter made the kill. They estimated the buck was in the 185-pound range field-dressed but with head intact. Working together, they pulled it out to a field and then the three-quarter mile across country to the road. Slick, cold snow made skidding the big buck a bit easier.

It was still early enough to run additional drives. These were true addict-type deer hunters. After stashing the buck at the road, they ran three patches of cover to the west of the little strip where the kill was made, but they found that as the day wore on, the whitetails lay even tighter in their beds.

They eventually flushed out a doe from a previously driven area. When the deer broke cover, it was three to four hundred yards away and leaving fast. Three of them tried long shots, spoiling the drive they were working and wasting precious time tracking the deer to see if it was hit. Other than the one buck, they were unable to put it together that day.

The successful hunter attributed his success to knowing the country and to having excellent, hard-working, knowledgeable drivers. The fact that the buck came across wind until it was too late also helped, as was the hunter's ability to hit a running target.

CHAPTER 21
SPECIAL TAG

HUNT CHECKLIST

Weather

Crisp, cool, and dry. Temperatures ranging from 30°F during the early morning to 45°F at midday.

Terrain

Steep, basaltic canyons with slopes sometimes covered with a thin layer of soil. Pine trees grew among chaparral brush, sumac, and blackberry. Very rugged country with limited road access.

Wind Direction

Out of the west, 8 to 10 knots.

Conditions Previous Day

Early- to mid-fall conditions prevailed, with no real change.

How Hunters Moved

On a line up deep canyon slope, down a ridgeline, then back to their vehicle, from which they shot the deer up the trail.

Clothes

Several layers of cotton pants and shirts, high leather rattlesnake-proof boots.

Rifle Caliber and Scope

.270 bolt-action with 3-9X variable scope.

Sex of Deer

Mule deer doe.

Time of Day

About 10:30 A.M.

Length of Hunt

Hunters started walking at 6:30 A.M. and shot the deer at 10:30 A.M.

Length of Shot

60 to 70 yards.

How Deer Moved

Two mule deer ran up out of a shallow, partly tree-covered draw. Shooter got one through the brush from a jeep trail.

Skill of Hunters

As a logger, he had spent several months working in the area. He and his wife were proven deer hunters on their home territory.

Not all successful deer hunts, as this case will illustrate, are well-thought-through contests wherein the hunter pits his superior intellect against the native instincts of the deer. This is true despite the large amounts of planning, replanning, and analysis that go into hunts. Successful hunters assume that, at times, all of the cerebral power in the world will have little to do with the final outcome of a hunt. Like missing an easy standing shot at a huge six-point buck, it often happens in real life—more often than most hunters ever care to admit.

This hunt really got its start in early spring when a rural couple decided to apply for an extra deer tag in a special drawing. If they won the lottery, it would allow them to shoot a deer outside their usual hunting territory at no penalty vis-à-vis their regular deer tags.

He was an avid deer hunter who kept his voracious family of teenagers fed on venison and elk. She often ventured out in the field on especially nice or especially vile days just for the sheer enjoyment of being out in the woods. She had killed a number of deer but preferred to do so close to home.

The state in which the couple resided occasionally offered special mule deer doe tags to the first 150 or so hunters who applied, good in a hunting area about 110 miles from their home. It was a device used by the state Fish and Game Commission (F&G) to thin out populations of less desirable animals. The tag allowed holders to take two deer that year in addition to what their regular deer tags allowed. It was this two-deer proviso, along with some hungry teenage boys at home, that enticed the man into ranging out of his regular territory.

To mitigate his uncertainty about hunting over entirely new country, he located a neighbor who at one time had worked as a logger in that region. The logger spoke glowingly of the many deer one could encounter there, urging the couple to put in for a tag. He told them he was going to give the lottery a try. The logger promised faithfully that if either of their applications was selected in the random drawing, he would accompany them to the hunting area to be sure they got their "extra" deer.

"Not much of a trick," he boasted. "We often saw twenty to thirty big mule deer a day."

Bucks in the region were heavily hunted as trophies. As a result, their number was out of balance with the does. Hunters, the F&G discovered, preferred to shoot the big mule deer bucks, leaving the overabundant does to die of starvation in the winter.

The country was a high, desolate plateau bordering on a deep, fast river. Deep canyons held the river in its place, leading on steep slopes to the plateaus above. Tens of thousands of narrow side gorges cut down through the area. Elevation differences were, in some cases, as much as 1,400 to 1,800 feet.

Grass grew on the steep slopes and in the deep canyons wherever Mother Nature was successful in turning the basalt rock into thin soil. Domestic cattle, sheep, and, at one time, wild horses grew reasonably fat chasing the grass. Alongside the domestic stock, mule deer also thrived.

Problems hunting the region related to the fact that there were very few roads. Even the few that punched through the area were extremely poor, little more than dirt tracks built to handle logging trucks on a temporary basis. Some wound tortuously along the rims of canyons so steep that the slightest miscue would send the vehicle plunging down hundreds of feet.

Those who won the drawing, including the lucky hunter, were notified by mail by the middle of summer. His neighbor stuck to his promise to personally guide him and his wife on opening day. They collected Bureau of Land Management and commercial maps of the area and made extensive plans regarding how they intended to hunt the region.

The three left their home at a pitch dark 3:30 A.M. for the two-hour drive into canyon country. As a result of the many glowing reports they had received, expectations for a quick, relatively easy hunt were high.

Quietly they inched their vehicle out on a track that followed a line between two deep canyons, arriving at the first gray of dawn. They parked at a wide spot in the trail virtually on the last foot of road that their four-wheel-drive would negotiate. Temperatures were about 30°F on what was to be a clear, dry day. As soon as the sun came up at 6:15 A.M., predicted highs of 45°F seemed possible. The three hunters wore several layers of cotton pants and shirts that could be peeled off as the day warmed. Due to the large number of rattlesnakes reported to be in the area, they wore high leather boots with cleated climbing soles. Early- to mid-fall conditions prevailed.

Knowing that they were in the midst of hunting country, they checked their rifles silently. The logger carried a .270 bolt with 3-9X variable scope. The tag holder had a .308 bolt with 6X scope, and his wife carried a .257 Roberts bolt with 6X scope. Their other gear included water bottles, binoculars, and a length of rope.

After testing the wind (out of the west at about eight to ten knots), they walked over a relatively flat but boulder-strewn field to a deep, steep canyon dropping away in almost dizzying fashion. Ahead was a soil slope falling an estimated one thousand feet. In places along the slope there were a few thin patches of sumac and chaparral brush intermixed with anemic stands of second-growth lodgepole pine. The country was so steep that the trio could look across the canyon to the opposite slope. Dark green leaves remained on the brittle chaparral brush, but otherwise the broadleaf brush was bare.

The crew spread out about fifty yards apart, slowly working up the canyon. It was tough for them to imagine that any deer could hide anywhere on these slopes, as everything was out in plain sight. From up high, they imagined they could see virtually everything. As much as was possible, they glassed ahead and on the opposite slope with their binoculars.

The logger first spotted a suspicious gray-colored rock feature. They were only on the slope fifteen minutes but he stopped dead still, signaling to the others to be on the alert. The other two also brought their glasses to bear on the suspicious object. After awhile it moved slightly. Observed from three angles, they confirmed that it was a mule deer nibbling on dry grass. Winds held steady out of the west uphill across the canyon. Even given

the fickle nature of the winds, it seemed unlikely that the deer would smell them.

Being seen by the critter was a different matter. There was absolutely no place to hide. Not a tree or bush over eighteen inches high was available from which they could put the sneak on the deer. Slowly, almost hesitantly, they advanced in a line. After perhaps fifteen minutes they were able to cut the distance to about two hundred yards, half of the distance from when they first saw it. With its back to the hunters, the big muley seemed unconcerned except for its next bite of grass.

Suddenly, something—probably ahead—excited the deer. It threw up its head, looking up the hill. It obviously was a huge mossy-backed buck for which the crew had no permit. The logger waved his finger signaling no, it was not a shootable deer.

They continued on, clinging to the steep slope. Their ankles and calves ached from the effort after only thirty minutes. All three glassed opposite their position on the facing slope and saw the next buck simultaneously. As they watched it eating, another deer higher on the hill came into view. They could not believe their bad luck—they were both nonshootable bucks.

Mule deer seemed to rise up out of the ground like ghosts. One minute there was nothing, the next there were several deer—a syndrome made more mystifying by the fact that the first buck suddenly became invisible. No one saw it run off; it simply disappeared.

The logger/guide grumbled to himself that if they had had a buck tag, all they would have seen would have been does. "Little justice in this guiding business," he mused. Ahead, standing on a prominence, another muley came into view. This one took much less time to identify—it was yet another buck with an absolutely massive rack.

The logger signaled for his neighbors to join him at the top. Wrong time and/or wrong place, he told the couple. Mule deer migrate; bucks separate themselves from the does till later when the days are shorter and the snow flies. "We had best clear completely out of here and find some new country at a different elevation where does are hanging out," he suggested.

They walked back out, past their vehicle, and a mile or more to the very end of the ridge where the two side canyons completed their encroachment, pinching the ridgeline down to thirty feet or less in width. From that point the ridge fell steeply toward the main river two miles or more in the distance.

They hiked over the steep ridge at least a mile till they came to a series of smaller ridges running out at right angles from the main ridge they were on. It was wild, wooly country with nary a soul that they could imagine within ten miles or more.

They picked a more prominent side ridge and walked out on it five hundred yards. Even going downhill in that country proved to be a chore. They stopped for a few minutes for a swallow of water and a sandwich and discussed their situation.

While thus engaged, another deer appeared out of nowhere. Like most of the others, its sex was in doubt. It stood at least a mile downhill under a scraggly pine. Almost reluctantly they set off downhill toward it. After walking another twenty minutes, they were close enough to determine its sex.

Fate was with them this time. It proved to be a giant, old mule deer doe, for which they had the appropriate tag. The only caveat was that the deer might as well have been on the dark side of the moon. They were fully half a mile from the high ridgeline and another mile from the top. Including the half mile to the doe and the half mile to the vehicle, they were looking at packing a two-hundred-pound critter two and a half miles up over at least six to eight hundred feet of elevation.

"I suggest we put our binoculars back in the case, take our rounds out of our rifles, and forget that deer," the logger suggested. His two companions complied without saying a word or wasting any time. No one wanted to risk someone changing his or her mind.

Immediately they lined around, starting the long trudge back uphill. By contouring uphill a bit they were able to top the ridge in close proximity to their 4WD. It was 10:00 A.M. They saw nothing on their way up.

After 10:00 A.M. mule deer usually bed down till about 3:00 P.M., their guide opined. "Never

have shot one from now till 2:30," he added. As a result, the three hunters decided to drive around in an attempt to learn more about the roads in the area.

The tag holder drove the jeep, his wife sat in the center, and the logger hung out the window to the right. They backed around, turning toward the place where the trail made a giant U across the top of the canyon in which they had just seen the four big bucks.

Their vehicle lumbered slowly and relatively quietly up the road about a hundred yards from the sharp left turn they were about to make. The rough, unkept road full of potholes precluded speeds greater than eight to ten miles per hour.

"There they go!" the logger shouted. Two doe mule deer, a large fawn and her mother, jumped through the spindly, tall lodgepole pine at the side of the road. The driver popped the clutch, stalling the vehicle with a clunk. Without thinking he pushed his door open with his left shoulder.

Both deer ran down the shallow draw at an angle, taking them through the few trees and up the other side and away. Perhaps the noise from the vehicle croaking or the two passengers frantically tearing through piles of gear for rifles confused the deer. They stopped about sixty yards out, standing on the opposite side. The hunter hurriedly grabbed the first rifle shoved at him and bolted a round into the chamber.

It was the logger's .270. He kneeled at the side of the jeep track, peering through the scope. Quickly he picked out a single deer in the crosshairs. As it started to move again, he squeezed off a round at what he supposed was the middle of the deer.

Somehow the speedy little bullet found its way through the brush, catching the smaller of the two just behind the front shoulder. At the time of the shot, the shooter was uncertain which of the two he had targeted. It fell instantly but tried to regain its feet and run. After wobbling on for twenty feet, it fell in the place where they eventually field-dressed it.

The mule deer was a one-hundred-pound coming one-year-old doe. Their extra tag was now filled, but certainly not in the manner in which

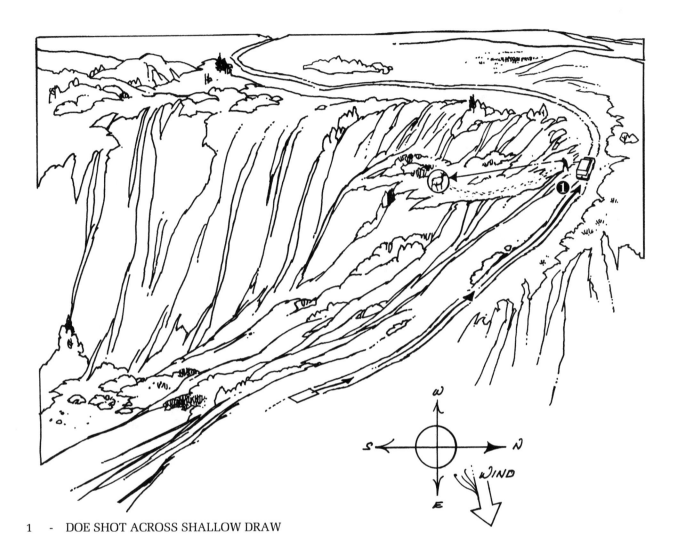

1 - DOE SHOT ACROSS SHALLOW DRAW

they thought it would be. It was about 10:45 A.M. after they finished field-dressing the deer.

The hunter attributes his success to his taking the only quick shot available, having no trees or brush to deflect the bullet, and being wise enough not to try to kill a doe spotted earlier deep down in the canyon. The fact that they kept alert when all looked hopeless was also a material benefit. Other than the above, nothing on this hunt went according to plan.

CHAPTER 22
UNLIKELY DOUBLE

HUNT CHECKLIST

Weather
Cool but not cold, 38°F, with fall definitely in the air.

Terrain
Gently rolling to almost flat in places. Some farmland in area. Dips and swales covered with patches of brush. Occasional groves of aspens with most leaves fallen. Country was mostly brown.

Wind Direction
Out of west, 12 to 14 knots, often gusting higher.

Conditions Previous Day
Very dry, slightly warmer. It was getting into serious fall and winter weather.

How Hunter Moved
Crossed about a mile of farmed fields, encountered patches of scrub, and walked through these on downwind side. Ran out two deer when he walked up a small rise.

Clothes
Jean-type pants, flannel shirt, jean jacket, leather boots.

Rifle Caliber and Scope
.308 bolt-action with 4X scope.

Sex of Deer
Two coming 2-year-old fork-horn bucks.

Time of Day
Started about 2:00 P.M.; shot deer at 4:00 P.M.

Length of Hunt
Including carrying the deer out, it was a 4- to 5-hour hunt covering about 6 miles out and back.

Length of Shot
About 80 yards, slightly downhill.

How Deer Moved
Lay in a patch of aspen till hunter walked past, then tried to sneak out in the other direction behind hunter.

Skill of Hunter
Hunter was a lad who enjoyed roaming the hills around his home and was addicted to whitetail hunting.

A teenaged boy lived in a place where white-tails were very numerous. From the time the lad could first purchase a license legally, he spent as much time as possible out in the field. By his mid-teens he was addicted to deer hunting. Even during the off-season he spent hours and hours wandering the hills near his home.

He often rode the family horses as far as eight miles out from his rural home. The delight of the boy's life was to ride up over the next rise checking to see what the deer were eating, where they were sleeping, and how they were moving. He was fortunate both that so much country existed over which he could roam and that the concentration of whitetails in that country was so high.

As a result of spending hundreds of hours out on the land, he always had a pretty good idea what the deer were up to. He knew what they would be eating, how they wintered, and even the number of twins and triplets the does had dropped in spring. His knowledge was workable for all but the last few weeks of hunting season, when it was too cold to ride his horse and the deer seemed to disappear into deep snowy cover. At that time he simply gave up caring about tracking them down at that time of year.

The countryside over which the lad roamed was gently rolling to almost flat. In places where little draws and rills cut across the land, fairly heavy patches of ninebark and blackberry bush grew in tangled profusion. In other places, poplar grew in tight little groves. On some of the rougher ground that the farmers had not gotten around to clearing, occasional lone ponderosa pines still grew. Some of the land might have been farmed eighty years ago, but it was now reverting to native scrub again.

During most of the year when the young hunter simply patrolled, he seldom bothered to carry a rifle. When he did it was to practice shooting an occasional groundhog or pine squirrel. He used a .308 bolt-action rifle with a 4X scope, the same rifle he carried the first day he went deer hunting. At times he went out with his father or an uncle, but his favorite expeditions involved wandering through the woods by himself. At the time of this hunt he had already bagged numer-

ous deer as well as coyotes, fox, bear, and the usual variety of small game.

He left the house on a cool, bright fall afternoon with enough frost around to suggest that the weather was starting to consider serious changes. It was about 38°F well after the noontime high, which had not quite reached 40°F. What frost that covered the low areas that morning was just about melted off by the time he departed. Rains last had fallen at least twenty days prior to the hunt, leaving the ground dry to almost powdery. Grass and brush over the hills also were dry and rattly. Most of the leaves had fallen from the broadleaf trees and bushes.

Winds were out of the west at a relatively vigorous twelve to fourteen knots, gusting at times to twenty. The hunter remembered the country as being windswept that day. As a result, he wore cotton blue jeans, long underwear, a flannel shirt, and a black leather jacket. His boots were simply high-top farm shoes.

The young hunter headed due west on a gravel road. After half a mile, he turned left (south), passing through an old harvested wheat field. After approximately another two miles of hiking, he entered an area of scrub brush and grass-covered hills. He continued through this little landform, maintaining his south bearing. At times gusty winds hit his right shoulder with vigor.

He moved on through three or four patches of heavy brush that he felt should have contained deer. He saw nothing but multiple layers of tracks on the trails. Because of the dry conditions, their age was questionable. Even for an old, experienced deer hunter, it would have been difficult to determine which were recent.

The boy pushed on, moving along perhaps faster than he should have. Like all young, enthusiastic hunters, he had plenty of energy. He was approaching three miles from home, but he felt no signs of tiring.

Now he passed through eight or ten patches of poplar and blackberry. Historic deer trails cut through the scrub, making it somewhat easier to walk. He knew of these trails from his many forays on horseback.

As a general rule, he worked through these

patches on the downwind side. He calculated that the westerly winds hitting him squarely would blow through the cover, scaring deer out the other side. It was a technique more reminiscent of pheasant than deer hunting. In general, the country sloped uphill to his left. Deer might have run out unobserved, but their holding tight till danger passed was the real problem. The kid regularly killed deer on the run and pheasants on the wing, so he was a bit overconfident.

The lad pushed his way through the most tangled stand of poplar he encountered that day. On the far side, he found a patch of low-growing blackberry bushes through which he also had to fight. After the thorny, sticky bushes, there was a relatively sharp twenty-foot hill to climb. Silently he pushed on up the grade, angling a bit to his left so as to take the terrain at an angle. At the top he deployed a technique he learned both from hunting with his father and from riding his horse.

As soon as the trail was clear and he knew he would not trip and fall, he turned around and walked backward. On his horse he would throw his leg over the horse's neck, riding along sidesaddle. By so doing he swept the country over which he had just come. On past hunts he had caught many deer sneaking out behind him when they thought the danger had passed.

In this case his efforts were rewarded again. Two coming two-year-old bucks with spike horns were trying to sneak off in single file. Evidently they had been lying at the edge of the path in the dense brush through which he had just come. The hunter was as much surprised for having missed them as he was for their boldness in filing out in plain sight behind him.

As a result of his many hours plunking running ground squirrels, he knew that if he shot the last critter in a running string, the ones ahead would seldom notice. Done this way, the shooter often could get a second aimed shot and perhaps a second or even a third kill.

Both deer moved along, head to tail, sneaking very slowly. They were plainly visible in the sparse brush that barely came up to their knees. They followed the trail, turning a bit so they were now parallel and broadside to the hunter. Range

was eighty yards at most.

He sucked in a breath, put the scope's crosshairs in the middle of the rear deer just behind the front shoulder, and squeezed off a round. The sound from the shot seemed to slap the deer down. It fell sideways toward the hunter, lying lengthwise on the trail. The round entered squarely through the right lung, punching out significant pieces on the left. The hunter had only three rounds for his rifle, one of which was expended.

The forward deer turned its head toward the hunter, swinging its ears around. It acted as though it would bound off at any moment, but it continued to stand there, twitching its tail, nose, and ears. Like western gunfighters, "Take your time in a hurry," the lad's father often told him. He bolted a second round into the chamber, aimed, and squeezed.

Deer two fell within five feet of its companion. Both lay there in the prickly brush, nose to tail. Like the previous deer, it was shot through the lungs. The shooter cannot recall if either deer moved a muscle after they were shot. He believed the rounds had knocked the wind out of them.

He ran through the brush over to the downed deer. They were not his first, or the excitement overload may have reached critical mass. Much to his surprise, the deer were not identical. Both were spikes, but one was 20 percent larger than the other.

As soon as the young man was certain both deer were dead, he started on a run for home. He knew that there was no way for him to move both animals around to field-dress them. He also realized that he had a problem until he could get back with his sister's tag. It was about 4:00 P.M. when he shot; full dark would arrive at 4:50 P.M.

He made it home before dark but, much to his alarm, no one was there. A note advised him that his family was having dinner at the neighbor's house and that they would expect to meet him there. It was a five-mile drive on the county road to the neighbor's house, but only a mile and a half from there to the place where the deer lay.

He raced his motorcycle to the neighbor's. It was dark when he got there, but at least help was at hand. His father borrowed a kitchen knife, stone, and flashlight, and dad, mom, and hunter set out

117

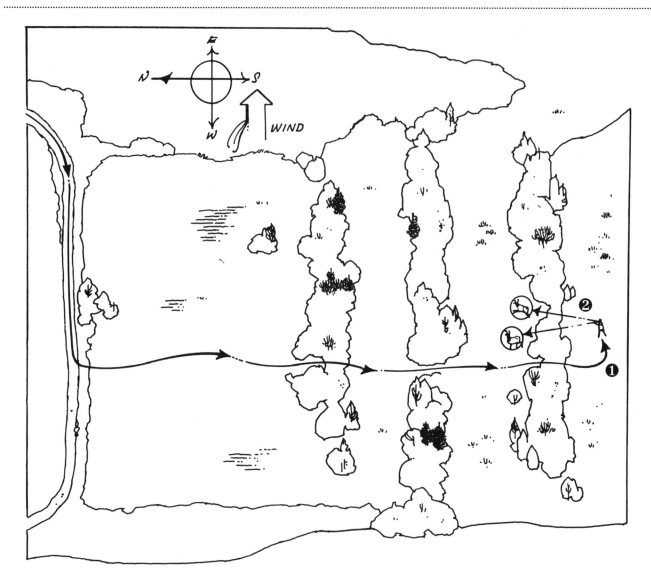

1 - HUNTER WALKS BACKWARD
2 - HUNTER SEES TWO BUCKS SNEAKING AWAY; SHOOTS BOTH

across country searching for the downed deer in the dark. Later, they claimed it was as black as the inside of a cow, but the hunter knew every fence post, lone tree, and rock in the region. He more or less walked straight to the pair of bucks.

His mother held the light while the men field-dressed the critters. It was 6:30 P.M. when they started packing the deer. Dad carried one critter while the lad and his mother dragged the second one. Father dropped the deer in their truck and then headed back up to help gather in the second critter.

By 7:30 P.M. they had both deer packed out and in their pickup. Temperatures dropped to the high twenties that night. They enjoyed a leisurely dinner with their friends before going to work skinning and hanging the meat.

The young hunter attributed his success to his knowledge of the country and where the deer were likely to lie, his technique of walking backward, and his hours of practice shooting ground squirrels. He also thinks that, in this case, he stumbled onto a pair of unusually dumb deer.

CHAPTER 23
SWIMMING DEER

HUNT CHECKLIST

Weather
Snowy, wet, raw conditions. Temperatures in the mid-30s.

Terrain
Long, thin lake with some high, tree-covered hills surrounding the water and coming to the water's edge in places.

Wind Direction
Down the lake, generally parallel to shore, not over 4 knots.

Conditions Previous Day
6 inches of new snow fell on the hills surrounding the lake.

How Hunters Moved
Hunted on the lake till they saw two deer. Made a land stalk, wounded a deer, and drove it into the icy water.

Clothes
Wool shirts, wool pants, and wool jackets covered by heavy nylon slickers.

Rifle Caliber and Scope
.338 Winchester Magnum bolt-action with 6X scope.

Sex of Deer
Older, large whitetail doe.

Time of Day
About 2:00 P.M.

Length of Hunt
They left home 2 1/2 hours before daylight, returning shortly after sundown.

Length of Shot
About 300 yards.

How Deer Moved
Deer crept along edge of clearing in open, wooded area. Hunter was so far away he thought he was shooting at a fawn.

Skill of Hunters
They had hunted this lake for many seasons, perfecting the technique of getting deer there.

Two avid deer hunters discovered that they could best find whitetail deer by cruising the shoreline of a large lake in their area. Over the years they had become quite good at using this technique. Just as hunters on land learn the territory, this pair learned how to hunt the water for the critters. As a general rule, they were every bit as successful as their family and friends who stuck faithfully to firm earth.

The two men felt that they had uncovered a great advantage or they would not have continued with their system. Close analysis suggests that good opportunities existed, but that the two had to overcome a batch of impediments.

The best time to hunt, they claimed, was at the tail end of the season after nasty weather in the hills around the lake drove the deer down to the water's edge, where they were easily shot. Meeting these criteria was not simply a matter of waiting till the last week of the season, however. In years past, they sometimes found themselves looking at a solidly frozen lake while their deer tags languished in their pockets. Another problem involved the difficulty of trailing their eighteen-foot boat to the lake when there was snow on the ground. Even when done slowly and cautiously, it was a harrowing exercise.

Snow on the boat ramp presented an additional problem. They hoped that if the pull rig ever slipped on the steep incline, it would regain its footing before sinking out of sight into the dark waters.

Hunting on the lake generally was not very good except an hour after daylight or an hour before dark. Also, shooting from the rocking, drifting boat was impossible. The hunters found that they had to beach their craft and make a credible stalk to the critter. At most, they could organize two or three stalks before it was too late in the morning or too dark to see.

The lake they hunted was a long, thin fifty-four miles. It contained more shoreline than the pair could ever hope to cover in one season.

It snowed six inches the day before the two pulled out for their annual boat hunt. It wasn't quite the end of the season, but conditions were definitely as good as they were going to get. A friend at the lake had reported by phone that temperatures were in the mid-thirties, with good snow cover down to within a hundred yards of the water.

Towing their boat to the ramp proved to be uneventful. What little snow remained had been plowed or had melted away by the time of their departure at 4:00 A.M. Sunup was expected no earlier than 6:30 A.M. It took them about two hours to drive the ninety miles to the boat launch.

It was a dull, foggy, damp, gray morning when they slipped their boat into the icy, black water. They had the ramp and parking area completely to themselves. No other boats were on the water—both reassuring and distressing. No other hunters were there to foul up their plans, but there was no one to render assistance should they require same. They took some comfort from the fact that their lone truck and boat trailer would draw attention if they were there overlong.

The hunters wore heavy wool shirts and thick wool jackets. Boots were knee-length rubber types over two pair of wool socks. They also wore heavy nylon windbreakers and warm wool caps. Both reckoned that a spill into the lake's icy water would be fatal but, nevertheless, carried extra dry clothes in rubberized emergency duffel bags.

Winds on the lake blew down from the east parallel to shore. Although they were changeable, they seldom blew in toward shore, alerting the game. Whenever the hunters saw shootable deer, the first determination was to find a downwind beaching area.

They motored gently up the lake at about eight knots till the engines warmed. They stayed out about a hundred yards from shore, scanning the land as they passed. At that range, deer seldom took much note of their passing.

As much as ice would allow, they investigated every bay and estuary. In some the ice was sufficiently thick to preclude their travel. Whenever it seemed appropriate to motor up to the very end of a creek inlet that was ice covered, the men simply ran along the edge of the ice, creating a wake wave that washed into shore, cracking it. It was then possible to turn and motor through the shattered ice field. Cracking, screeching sounds from the ice scraping the vessel probably alerted every deer in the region, so it was a technique they seldom employed.

Full daylight on the lake seemed to arrive rather quickly. They saw absolutely nothing but continued running on up the water. By noon they were about fourteen miles from the landing. It now seemed apparent that they would not see deer from the water till shortly before dark. They were somewhat encouraged, however, by the dull, gray, overcast skies. All other things considered, sunset that evening would be long and laborious, providing extended opportunities to see and stalk deer.

As an interim strategy, the pair elected to beach their boat in a sheltered cove where they were aware of a large meadow. In the meadow itself they encountered millions of deer tracks. Obviously the critters were yarded up some place near at hand! It appeared they were coming to the meadow to dig in the slushy snow for fresh grass.

The hunters circled the meadow in opposite directions, keeping fifty to eighty yards inside the line of trees. Their strategy, as well as execution, was faultless. However, forty minutes later when they met going in opposite directions, they agreed that the largest herd of deer in history had come through but was not there now.

It was now 1:30 P.M.; at least two hours still remained before hunting could be expected to become productive again. The pair decided to use the time to motor to the far end of the lake to an area they seldom hunted. It was something of a traumatic choice, given the fact that they could expect to finish hunting after dark, at which time it would be necessary to motor a long distance across some open water at a time of year when conditions could change dramatically. They were also less than thrilled about loading the boat at the landing in icy water at a time when it was pitch black.

Gathering up their pluck, they headed out at half throttle. From a bit farther out they could still check out suspicious rocks and stumps. They hoped they wouldn't inadvertently pass game.

Perhaps three miles beyond the meadow, they spotted something brown standing on shore. Gradually they cut power so as not to alarm the potential deer. Closer examination confirmed its status as a large, whitetail doe.

Moving along now at five miles per hour, they angled in toward shore. About fifty yards out they cut the motor and drifted. Steam from their breath confirmed that the slight breezes were moving parallel to shore at not more than four knots.

Waves from their wake rocked the boat as they peered through their scopes at the critter. One man carried a .300 Winchester Magnum with 3-9X scope; the other had a .338 with 6X scope. From the boat it was extremely difficult to hold the crosshairs on the deer, as even the slightest movement threw the sights off. As a result of their spending so much time peering through their scopes, a second deer had time to appear. It raised its head almost directly behind the first one.

It took an additional minute or so before both critters were plainly visible. "If we can get this boat even steadied down," the first hunter whispered, "I can kill two deer with one shot!"

Two hunters trying to shift and sight from the gunwales was impossible. Realizing this, the second hunter sat down in one of the boat seats where he remained, creating a minimum amount of movement.

The two hunters believe they sat there on the water for twenty minutes or more waiting for the deer and the scope's crosshairs to line up. It was a much greater problem then one who has never tried it can ever imagine. Finally, the shooter squeezed the trigger. Nothing happened. The hammer slid forward with a long, greasy *thunk*.

He had cleaned and oiled his rifle the night before. Apparently the bitter cold solidified the oil, preventing the firing pin from falling with enough vigor. He lifted the bolt and tried again. The deer were no longer lined up, but it didn't matter—the rifle still refused to fire.

The hunter immediately sat down in the middle of the boat, pulled the bolt from the rifle, took it apart, and started wiping with his handkerchief. Eventually he was able to clean the bolt sufficiently so that it appeared likely to function. He got it back together without losing any pieces. Unfortunately, the clambering around in the boat distressed both deer to the extent that they pulled back from shore

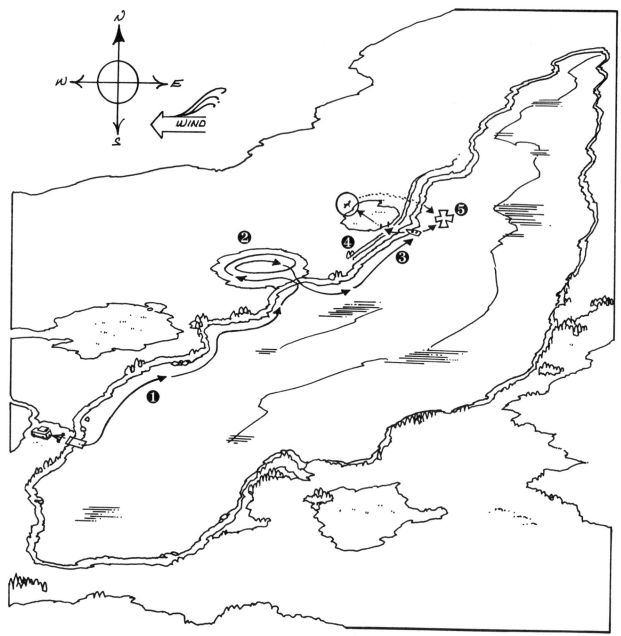

1 - HUNTERS SCAN SHORE FOR DEER
2 - HUNTERS SEARCH FIRST MEADOW
3 - TWO DEER SPOTTED ON SHORE
4 - HUNTERS SHOOT DOE ACROSS MEADOW
5 - DOE SWIMS OUT INTO LAKE AND DIES

into heavy shoulder-high underbrush.

The hunters glided their vessel into shore, where they tied to an old stump. They worked their way up the bank, hoping to surprise the deer in the underbrush. After sneaking about fifty yards, they crossed an old logging road. Only traces of the straight line it cut through the timber were still visible.

Ahead, a steep, tree-covered hill rose behind a medium-sized meadow. Neither man had the slightest idea that the meadow existed, as it was completely obscured by the trees and underbrush along the lake. At the edge of the meadow they spotted a small deer on the other side. It was among trees with mostly bare trunks, perhaps fifty feet in from the edge of the clearing.

In hushed whispers they discussed taking a shot at so small a deer. Because hunting on the lake had been less than outstanding, the hunter with the unoiled .338 decided to try a shot. He placed the vertical crosshair in the middle of the critter, keeping the horizontal line parallel with its back, and squeezed off a round.

He saw the deer bound off to his left and assumed that he missed the small target. They paced the distance from the shot to the place across the meadow where the deer stood. It was an astronomical 298 long paces! Apparently the country was far larger than they had thought. Subsequently, the deer was probably a full-sized critter, not a coming one-year-old as they had first supposed.

It was too long for an offhand shot, the shooter reckoned, but much to their surprise, they found blood splattered all over the snow. It was on the bushes, tree trunks, and a little rise behind. However, no downed deer was in sight.

Immediately they started circling, looking for bloody tracks and/or the dead critter. From the looks of the impact area, the deer could not have gone far.

As soon as they separated, a deer jumped up on the left, running in front of the two toward the east. The hunter nearest the deer did not shoot. The second man took a quick, running shot before the deer ran into the shoulder-high brush at water's edge. There was no tracking snow in that brush. The shooter ran two hundred yards east into the brush in an attempt to prevent the deer from running on up along the lake.

He was uncertain if the animal he was after was the wounded one.

The second hunter continued tracking the wounded critter. When he saw the tracks disappear into the brush where the snow petered out, he cut hard right in an attempt to keep the deer between the two. They both worked through the brush for a few minutes till they heard a loud splashing in the water.

Both men ran down to the water to see a full-grown whitetail doe swimming sixty feet from shore. They were about to try a shot when the deer simply stopped swimming. It floated in the water with its head below the surface.

The animal had just died in the icy water. As fast as they could, they ran to the boat and pushed out with great enthusiasm to the deer. One hunter threw a rope around its neck, snubbing it to a cleat. Together they pulled it to the shore, where they beached and field-dressed it.

They found that the .338 round had blown a softball-size wad of large intestines out of the deer's right flank. The shot would have eventually killed the animal, but it might have lived up to eight hours had it not tried to escape by swimming in the icy water, where it was shocked and killed by the cold.

After loading the deer into the boat, they hunted the shore till dark and then motored back to the landing.

The two hunters concluded that they were successful because they picked an ideal day to hunt the lake. They then found an area that probably had never been hunted before, working it properly regarding wind and terrain. However, the most significant factor, according to these hunters, was that their rifles were large enough to get the job done, even if the rounds were not well placed.

123

CHAPTER 24

CHERRY BOWL WHITETAIL

HUNT CHECKLIST

Weather
About 28°F, very cool and dry. Frost layer in low areas persisted through the day.

Terrain
Almost perfectly formed bowl with 5-acre clearing in the center of a thickly wooded area.

Wind Direction
Out of the west across bowl at about 5 knots.

Conditions Previous Day
Cool, dry, and overcast with fall-type conditions.

How Hunter Moved
Hunter walked up to top rim of bowl, threw rocks into woods on either side, then sat down to wait for a deer to cross the opening.

Clothes
Cotton jeans, flannel shirt, light cotton jacket, and common low-cut leather work shoes.

Rifle Caliber and Scope
.257 Roberts bolt-action with 6X scope.

Sex of Deer
3- or 4-year old doe, apparently barren that year.

Time of Day
Deer was killed at about 4:45 P.M.

Length of Hunt
About 3 hours start to finish, including packing the deer out. Hunter walked about 3 miles.

Length of Shot
About 125 yards, perhaps more. Estimates in this case were unreliable.

How Deer Moved
Came out of heavily wooded patch into a clearing, where hunter spotted it.

Skill of Hunter
Hunter was modestly skilled, having killed some deer in the same general area.

The hunter in this case went out on a modestly successful cottontail hunt that a month later led to a situation wherein a nice, fat whitetail doe fell to a long, well-planned shot. He used his prior on-the-ground experience in an analytical manner to put together an unlikely but successful one-man drive.

The man was a reasonably successful recreational deer hunter who usually spent nine or ten days a year searching for deer. He had observed that other, more successful hunters often spent more time and energy than he did analyzing their own situations, leading, in each case, to easier, more effective deer kills. He soon ascribed to being a thinking, analytical deer hunter rather than one who simply bulldozed through the bush.

In that regard, he found he had about three hours of daylight remaining one mid-week afternoon after coming home from work. It was only 3:30 P.M., so he grabbed his shotgun and headed out the door across the fields behind his home in a small rural town. He told his wife he was going for a rabbit for supper. Nevertheless, she put a package of burger in the microwave.

The terrain over which the hunter ranged was hilly to steeply hilly. About 50 percent was cleared and used as pasture; the remaining half lay in intermittent lots covered with second- and third-growth fir, pine, cedar, poplar, scrub oak, and maple. Some of the woodlots were filled with tangled, blown-down timber. Neither man nor beast was able to cross these areas without expending a great deal of energy. The only other impediment to travel out in the fields was the steep hills. It was out in these relatively open pastures among the little patches of brush and weeds that the hunter hoped to scare up a cottontail.

He walked about a mile from home up over a forty- to sixty-foot hill, exploring as much as he was hunting. At the crest of the hill, he circled to his left till he walked out to the rim. He continued walking the rim till he was looking out over a deep, bowl-like land structure. It was a peculiar landform filled with similarly unique vegetation.

The ground itself fell away steeply, circling around almost like a cupped set of hands. Heavy dog-hair stands of second- and third-growth pine and fir grew on three sides of the bowl up to the place where the land rose sharply. Only sparse, low brush grew in the bowl, but the tops of large fourteen-inch fir trees that once grew there were scattered around like a handful of giant toothpicks. It appeared to the hunter as though a strong wind had come through, breaking all of the tops at the twenty-foot level and scattering them around on the ground.

Most of the smaller trees that still stood were stripped clear of lower branches. Little tufts of green stood atop spindly, thin trunks along with the broken bare tops of larger trees. The ground was littered with fresh and decaying logs.

The most unique feature of the bowl's ground cover was the fact that most of the underbrush was wild cherry, which, at that time, was just past bloom. Cherry seldom grew wild in that country. The fact that it grew there in profusion caught the man's eye and aroused his interest. He concluded that anything bigger than a raccoon would have difficulty crossing that bowl even though a minimum of brush grew there. Nevertheless, he decided to hunt there come deer season.

The hunter took note of the situation on the ground, swung around, and hunted his way back home. Although he cannot recall with certainty, he believes he ate hamburger for dinner that night.

Deer season rolled around about a month later. While he enjoyed small-game shooting, the thought of filling a freezer with only a shot or two was much more on his mind.

The hunter finished work at 3:00 P.M. on a Wednesday. He was home by 3:20 P.M. pulling on his old Levis and flannel shirt. His shoes were simple, low-cut leather work shoes. He figured it would be a brief hunt, not requiring elaborate clothes and equipment.

By 3:30 P.M. he was out the back door. Full dark was expected about 5:15 P.M. Having mulled over his options for the last four weeks, he concluded that his best alternative was the little cherry bowl discovered on the rabbit hunt. With his .257 bolt with 6X scope, a knife, and a stone, he headed out across the hills.

The temperature was a crisp, dry 28°F in the late afternoon. Ground was relatively bare, but in some sheltered places frost persisted through the day and into the evening. In these places it was possible to track deer.

Winds were a relatively gentle four to six knots out of the west. His path to the bowl took him north across the wind. When he ended up at his destination, he was above and downwind of potential game. He found that except for some isolated patches of greenery, most of the leaves had fallen off the brush, revealing more fallen trees and logs lying about. Litter in the bowl was far more formidable than he had remembered.

On his way up the hill to the bowl, he had filled his pockets with about fifteen hen-egg-sized rocks. Like any rational person, he hated to pack them uphill, but he had a specific plan in mind.

At the top of the hill overlooking the bowl, the hunter found an ancient stump. It was almost exactly in the center of the rim at a place where he could see 95 percent of the bowl below. If need be, he could sit and wait for hours in this ideal place. Winds were still out of the west, blowing into his face.

He slowly and quietly crept to his left along the rim until he came to the transition area where heavy tree cover took over from the more open bowl. Standing out on the rim as far as possible, he lobbed the stones out into the woods about forty feet from the edge of the clearing.

The relatively large rocks rattled from one tree trunk to the next and then down through the dry brush. Because of the height from which he launched them, the rocks sailed inordinately far out into the woods, making lots of noise as they fell.

Having stoned the left side, the hunter retreated back fifteen feet from the rim and then over to the tree line on the right. He launched three more missiles out into the trees from that position. Content that he probably had alerted any critter in the area, he quietly worked his way back to the stump and sat down.

It was about 4:30 P.M. He remembers thinking that if he had been forced to sit where frost was starting to form below, he would have been much colder. He sat patiently, intending to keep his vigil till full dark if necessary.

After about fifteen minutes, he heard a distinct clacking sound below. It sounded as if someone was beating a dry stick against a log and a piece was cracking off now and then. When he finally zeroed in on the sound, he was chagrined to see a big doe picking her way in plain view, heading left to right in the log-strewn bowl. She seemed to have appeared out of thin air and was making about as much progress as a human would in those circumstances. She was making quite a rattle of things but probably less than the hunter would have in the same place. He was hearing the deer's hooves striking the fallen trees.

The hunter eased off his stump and crouched down behind it with his rifle resting on top. The deer was too low below the rim for him to get a view of it through his scope while resting the gun. She had no idea he was behind the stump looking at her through the scope. For some reason, he was alert to the possibility that another deer would come through from the other side and that they would cross in the middle, but one deer was all that he saw.

Carefully he placed the scope's crosshairs on the lung area. The doe continued moving slowly, picking its way through the forest wreckage. The hunter estimated the range at about 125 yards, but because it was out over a straight line from the rim, there was no way to be certain. Lengthening shadows from the approaching night caused him some grief as he worked at picking out the deer and then getting the black crosshairs centered.

The hunter gently tapped the trigger. He remembered that it seemed to take a long time for the bullet to get to the deer. When it did, it splattered the animal over like it was hit with a rubber wrecking ball. He watched quietly from the stump for signs of a second deer and for any indication that this one would regain its feet.

The deer got up, stumbled a few feet, fell down, and then flailed the air with its feet before lying still. He marked the exact spot with precision, resulting from his extensive experience in the field. On the way down to the critter, he passed through a line of heavy underbrush, where he lost contact with the downed deer. The brush did not look nearly so high or tangled from above. It took him at least ten min-

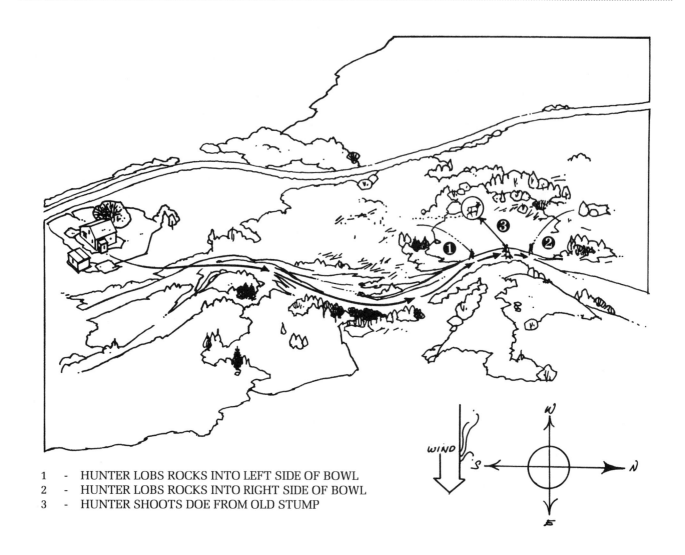

1 - HUNTER LOBS ROCKS INTO LEFT SIDE OF BOWL
2 - HUNTER LOBS ROCKS INTO RIGHT SIDE OF BOWL
3 - HUNTER SHOOTS DOE FROM OLD STUMP

utes to navigate the fallen logs and trees through the little bowl.

The hunter came to the place were he thought his deer should be. It wasn't there. He knew the deer was down, but if he had to wait till morning, the meat would be spoiled. He really could not circle because of the many fallen trees.

The hunter then recalled a peculiar broken tree and its alignment with some low brush at the back of the clearing. From there, he reckoned that the deer was to the right of his current position, perhaps behind a double stand of fallen logs. His last-minute calculations proved correct. He scrambled over the tree bodies and found the dead deer stacked up behind.

The single shot from the .257 entered the critter on the right side about four inches down on the center of the shoulder. It angled down, exiting about eight inches low on the opposite shoulder. In the process it shattered the thin shoulder bones and the base of the neck. The hunter wondered how the deer even got up after the shot.

Later, he found that the tops of the shoulder were hit "pretty good." Quite a lot of the meat was bloodshot, requiring patient washing before it was fit even for hamburger.

He field-dressed the doe in the failing light, leaving head, feet, and entrails in the woods. A gravel road came within four hundred yards of the bowl. It was night time before he was able to drag the doe to the road.

He walked down the road to get his truck at home. In less than an hour he was back at his house with the deer, where he skinned and halved it. He wished he had hit it where he aimed but was satisfied given that it was probably taken over a greater range than he first supposed.

The successful hunter concluded that he got the deer because he scouted the country, thought through a number of potential hunt options, and picked a valid strategy for that exact piece of terrain. Patience also helped. His shot still puzzles him, as it definitely didn't strike where he aimed.

HUNT CHECKLIST

Weather

35-45°F with gray, overcast skies.

Terrain

Worn mountains with covering of forest soil that supported extensive growth of pine, fir, aspen, poplar, and scrub oak.

Wind Direction

Gentle out of southwest, 4 to 5 knots.

Conditions Previous Day

About the same, with rains earlier in week.

How Hunters Moved

One man hiked up and around a large domelike mountain. The other hunted downhill to a creek, upstream to its end, then back uphill on a game trail. Deer were killed on the game trail.

Clothes

Light wool pants, shirt, and jacket, and rubber boot pacs.

Rifle Caliber and Scope

Deer were killed with two shots from a .338 bolt with 6X scope.

Sex of Deer

One 2-year-old buck and one 2-year-old doe.

Time of Day

Probably about 1:30 P.M. Packing them 400 yards took another 2 hours.

Length of Hunt

Started at daybreak. Covered about 5 miles each.

Length of Shot

From 70 to 80 yards downhill.

How Deer Moved

Came from below hunter across the trail he had first walked.

Skill of Hunters

Both men were experienced deer hunters. However, the man who killed the deer had scouted out the countryside and was considered very lucky, while the other was considered the better shot.

The deer chasers in this hunt were an unlikely pair who hunted together regularly for eight years. Both were raised on old-fashioned family farms in different parts of the country, where they were started deer hunting at an early age. They both had killed numerous deer back on the farm and in their current place of residence. Somehow fate conspired to throw the two together, as in many regards they were not predictable partners.

Upon arriving in the small town, they shared a lack of knowledge regarding local opportunities. One man threw himself enthusiastically into learning all of the local paths and trails. He soon knew every road in the county and had talked to virtually every deer hunter and anyone anyplace about shooting deer. He spent countless hours walking over the hills, looking at deer feeding, evaluating the fawn drop, and studying their migration patterns.

The second hunter put most of his considerable energies into his job. He labored at his desk for long hours, seldom taking time to be afield except during deer season. Of the two, he was decidedly the better shot; he could consistently kill running coyotes at two hundred yards. His problems with deer hunting were that he seldom saw deer and, when he did, something always seemed to go wrong—another hunter spooked the deer he was stalking, the critter got out of sight too quickly, he blew a sapling in two, or his rifle malfunctioned. Because of this, he seldom hung deer and was judged by his peers to be an extremely unlucky hunter. He did manage to kill an occasional deer, bear, or coyote—principally because he was such an excellent shot.

By contrast, hunter one, the scout/explorer, always seemed to stumble into groups of deer. He generally had a pretty good idea where they were, especially after hunting pressure and weather confused the issue late in the season.

It was about a forty-mile drive from the rural burg in which the two resided to the place where this hunt took place. The terrain was old, worn mountains covered with at least a foot of soil. Steep reliefs characterized some of the country, but there were virtually no rock outcrops or large bodies of rock in the region.

Most of the big timber had been cut twenty to thirty years ago. In its place, second-growth jack pine, fir, scrub maple, poplar, aspen, and some birch grew in profusion. Lower ground cover was comprised of scrub oak, juniper, pawpaw, and hazelnut brush. Although solidly wooded with little farmland, the country supported a thriving population of whitetails.

Temperatures the day before started at a crisp 33°F, rising to the mid-forties by noon. Rains fell earlier in the week, turning the powdery, dusty roads into slick, muddy four-wheel-drive traps. They expected 35 to 45°F temperatures and overcast skies the day of the hunt. Light frosts had knocked some, but not all, of the leaves from the trees. For some strange reason known only to Mother Nature, some big, bright red and yellow leaves still clung tenaciously to the branches that bore them, while others on the same tree were still bright green.

Visibility in the tangled second- and third-growth and scrub underbrush was never more than seventy-five yards. Even then it was common for local hunters to refer to using one's "imagination" to look through the dense cover to see game.

The hunters left their houses the day of the hunt at 4:45 A.M. Sunup, expected at about 6:00 A.M., was just about on them as they turned their 4WD off the main haul road, through the mountains, and onto a little grass-choked logging road. The track contoured on around an especially high domelike landform.

The duo was aware that, by driving north on that trail, they would position themselves above an old rail spur that ran along a small creek. Originally, the spur was used to haul lumberjacks in and logs out, but it had been forty or more years since steel rails wound their way up that valley. Few visible relics of that era lay on the ground for people to see.

They motored in to their preselected parking spot as quietly as possible and climbed out of the vehicle with a minimum of fuss and confusion. Because they were in the middle of some excellent deer cover, they were extra cautious about slamming doors, talking loudly, or otherwise broadcasting their presence.

Winds were steady out of the southwest which, on that domelike mountain, made little difference. As soon as they walked around on the trails even a modest hundred yards, prevailing breezes would hit them from an entirely different direction. Their plan was to hunt through various areas up or downhill as the winds and ground conditions dictated.

At their parking area, the mountain rose rather steeply to their left. In some places, recent logging, thinning, and brush-clearing activities created openings that appeared to provide more opportunities to see deer. To the right, downhill into the creek valley, the underbrush looked very thick.

The unlucky hunter elected to walk up to the top of the mountain, hunting through little patches of standing scrub and timber. He reasoned that he could sneak along some of the old logging roads around the dome in hopes of getting a shot at any deer his partner scared out.

The second hunter thought he had little chance of getting a deer in the heavy brush below. He was happy, however, to chase one out for his friend. He resolved to hunt all the way down to some old beaver ponds on the creek, where he might surprise a critter or two. It was still early enough to catch a deer out eating or drinking. After parting, the pair were at most eight hundred yards apart the entire day, yet they never saw or heard one another till later that afternoon.

The second hunter headed for the rail spur and ponds carrying a .338 bolt-action rifle with 6X scope. The unlucky hunter used a .30-06 bolt with 4X scope. They wore light wool jackets and pants so as to better sneak around the heavy brush. Boots were rubber pacs more suited for late-season snows.

Both hunters were pleased to discover that it was still quite damp on the ground as a result of the recent rains. Noise in the brush was hushed considerably. The hunter below was optimistic that he might be able to stalk up on a deer. The hunter above was encouraged about the country and conditions he saw ahead of him. There was little likelihood that they would encounter other hunters that day.

The downhill hunter chose a deep, fairly open side draw with sparse underbrush in which to hunt down to the creek. His sight distance was between 100 to 120 yards. At about 8:00 A.M. he reached the creek and turned left, stalking along the rail spur. Winds that blew four or five knots by the road were nonexistent down below. Dandelion seeds that puffed into flight simply hung in space, drifting off in a lackadaisical manner.

He continued up the old spur, arriving at its terminus at about 11:00 A.M. He sat in a little clearing where lumberjacks once rolled logs and ate his lunch. After lunch, he retraced his steps back down the spur for about a mile.

About four hundred yards north of the side draw he used earlier, the hunter found a recently used game trail leading up to a small bench. He supposed that, as was common in that country, one little bench would lead to another and perhaps he would stumble into an opening in the forest.

Meanwhile, the hunter above worked his way around the dome and then down a small worm saddle that ran more or less parallel to the creek. He saw numerous deer tracks but not one of the crafty critters. Unknown to either of them, his progress north around the dome and then west on the saddle kept the two surprisingly close together.

As the lower hunter started up the game trail, he noticed scores of tracks in the soft, wet forest soil. Winds, changable in the mountainous terrain, hit him on his left shoulder and in his face. They were very gentle, so he hoped they would not be too much of a factor. Heavy underbrush closed in on the trail on all sides. Visibility was not great in any direction, but he tried to be especially vigilant in the changing winds.

He climbed up the fairly steep grade four to five hundred yards, stopping often to catch his breath and look around. At one of these stops, he heard a subdued snort and thumping behind him. Turning 180 degrees, he thought he saw a flash of buckskin virtually on the path he had just walked.

The hunter stalked cautiously off the trail to his left to a place where the brush favored a

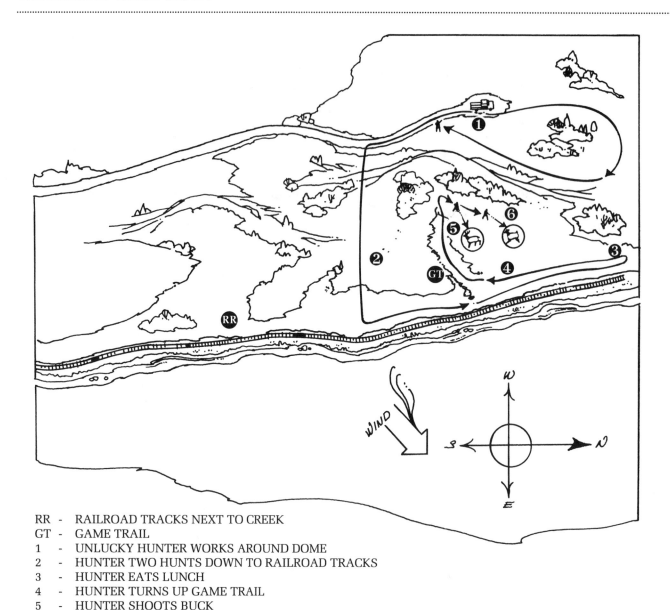

RR - RAILROAD TRACKS NEXT TO CREEK
GT - GAME TRAIL
1 - UNLUCKY HUNTER WORKS AROUND DOME
2 - HUNTER TWO HUNTS DOWN TO RAILROAD TRACKS
3 - HUNTER EATS LUNCH
4 - HUNTER TURNS UP GAME TRAIL
5 - HUNTER SHOOTS BUCK
6 - HUNTER SHOOTS DOE

straight view downhill some eighty to one hundred yards. Through his scope he picked up a fork-horn buck trying to sneak away to the south. Every now and then the buck jumped a few feet, obviously nervous over the fact that, due to the crossing winds, it could not positively identify the man or his location.

The hunter lined up the scope's crosshairs through the brush as best as he could. He remembers that a lot of big green leaves obscured his view, but that he could plainly see the deer's head as well as one of its dark brown eyes. He placed the crosshairs at a spot in the foliage behind which he knew the buck's body was. It was about an eighty-yard shot.

At the shot, the deer rolled violently sideways downhill. Despite the recoil, he remembers seeing white belly hair and legs flailing through the underbrush.

He bolted another round into the chamber and started working his way down toward the deer. It was well north of the game trail and much farther down than he would have chosen had he had the option.

As he stalked, the shooter saw and heard a deer to his left moving through the underbrush. He could not see the first buck but assumed it had to be a second deer. Deer seldom get up and walk around after being rolled over with a .338, he figured.

The hunter froze, searching the brush with his scope till he spotted a doe stretching its neck up over some brush. It was trying to wind or see him, but it was far enough left and downwind that it could not.

Again he estimated the location of the critter's body cavity and touched off a round. The animal fell forward on its nose as if someone had knocked its front legs out with an iron bar. He did not reload after that shot but continued on down to the buck, which he found lying in a clump of brush. The doe was down still farther to his left at least sixty yards. Like the first shot, this one also figured to be eighty yards.

Since it was at least another four hundred yards uphill to the logging road, the successful hunter was thankful that the doe was a bit smaller. He field-dressed it, taking legs, head, and even tail off in an attempt to lighten his load. He placed the deer uphill, sat below it, and pulled it onto his shoulders as he stood. Thus loaded, he carried it about eighty yards beyond the fallen buck, then dumped it at the approximate place from which he had first fired.

His breath and energy revived a bit as he walked back down to the buck. The horns, he concluded, were too small even to make buttons, so he left the head with the guts and feet. Hoisting the buck was a rerun of the doe except for its greater weight and body size.

With a great deal of effort, he carried the deer uphill two hundred yards past the doe. Fearing he would not be able to find the doe if he went further, he dumped the buck and went back down. Energy and enthusiasm for the project only partially returned as he made his way downhill.

Expending a great burst of energy, the hunter managed to pack the doe up to the logging road. The road cut was chest high above him and lined with undergrowth. He wiggled the deer through the brush and onto the level road.

After hollering for his partner at the road and receiving no response, he went back down for the buck. This time he dragged the deer rather than packing it. It took just as much effort, but it was easier to stop and rest.

At the top again, the hunter/shooter/packer found his friend standing on the road looking at the doe. The two dead deer were the only ones he had seen all day. He walked back about six hundred yards for their truck. The successful hunter was so pooped that all he could do was sit on a water bar and wait.

He brought the rig up and they loaded the deer. It was about 3:30 P.M.; dark was expected about 5:00 P.M. The successful hunter was covered with blood, so he pulled off his light jacket and one shirt and got into a clean pair of coveralls that he carried in his vehicle. They both agreed that they had had more than a full day so they left for home.

The "lucky" hunter concluded that he got the deer because he analyzed the country through which he was hunting on an ongoing basis. He followed a good game trail, kept track of the wind, and carefully calculated the location of the deer in the brush. His rifle was large enough to punch through the brush when making a shot where he couldn't see the deer but knew positively where its body was located.

CHAPTER 26

BUDDY HUNT

HUNT CHECKLIST

Weather
Bitter, cold, crystalline snow blowing sideways. Temperature about 20°F.

Terrain
They hunted in a fairly deep draw covered by large old timber with little understory. Country in general was gently rolling with only a few larger, deeper landforms.

Wind Direction
Out of north, 10 to 12 knots.

Conditions Previous Day
Cold, but this was first indication of real snow beyond heavy frosts.

How Hunters Moved
Hunters stalked up through a tree-covered draw, keeping about 50 yards apart. One hunter was a bit too far east and out of the hunt till the deer ran over to him.

Clothes
Heavy wool pants and shirts, long underwear, insulated boot pacs.

Rifle Caliber and Scope
.300 Winchester Magnum with 3-9X variable scope, .308 bolt-action, .338 Winchester Magnum bolt-action with 6X scope.

Sex of Deer
Doe whitetail.

Time of Day
About 7:30 A.M.

Length of Hunt
About 3 hours total.

Length of Shot
Various shots taken first at 125 yards, then 100 yards, 10 yards, and last at about 200 yards.

How Deer Moved
Deer tried to sneak up draw away from two hunters who scared it over to a third man, who also shot and missed.

Skill of Hunters
Two old-timers who spent a great deal of time in the country, along with a third man who had killed several deer but lacked the many years' experience of the first two.

wo old-timer deer chasers hunted together on an irregular basis. Some years they went out only two or three days. Other years their time in the field totaled two weeks or more. Both knew the country well from having hunted over it for most of their lives. They got on well, but one man was an addicted deer hunter while the other was content to call it quits when his freezer was full rather than trying to fill the neighbor's freezer as well.

The year of this hunt was skewed a bit by the fact that an advanced novice added himself to the crew. In times past, the new fellow had bagged his share of deer, being anything but a greeny. However he did not have anywhere near the miles or the total deer killed as the first two.

The two old duffers collectively had killed a huge number of deer. Going back twenty years when they could legally take four deer per season, they probably killed close to 150 deer each in their lifetimes.

This hunt started at a cold, miserable, pre-dawn 5:30 A.M. on a windswept gravel road a few miles from their homes. Sunup was expected at 6:45 A.M., at which time the three hoped the powdery, bitter cold snowfall would stop or at least moderate. The temperature was about 20°F with a nasty ten- to twelve-knot wind blowing out of the north. It had been very cold the previous week, but this was the first snowfall.

Climbing into one rig, they sat discussing the state of deer hunting and wool shirts. They agreed that conditions on the ground were tough and that any hunt outside sheltered heavy timber would be truly miserable. In addition, they knew from long, tough experience that deer would not drive in the conditions in which they now found themselves. "Best we can hope for is to walk up on them while they lie tight in the heavy brush," one old-timer suggested.

After discussing the pros and cons of many theoretical hunts, including the option of going home to sit in front of the fire, they hit on a plan that entailed a fast, heart-pounding, strenuous stalk through heavy timber.

Their agreed-upon plan was to stalk through heavily wooded areas, preferably in deep draws, moving through about fifty yards apart. By so doing, they hoped to jump deer, which they would shoot on the run. All three were able running shots, having taken numerous critters in that manner during prior hunts.

Having agreed on a plan of action, they motored to a sheltered draw that they knew from past experience harbored deer when the weather was stormy. It took them no more than ten minutes to travel the three miles to their targeted woods. By the time they parked, the black sky was showing some signs of light. Unfortunately, neither snow nor wind showed any sign of abetting.

They sat in their truck a few minutes longer till it was ghostly gray in the woods. There was enough light to walk but certainly not enough in which to shoot accurately.

The woods were comprised of pines and firs twenty to thirty inches in diameter. In many places, all underbrush was shaded out, but in the very bottom of the draw, some elderberry, vine maple, and ninebark still managed to find enough water and sunlight. In a few places where older trees had died or were blown over, new groves of smaller pines and fir flourished. Other than these groves, there was no fresh growth in the area.

All of the leaves were off the brush and the broadleaf trees, providing, in most cases, 100 to 150 yards visibility. Heavy, matted and tangled underbrush bordered the woods along the road.

By twisting and brush busting, the three were able to work their way into the parklike area. "Park" was in fact the name used by locals to describe this type of country. Although the wind theoretically was at their backs, they found that once inside the woods among the high sides of the draw, little wind moved through the area. The figured they could easily outwalk the gentle air movement, staying even with or ahead of their scent. Deer, they reasoned, were more likely to spook from noise than from winding them.

All wore heavy wool shirts, long wool jackets, long underwear, wool hats, and rubber boot pacs. Fine powdery snow did not adhere to the brush in any great quantity, so the men were not wetted above waist level and very little above their knees. In that regard, they stayed a bit warmer and dryer than they had anticipated.

The wooded area they were in ran up a draw about seven hundred yards. Other equally deep woods surrounded the targeted draw. At the far end, the woods stopped abruptly at a grassy opening of about sixty acres.

They continued walking through as per their initial plan. The man to the far right (west) was on the draw's side hill about two-thirds of the way to the top. The hunter in the middle walked through the bottom on a game trail of sorts. The man to the east was over the edge of the draw into heavier cover. The two on the right should have been able to see their companion, but they often lost sight of him.

Moving somewhat together, they stalked the draw for about five hundred yards. At that point, the party started to encounter some heavier tangled brush. The man in the center stopped suddenly.

"Hey, isn't that a deer?" he hollered to his partner above him on the slope.

He then ran uphill, stopped, and looked down into the draw, then across to the other side.

"It's a deer! It's a deer!" he shouted.

The hunter on the right did not see the critter but ran uphill as fast as he could for about fifty yards. He hoped to get ahead of it, get a better view, or force it over to the third hunter to the east.

The hunter who originally spotted the critter looked at it through the 3-9X variable scope on his .300 Winchester Magnum bolt-action. He then stepped forward three long paces, sat down, and tried for a better, more accurate shot than he would have had standing. Range was about 125 yards. After trying for about thirty seconds to see the deer through his scope, he stood up again.

"Can't see it," he hollered. As he did so, a whitetail doe jumped from the brush, running up over the hill toward the east hunter. He took a single snap shot.

The far-right hunter finally saw the white tail waving to him as the deer ran uphill. He had a number of intervening trees to contend with but nevertheless tried a snap shot as well. Neither his nor his companion's shot had any visible effect. Range for him was a minimum of one hundred yards.

The deer bounded up the east side of the draw,

through a few low leafless bushes, and out of sight over the hill. Both hunters remarked at the incredible ability whitetails have of keeping any available trees between themselves and hunters, as well as their aptitude for picking the absolute shortest distance to get out of sight over a hill.

Hunter three was over the hill and in the general area into which the deer was headed. Quickly the shooters called him on their walkie-talkies, informing him that a deer was on its way. They received no answer—an encouraging sign, they thought.

Perhaps overoptimistically, the first two assumed their friend had the deer in his sight and was getting ready to shoot. Under those conditions, there is no time for radios. After a minute they heard the transmit button snap twice, indicating everything was as they had supposed.

The two unsuccessful shooters climbed down into the draw and back up the other side looking for signs that they may have hit the deer. Both hunters had large rifles. Any deer touched by these calibers virtually any place could be tracked and killed, they figured.

They found nothing on the hill except the tracks of the bounding doe in the powdery snow. There were no signs of blood or of any faltering on the deer's part.

In retrospect, all three hunters were surprised at the length of time it took the doe to get over to the east hunter. They speculated that perhaps it ran over the little rise and out of sight, where it started sneaking again. The pair checking the trail for blood may have jumped it again.

A minimum of five minutes elapsed before the deer came bounding at hunter three. He assumed he was prepared but apparently the sound of the shooting, the overlong wait, and then the sight of the deer bearing down on him were unnerving. The fleeing animal seemed intent on following along the exact game trail on which he waited.

He fumbled with his gloves, the radio, and his .308 bolt-action rifle. The intense cold was a real hindrance. Finally he got a shot off at a range of no more than ten yards as the doe bore down on his position.

At the shot, the deer spun to its right and headed out toward the meadow directly away from

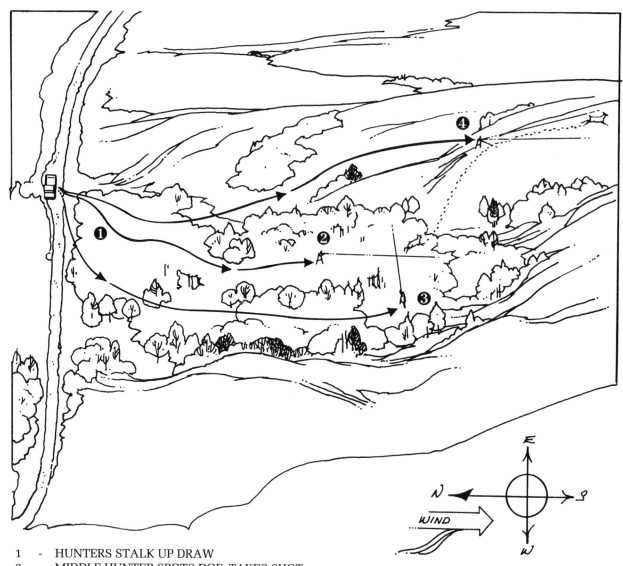

1 - HUNTERS STALK UP DRAW
2 - MIDDLE HUNTER SPOTS DOE, TAKES SHOT
3 - WEST HUNTER RUNS AHEAD, TAKES SNAP SHOT THROUGH TIMBER
4 - HUNTER THREE TAKES THREE UNSUCCESSFUL SHOTS

the hunter. He fired a second shot. When that had no effect, he bolted a third round into the chamber. The deer was now about two hundred yards out and really carrying the mail. His third round also missed, kicking up frost and snow ahead of the bounding deer. At three misses, he decided to call it a day. He could have taken a fourth shot but elected to stop wasting ammunition.

The deer ran into a wooded patch across the meadow, disappearing forever. As far as the three hunters know, that doe had triplets the following spring. They hunted around in a desultory fashion for the remainder of the day but saw no more deer.

All the hunters went on to bag deer that and subsequent seasons. They reasoned that they had hunted wisely that day, given the weather. The critter demonstrated how cleverly evasive deer can be trying to sneak off in virtually no cover and then running in a manner that prevented hunters from getting a good shot. No one agonized over the failed hunt or gave it much consideration past dinner conversation with the family that night.

CHAPTER 27

HERMIT BUCK

HUNT CHECKLIST

Weather
Overcast, drizzly day of about 40°F.

Terrain
Fairly flat to gently rolling. Government fields mixed in with numerous small patches of timber.

Wind Direction
Quite gentle out of southwest.

Conditions Previous Day
Rain and cold, much the same as it was the day of the hunt.

How Hunters Moved
Drove through three large patches of brush and timber without results. Picked a tiny, unlikely patch of woods along the road and drove a huge buck from it.

Clothes
Mostly worn old work clothes, whatever hunters could conveniently find around the house.

Rifle Caliber and Scope
Deer was shot with a .30-06 commercial semiauto with 4X scope. Other rifles in the group included a variety of mostly cut-down military-type guns.

Sex of Deer
Huge whitetail buck with 6-point (western count) rack.

Time of Day
About 1:30 P.M.

Length of Hunt
The crew was out the entire day, sunup to sundown, probably walking 6 or 8 miles total.

Length of Shot
About 60 yards.

How Deer Moved
Deer was lying in a small thicket covering a little gully. It ran out, where a stander dropped it.

Skill of Hunters
Shooting hunter was skilled and experienced, having hunted over that country for years. Drivers were mostly young men.

Three long-time hunting companions form the basis of this case. One of the men had three boys who, as they grew older, were added to the hunting crew. Since half their group was young and full of energy, the crew usually worked a great deal more country than one would expect during the course of a normal day's hunting. Among local hunters, they had a well-deserved reputation for being smart and energetic hunters who usually did things in an effective manner.

The territory in this case was a mix of farmland, set-aside government acres, and wooded patches. About half the fairly level ground was farmed for wheat, oats, barley, or peas. All crops were long harvested by early winter when deer season normally kicked off. Other than cropland, the area was interspersed with varying-sized patches of woods from 5 to 250 acres or more, where pine, fir, and aspen grew.

The trees that covered the patches often hid small rock outcrops, old erosion gullies, and, in a few cases, some fairly deep ravines. Hunters in that general area customarily sent drivers through as many of these patches of cover as they could manage in a day. Standers on the other side, where they knew from experience that deer would jump, got most of the shots. Wind, snow, and on-the-ground constraints dictated which of the patches they ran as well as exactly how.

It was drizzly, overcast day of about 40°F. Weather the previous week had been damp but not much colder. Winds out of the southwest were of limited intensity. Since in any given year the group managed to drive virtually every woodlot and brush meadow within thirty miles, they usually spent a relatively long time each morning discussing where they intended to hunt that day.

Because the group usually found deer to shoot at, they attracted a continual string of friends, acquaintances, school chums, and assorted camp followers to their weekly outings. As a general rule, those in the original group did not object, as valid, unused tags were always in short supply. Toward the end of the season, it was not unusual for three or four desperate extras to show up in hopes that they would at least see a few shootable deer.

As can be imagined, given a group comprised to a great extent of miscellaneous teenaged boys, weapons as well as hunting clothes were anything but standard. Rifles tended to be less expensive, more rugged, cut-down military types. Some of the young men who had hunted seriously over the last few years had saved their money to purchase modern scoped rifles, but for the most part their armament and clothing were fairly ragtag.

Most of the men wore clothes that showed no thought for slipping through the woods silently or being able to withstand long stretches on a cold stand. They generally wore whatever was available as they ran out the door. Economic realities in their little rural community precluded purchase of comfortable utilitarian wool jackets, pants, or shirts. As one would expect, their boots were whatever they commonly wore to work or school.

No one remembers exactly how many bodies presented themselves for duty other than the three old-timers and the three sons that day. Their hunting techniques made being in the woods at first light unnecessary, yet they usually collected, argued, and discussed early so as to leave as much daylight as possible in which to hunt.

They ran their first patch just at sunup, or about 6:30 A.M. It was a heavily wooded patch no more than three hundred yards wide but more than a mile long. A county road bordered the long, thin strip on one side; a harvested wheat field delineated the other side.

The patch of cover was so wooly and overgrown that few, if any, conventional hunters ever ventured there. For single hunters, the deer just sat tight, as they could not be seen at even fifteen paces.

At least four drivers were dropped off at the south end of the strip. Two standers waited in a thirty-yard-wide clear-cut hacked out by the power company for their line. The cut ran at right angles across the strip about halfway to the other end. Several other standers drove a pickup down to the far end where they waited.

The plan included having the drivers beat through the brush to the power-line cut. At that time one of the standers would also drive while the other headed out into the wheat stubble lest any deer break cover trying to escape cross country.

The terrain they were dealing with was flat to slightly undulating. There were a few widely scattered draws, but these were never much of a factor in their hunts. Winds for the drivers were quartering from behind and left, just enough so that the deer would be unlikely to wind them.

On this, the first push of the day, they ran a large deer of unknown sex out across the county road east. One of the drivers saw it briefly from afar as it bounded down the road and cut across the gravel onto the other side. Two of them followed the track in the soft gravel but lost it when the deer ran across a much-trampled pasture.

A second smallish doe left the strip of cover halfway between the power-line cut and the far north end. It ran out across the stubble field right out in plain view. For some reason, the stander in the field who was about two hundred yards away did not attempt a shot. He simply reported seeing the deer run away.

All of the drivers reported numerous tracks in the soft, muddy ground within the strip but, at the end, they came up with nothing except the two escapees.

Two sixty-acre wooded areas lay ahead and north of the crew perhaps another half mile. Walking together, they crossed the open farm fields, splitting up only at the last. Three standers cut west half a mile from the first patch, walking around till they were on stand on its west end. The remaining drivers literally beat their way through the dense underbrush.

Winds for the drive may have been slightly adverse, but given their sheer numbers it was not unreasonable to expect something to scare out someplace. Nothing jumped, there being only a few fresh tracks in the thicket.

They moved directly to the second sixty-acre patch to the immediate west. In this case the standers split off early and walked round to the other side in a very lengthy, circuitous fashion, taking them well to the north. They did everything they could not to alert the critters.

When the main gang of drivers stormed through the patch, the results were painfully typ-

ical for the day. They pushed nothing out of the woods and were, when they finished, at least two miles from the nearest vehicle and three miles from all of the others.

Some hunters brought their lunches. It was 11:30 A.M. so they broke them out, eating as they walked back to the pickup truck parked north of the first strip they had driven in the early morning.

As one would expect, the question asked over and over again was "Where are the deer?" They beat the issue to death, yet no one had any good answers. The old-timers were perplexed and the kids were anxious. The discussion continued hot and heavy as they loaded into the single pickup for the ride back to the other vehicles. At the main group of vehicles, there was still no consensus as to what would constitute a next smart hunt.

"Let's just drive around to the other side and see if we get any bright ideas," an old-timer suggested.

Driving around involved following a set of county roads that were laid out much like a giant egg. It was about two miles across the egg, two and a half or three end to end, and about seven miles all the way around.

With three trucks running in tandem, they headed around to the other side. As they came up the west portion of the grid, one of the old-timers noticed a small wooded patch of pine, fir, and poplar. They had never run that piece before, but he suggested that today might be a good day to do so. It was at most six to eight acres.

"Far too small," his peers piped up. "Can't be any deer in there!"

After a brief discussion, they turned their vehicles around and drove back for another look. The patch lay at an angle to the road, strung out for about two hundred yards. Numerous dead, broken trees and limbs covered the floor of the woods.

They neither stopped nor slowed as they passed. About two hundred yards on past, one of the old-timers quietly jumped out of the truck to start walking into the open field behind the patch. Winds were crossing slowly in a bit of an unfavorable direction. He kept well away from the woods till he was passed them and the winds could blow harmlessly beyond.

143

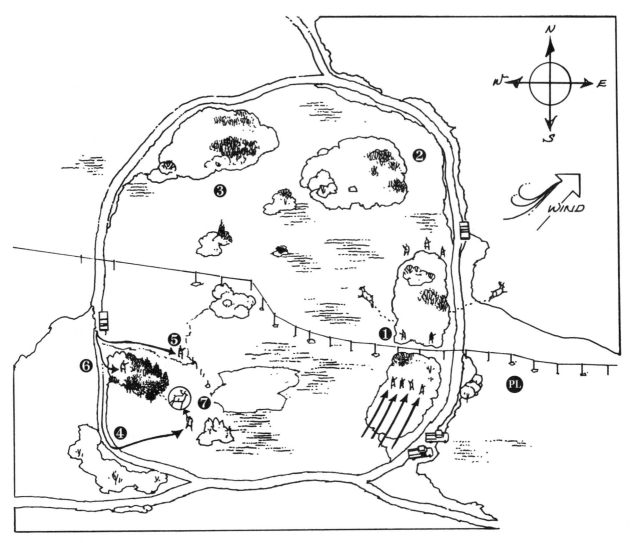

PL - POWER LINE
1 - FIRST DRIVE; TWO DEER ESCAPE
2 - SECOND BRUSH PATCH DRIVEN WITHOUT RESULT
3 - THIRD UNSUCCESSFUL DRIVE
4 - STANDER JUMPS OUT OF TRUCK, TAKES UP POSITION
5 - SECOND STANDER TAKES UP POSITION
6 - DRIVERS PUSH THROUGH PATCH
7 - STANDER SHOOTS BUCK

The others turned around, driving back to the north side of the targeted patch. They moved slowly due to the great distance the stander had to travel.

Another stander walked due east from the parking spot along an old fencerow. The drivers waited another five minutes till both standers were definitely in position.

The first stander carried a commercial .30-06 semiautomatic with 4X scope. The second stander used a cut-down .303 Enfield that was probably new in World War I.

Four drivers walked down the road. They recall that some of the party had elected to stay in the trucks. The assumption was that they would be rubbing shoulders in such a small patch and there wouldn't be anything there anyway.

The drivers were barely in the woods when a single shot was heard from behind the patch. It sounded very much like a meat shot, but even though the woods were only six or eight acres, they could not see through to know what, for sure, was going on.

As instructed, they ran the area out cautiously and completely. They were close enough together that they could discuss the shot in a normal tone of voice.

Upon walking out the other side, they found the first stander perched on top of a huge gray-brown six-point buck. It was the largest-bodied and -racked whitetail most of the men had ever seen.

The stander had hit it once through the brisket at a range of about sixty yards. The heavy .30-06 bullet traveled the full length of the critter's body cavity, coming to rest against its backbone about four inches from the tail. After being hit, the deer continued to run up to within thirty yards of the stander before it collapsed. Thinking another deer could emerge, he walked over and stood on the body to get a better view of the country.

After field-dressing it, the crew dragged the deer the three hundred yards to the road, where they loaded it into the truck. Most estimates assumed a weight of three hundred pounds or more.

They went on to drive the first long strip of woods again. No one believed that additional deer had moved in during the last five hours, but they did manage to get two more out this time.

One was a nice spike buck. It broke cover in the middle of the drive and was able to get over a little rise to the east before anyone could get a shot. A doe popped out of the strip, ran into the stubble field, and ducked back into the brushy strip and was never seen again. After that, they gave up for the week.

The hunters later concluded that they got the solitary buck because they tried a seemingly nothing drive on a hunch. Even so, they drove the woods carefully and properly, taking nothing for granted. Obviously the buck was ready to vacate its premises immediately. Had they not set up adequately, they would have missed it.

No one knows why the senior member of the group thought a deer might be hiding in the little patch. They do realize that his ability to remain cool contributed to his getting the deer. One of the younger hunters might simply have shot up the open space around the buck. All agreed it was the best deer they had killed in many years, taken out of the smallest, most unlikely piece of cover.

CHAPTER 28
BEACH BLACKTAIL

HUNT CHECKLIST

Weather
Cold, miserable, and damp. 38 to 40°F day with penetrating wind.

Terrain
Steep northwest coastal mountains, dropping sharply to the ocean.

Wind Direction
8- to 10-knot wind out of northwest, with gusts to 15 knots at sea.

Conditions Previous Day
Snowed extensively in the mountains and had stormed at sea.

How Hunters Moved
Motored boat up coast to a long, thin fjord, which they hunted to the river feeding it, where they found the deer grazing on kelp.

Clothes
Nylon, cold-weather flotation/survival suits over several layers of thermal underwear and wool shirts and pants.

Rifle Caliber and Scope
.338 Winchester Magnum bolt-action with 4X scope.

Sex of Deer
Spike buck.

Time of Day
Deer was shot about 9:00 A.M. Hunters stayed out all day.

Length of Hunt
About 40 minutes from the time they suspected they had a deer in sight to the time hunter shot it.

Length of Shot
About 140 yards.

How Deer Moved
Deer came out of poplar grove to eat kelp on the shore of a bay.

Skill of Hunters
Hunters all had extensive experience operating boats and hunting in coastal waters for blacktail deer.

This seemingly straightforward case wherein the hunters stalked coastal blacktails graphically illustrates the necessity and difficulty of integrating weather, ground conditions, stalking techniques, and—most of all—modern equipment and technology. Because one sees a critter while riding in a truck, boat, or plane does not automatically mean that it can be stalked successfully and killed.

This example occurred in an area where tangled, thick, impenetrable Pacific rain forests harbored huge numbers of elusive coastal blacktail deer. Access to the area was limited to use of boats to drop hunters off on the infrequent little pebbly beaches. Penetration into the forest for any distance on foot was extremely difficult to virtually impossible.

Because of the rocky, mountainous terrain cut through by hundreds of small ocean fjords, road building was prohibitively expensive. Few roads, paths, or even trails crossed the area. The few that were punched through ran inland at places where the terrain was less inhospitable.

Although thousands and perhaps even tens of thousands of coastal blacktails inhabited the area, few were ever taken. The combination of the deers' stealthful nature and the extremely thick stands of Sitka spruce, cedar, and giant ferns growing on the rugged terrain conspired to keep the deer safe from hunters.

Those who regularly hunted blacktails in the region found that the only rational method of doing so was to wait till late season snows pushed the critters down onto the shoreline. At this time, one could attempt to hunt them from boats. However, even this method was perilous.

Sly blacktails seldom left the shelter of the forests unless recent storms created large waves that threw fresh kelp up onto the pebbly beaches. Successfully hunting these deer involved a combination of watching for severe snowstorms in the mountains followed by heavy storms at sea the previous day and a calming the day of the hunt, permitting one to operate a boat along the coast. Needless to say, this combination of conditions seldom occurred, but even when it did, hunting was far from simple.

Temperatures the day of this hunt were a cold, damp, raw 38 to 40°F. Eighteen inches of new snow in the mountains rising from the water's edge pushed the deer down to the last hundred yards of cover. The terrain looked clean, neat, and tailored with the exception of the water's edge, which looked muddy and trashy.

Two-foot waves along with a vicious northwest cross chop washed against the shore. It was as calm as it was going to get that time of year. A bank of thick, greasy, rapidly moving fog hung on the water, causing even greater concern for those who might venture very far from land.

Blacktail hunting is not a sport for the faint of heart, the three hunters reminded each other as they pulled out of the shelter of the levee. They set out just before first light, about 7:30 A.M. They intended to cruise the shore from the first hour of daylight till full dark at about 3:30 P.M.

Although there was a certain amount of safety in their 240-horsepower, twenty-two-foot offshore fishing boat, each hunter wore a bright orange cold-water flotation/survival suit. Under these suits they wore several layers of thermal underwear as additional protection against the cold, damp, eight- to ten-knot wind. Boots were rubber pacs that they wore untied so that, in an emergency, they could be kicked off.

The hunters—who had extensive experience operating boats on coastal waters—motored north from the boat landing for about thirty minutes, covering about three miles. They carefully glassed the fresh, green line of kelp recently thrown on shore. Until full light, they stood offshore one hundred yards lest they get into the whitecaps and rocks.

As a result of both the bobbing boat and the great distance, they may have missed some of the diminutive deer along the shore. As soon as there was enough light in the gray, leaden sky, they pulled in closer.

After a half hour's travel north up the coast, they came to a relatively long arm reaching back toward a river flowing out of the highlands. Cautiously they motored up the estuary, encountering small patches of fog hanging among the steep cliffs. The rock shore was sufficiently steep and rugged in places so that any deer would have had to rock climb to approach the kelp.

Perhaps a mile into the arm, the hunters spotted where the river pouring down from the mountains met the ocean. Thick stands of poplars grew in the little dished-out valley formed by the river. Snow covered the ground down to within a hundred yards of the river's termination at the ocean.

As they approached the wide, troughlike opening, winds previously held back by the high mountains started to hit the more open waters. Almost as if an invisible hand drew a line on the water, the vessel ran into a patch of vicious chop.

About this time the two spotters thought they saw a chocolate-brown to almost black dog-sized animal at the bright green kelp line on the gravel bar formed by the rushing river. Unfortunately, no amount of steerage could steady the boat sufficiently so that they could confirm what it was they saw.

They throttled back until the vessel just maintained its heading. Winds blew down from the left (approximately northwest) across the river on an angle over the position of the suspected deer.

Beaching the boat in the high, cold waves washing across the shallow beach was more trouble than anyone who has never tried it can possibly imagine. It still wasn't certain whether they had a deer spotted, but one man decided to go ashore downwind to have a look from land.

Landing might have been easy during summer, but in the icy 35°F water it was a most rigorous exercise in survival. So that the vessel's prop might not be bent or the hull damaged, the hunter slid off the bow into eighteen inches of water. It quickly filled his loosely laced boots but crept up into his flotation suit much more slowly.

The hunter waded to shore holding his .338 bolt-action rifle with 4X scope high above his head. The others backed the boat out into the waves, standing offshore till he needed them. Even the stalking hunter wondered at the commitment necessary to be out in such horrible, dangerous conditions wading around in water that was almost a freeze bath.

He slogged on to shore and crouched down, attempting to stalk up on an as yet unknown target across country as open and desolate as the surface of the moon. In addition, he was continually mindful of the constant threat from marauding bears, explaining the large-caliber rifle he carried for a critter that certainly could be taken with a .22 rimfire!

After crawling about two hundred yards, the hunter assumed a half-crouch, looking through his scope. He confirmed that a deer actually was eating at the kelp. With its head down, only the main body was exposed. It was a very small target to identify positively.

He crawled back closer to the surf, where the natural drop to the water provided some relief in which to hide. He worked on around another eighty to a hundred yards till he moved uphill onto the river delta again.

Now he could see the deer plainly without the scope. It was fighting with a long piece of kelp, pulling it this way and that.

The hunter estimated the range at 175 yards. He duck-walked onto the beach another forty yards, where he sat down. For several minutes he watched the deer through his scope.

It was now angling a bit away from him but, for the most part, he had the best broadside shot he was going to get. Coldly and stiffly he wiped the scope one more time, bolted a round into the chamber, put the horizontal hair level on the animal's back, and touched the trigger. When he looked again, the critter was gone.

The hunter bolted another round into the rifle, got up, and started walking toward the deer's location. He realized he had a cold, deep, freshwater river running between him and the spot. Now he could plainly see the little deer lying crumpled on the other side.

On his way to the river bank, the hunter laced his boots up tightly, zipped up his flotation suit, and unloaded and slung his rifle. He looked around till he found a stout, clean cedar pole about eight feet long lying among the flotsam on the gravel bar.

The freezing water piled up almost to his hips. Had it not been running so fast, he assumed it would have been frozen. He had to cross as quickly as possible before the icy water leaked through his suit, freezing his legs so he couldn't move.

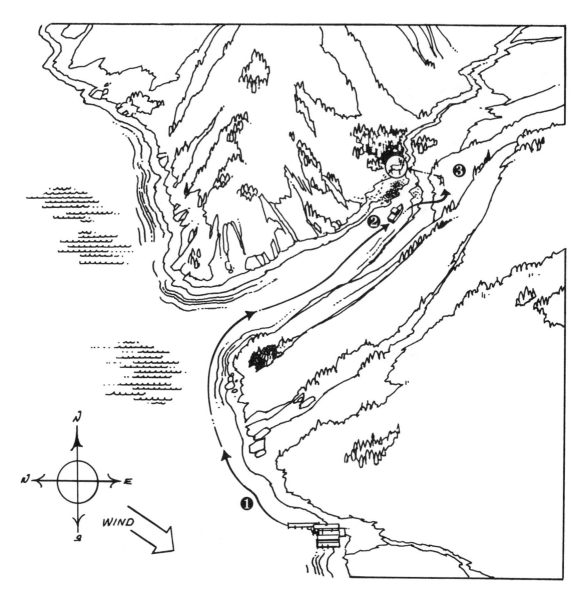

1 - HUNTERS MOTOR UP COAST LOOKING FOR DEER EATING KELP
2 - HUNTERS SPOT DEER ON GRAVEL BAR
3 - HUNTER STALKS ASHORE; SHOOTS DEER FROM ACROSS RIVER

He field-dressed the deer as quickly as possible. It was a spike buck, weighing at most seventy-five pounds. He cut through the skin between the hock tendons and laced a piece of cord from one foot to another. Thus secured, he draped the little deer over his shoulders like some sort of grotesque scarf.

Carrying deer, rifle, and wading pole, the hunter waded out into the little bay. By running the boat up the slightly deeper river channel and using poles and paddles, his two companions were able to get in relatively close to shore. At the boat, the hunter turned and held the deer so that his buddies could lift it from his shoulders.

He jumped backward into the boat, falling off the gunwale and into the boat's center. He had a change of thermal underwear and socks in a duffel bag, which he substituted for the wet set he wore.

150

They patrolled the shore for another two hours but could not confirm another deer. About one hour before dark they headed back to the harbor, not wanting to risk being caught out in rough water in the dark or be swallowed up by a bank of fog.

The hunter attributed his success to plain old stubbornness in that he even considered going deer hunting on such an awful day. He also believed a basic immunity to pain and suffering helped. Most hunters would not have considered wading through the icy surf, crawling across the rocks, and then crossing the river. He is not sure whether this case demonstrates anything other than that conditions can get so tough that no amount of money could ever entice someone to go deer hunting had he no sporting reason to do so.

CHAPTER 29
CHURCH DEER

HUNT CHECKLIST

Weather

Cold, dry, 20 to 25°F. Skies were gray and leaden.

Terrain

Gently rolling hills with a few severe, deep canyons and high hills covered with second-growth pine and fir and intermittent patches of poplar.

Wind Direction

Very little wind. At final brush patch, winds were 2 to 4 knots out of the west and not a factor.

Conditions Previous Day

Snow from previous week was mostly evaporated by cold, dry winds. Some snow remained in sheltered woods and in the lee of little hills.

How Hunters Moved

Hunters circled through three brush patches surrounding an apple orchard. In fourth patch they got up two deer, which driver shot.

Clothes

Several layers of wool clothes so that they could stand as well as drive and stalk quietly through heavy brush.

Rifle Caliber and Scope

.338 bolt-action with 6X scope. Two shots were taken.

Sex of Deer

One very nice doe and one exceptional 5-point (western count) buck.

Time of Day

Sunday about 11:30 A.M., the third weekend of deer season.

Length of Hunt

Hunters started at daybreak, going till the middle of the afternoon.

Length of Shot

Both were about 35 to 45 yards.

How Deer Moved

Driver entering woods on east scared two deer to stander on west, who scared them back to driver, who shot them.

Skill of Hunters

Both hunters were skilled old-timers who had hunted deer together almost forever. They knew from vast experience what each was likely to do in any given circumstance.

The case in question involved two extremely able, terminally addicted deer chasers. Together they spent almost every daylight hour of the season out in the field. The two men had hunted together so long that they virtually could read each other's mind. They knew how the whitetails usually reacted to their hunting tactics, where the deer would lie up during various types of weather, and exactly how the other would handle each situation.

When recounting various kills, the men could and would start with various patches of timber, telling in great detail the number of deer taken out of each. Thus inspired, they moved around the country in their minds' eye till they recalled scores of successful hunts.

The terrain over which they hunted was mixed farm and forested land comprised of large tracts of cleared and uncleared pasture, wooded areas, and large grain fields. Often these fields covered a hundred acres or more without a fence or hedgerow.

Topography was gently rolling to fairly severe in a few places where high hills or steep canyons intervened. As a rule, the two hunters enjoyed their best successes working the fringe areas, where pasture and grain fields met heavier cover.

Woods in the region were inhabited by second- and third-generation pine and fir with some smaller patches of poplar. Short huckleberry brush covered the ground wherever tall trees did not shade them. Where sufficient sunlight filtered through the forest's top cover, dense, tangled patches of ninebark thrived.

County roads cut through the region in an irregular pattern. While it was never possible to predict their exact course, the two men could assume they were rarely more than two miles from some kind of road on which they could operate at least a four-wheel-drive vehicle. As a result of the heightened level of farming as well as the great many roads in the region, a number of residential and commercial structures dotted the landscape. The nearest large population centers were at least thirty miles away, but the significant number of people who called this basically rural area home were always a consideration for them.

During the deer season they expected competition from other hunters as well as the continuing problem of avoiding residents, office buildings, farmsteads, and other places where people were likely to be. As a general rule, citizens of that region understood hunting, but wise hunters maintained a low profile.

The day of the hunt was overcast but dry. Temperatures held in the 20 to 25°F range. Snow from the previous week was mostly gone, evaporated by the cold, dry wind except in isolated patches in the sheltered woods. Winds were so light they were virtually no factor.

The hunters wore wool pants, shirts, and jackets. Because they intended to alternate between standing and driving, they wore layered clothing that could be opened as needed. They knew from past experience that they might need to stalk deer virtually any time during the hunt. As a result, their external covering was all wool.

They parked their truck on the county road at first light on the third Sunday of the season. Together they moved up a gentle rise into a large, cutover wheat field till they reached a forty-acre wooded area. One hunter swung around the woods, coming toward it from the south, where he took up a stand at a place where a brushy fence line ran due east from the woods for about three-quarters of a mile into a similar wooded area.

The driving hunter plowed through the woods, moving with the slight wind on top of the hill. He made numerous zigzags, stops, and detours, but despite being a skilled, experienced driver, he was unable to get anything out of the woods. The pair was somewhat dismayed that they did not scare up a deer. An eighty-acre apple and plum orchard to the north a quarter of a mile almost always kept dozens of deer in the immediate area.

They moved along the overgrown fencerow east to the next patch of woods. As they had many times before, one man walked around the woods to the other side while his partner waited patiently for an all-clear over the walkie-talkie to start the drive. As soon as the stander was in place in a tall grass pasture, he called on the radio, setting the driver in motion.

The driver performed his part of the hunt in a thorough, professional, skilled manner but was again unable to find deer in the second patch of woods. Tracks in the soft, moist portions of the woodlot soil were conspicuous by their absence. At the conclusion of the second drive, they were south and a bit east of the apple orchard around which they were hunting.

A third wooded area lay north of their position, directly east of the apple orchard. It was somewhat different in makeup, being a heavily grazed wooded area. As a result of the grazing, all of the understory was gone and most of the trees' lower branches up to about six feet were also missing. Many of the trees in this area were smooth-trunked poplars. Visibility was often 150 yards or more.

Because horses and cattle were grazing in the sixty-acre patch at that moment, the hunters knew they had to exercise great caution. Rather than attempt to drive the patch, they concluded that a careful, slow stalk across the cover might be productive.

They spread out 150 yards apart and walked through the mostly rectangular-shaped patch. By so doing, each man could see the edge of the pasture as well as into the center of the woods. There was no way of testing the theory, but they thought their respective sight distances overlapped, and that one or the other would spot any deer trying to escape. Should a deer have tried sneaking between them, they intended to discuss the matter over their walkie-talkies before taking action.

As it unfolded, no deer tried to sneak between, ahead of, or away from them. As in the last two pieces of cover, tracks were few and far between and deer nonexistent. Even at the salt block, tracks were so few it was puzzling. The hunters thought that perhaps other hunters had come through the area ahead of them. However, there were virtually no human tracks around, leading them to believe that other problems existed that they were unable to identify.

They concluded that portion of the hunt when they arrived at the orchard at about 10:30 A.M. Fresh cultivating in the orchard made it possible to determine that a number of deer had passed through in the last few days. Yet the sheer number of tracks made it impossible to determine where the deer came from or where they were now.

A single fifteen-acre wooded area lay across the orchard to the west. The hunters could have reasoned either that no deer were in the woods because they failed to find any in the surrounding areas or that all of the deer they knew were around someplace must be there. They were reluctant to run the patch on this particular day, however, because of a small rural church that lay along the road on the far west end. Worshippers, they thought, who might be leaving services between 11:00 A.M. and 12:00 noon would be mightily disturbed by any deer shooting close by.

In retrospect, the hunters think they probably knew that there were deer in the patch but were looking for an excuse to go someplace different. They were fearful of drawing attention to themselves, which would certainly happen if they shot behind the church at that time.

After a fairly lengthy discussion, the two decided that they would go ahead and run the little patch. Obviously, addiction to anything is a heavy price to pay.

Basically, the woods ran in an east/west direction. What small amount of wind there was seemed insignificant as they stalked and drove through the area.

One hunter swung around to the north, walking about five hundred yards to a place where a little strip of unfarmed, weed-covered land ran into the northwest end of the woodlot. The stander was about three hundred yards northeast of the church.

The driver waited till he got an all clear on the radio before starting through the woods. About fifty yards into the heavy, tangled ninebark and elderberry, he heard something crash ahead and to his right. Although he never saw it, he assumed that it was a deer. He called the stander, who agreed to be especially vigilant but also reported that the driver's radio batteries were about used up.

The driver continued pushing through the heavy brush into a slightly lower area where large trees shaded the ground, dramatically reducing the amount of brush he had to contend with. Visibility was now up to fifty or sixty yards. Dead

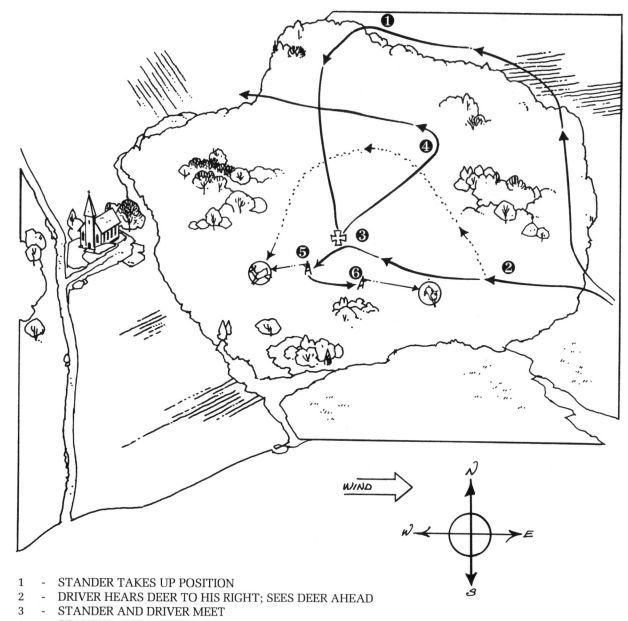

1 - STANDER TAKES UP POSITION
2 - DRIVER HEARS DEER TO HIS RIGHT; SEES DEER AHEAD
3 - STANDER AND DRIVER MEET
4 - STANDER, NOW DRIVER, HEADS OUT OF WOODS
5 - HUNTER SHOOTS BUCK
6 - HUNTER SHOOTS DOE

ahead he spotted a whitetail sneaking head down on a right angle to him. He tried to find an opening for a shot but was unsuccessful. Before he could determine its sex, the deer disappeared.

The driver did not have a lot of information such as size and sex, but he called the stander and reported another critter. His radio worked well enough to hear a transmission from his friend telling him that his message was unintelligible. He tried transmitting again, but the power light indicated his radio was completely dead. He was at something of a loss as to how to proceed unless it was to simply follow the deer through till it ran past his companion.

156

A few close deer hunting companions believe they can read each other's minds. Perhaps this case proves that hypothesis true. The driver was standing in a little opening covered with brown, dead ferns when the stander showed up on his right.

He quickly told the stander about the two deer he jumped. The stander told the driver to wait there, that he would swing around and drive them back to him. The driver remembers that he had little confidence that the maneuver would be productive.

Their roles were now reversed: driver was stander and stander was driver. The new driver ran out to the open field bordering the woods, then straight west along the field's edge. He reasoned that if either of the deer broke cover, he could get a shot at it. About three hundred feet northeast of the church, he reentered the woods at the northwest corner, not having seen the deer. From that point, he drove toward the stander.

The stander stayed where he was for about five minutes and then started ahead as quietly as possible. It was another five minutes and two hundred feet before he heard a critter thumping through the dead leaves and grass. He turned to see a giant buck slow to a cautious walk trying to move north to south thirty-five yards behind him.

He stepped over to a little bare-based pine, rested his rifle solidly on the trunk, placed the crosshairs in an opening ahead of the deer, and waited. As soon as he saw movement in the right of the scope, he jerked the trigger.

The hunter was using a .338 bolt-action with 6X scope. He saw the deer roll over at the shot. As he walked over to it, he could smell the gun smoke hanging in the air. He reached the buck and was about to start field-dressing it when he heard a snort behind him in the path over which he had just walked.

A huge old doe stood in the woods no more than forty-five yards away. The hunter grabbed his rifle, which had been resting against a tree, and bolted another round into the chamber.

He took an offhand shot at the doe as it stood looking around, trying to locate both the stander and driver. He saw the deer run off to the north and disappear. The shot was taken in the general area of the church, which was, at most, two hundred yards away. The white wood building was not visible because of the many trees.

The shooter encountered the driver again as he walked back to look for the buck. They found its track in the soft soil and followed it on about eighty yards to the critter, gasping its last with a hole through its heart.

Working as expeditiously as possible, they field-dressed the buck. They estimated its weight, less guts and legs, at between 275 and 300 pounds. While they were working, they could hear people talking, car doors slamming, and the sound of a church organ.

They pulled the giant whitetail over to the edge of the woods, rolling him into a little grassy depression. It may have been an illusion, but the sixty-yard drag away from the people gave them a heightened feeling of safety.

The doe was hit high and solid through the front shoulder. They field-dressed it, taking off the head as well as the feet. It was about 12:00 noon when they dragged it over to the same hide in the tall grass with the buck.

Rather than trying to hunt without radios over country they had not intended to run that day, the two lay at the field's edge watching cars from the church depart for home.

At about 1:00 p.m. they determined that they could load the deer without disturbing anyone. No cars had ventured out on the rural road for almost fifteen minutes. One hunter walked to their truck, brought it around, then backed it across the roadside ditch into the field. His partner pulled the deer out from the woods across the field two hundred yards or more. They got home within forty minutes, where they spent the remainder of the day skinning and splitting the deer.

The hunters concluded that they were successful because they persisted till they located deer they knew were in the general area, and because even with dead radios they knew how to drive deer out of that particular piece of country. They knew how each would move, and they knew how to shoot in heavy brush. They also believe it was appropriate not to disturb the people in church unduly.

CHAPTER 30
NOVICE HUNT

HUNT CHECKLIST

Weather
25°F with solid, low clouds blowing through. Snow looked imminent.

Terrain
Hilly, with relief difference of 400 to 600 feet in some places. Ground cover was pine and fir with an understory of hazel, ninebark, and huckleberry.

Wind Direction
Steady out of the west to northwest, 8 to 10 knots.

Conditions Previous Day
Snow the previous week, much of which had been blown off exposed hills into drifts in sheltered draws.

How Hunters Moved
Hunted up a draw running off a high hill. Hunter swung around a small brush field at the top, where he jumped two deer, shooting the second.

Clothes
Traditional wool hunting coats and pants. Cleated foul-weather boot pacs.

Rifle Caliber and Scope
.338 with 6X, .308 with open sights, and 12-gauge pump shotgun.

Sex of Deer
Mature whitetail doe.

Time of Day
Started after lunch about 1:00 P.M., hunting till just before dark at 4:30 P.M.

Length of Hunt
They walked about 3 miles each during the course of the 3 1/2-hour hunt.

Length of Shot
About 175 yards. Last 10 yards were through canelike brush, which failed to deflect the heavy round.

How Deer Moved
Out of bed in a little grass-covered bowl back into the edge of heavy timber, where hunter shot it.

Skill of Hunters
One hunter had been over that country for scores of years; the other two were just starting to hunt.

First-time deer hunters, as this case illustrates, usually fall into two distinct categories. Either they are wooden and unimaginative in their approach to the drama unfolding before them, or they run around the country in an unpredictable and unproductive manner. Experienced deer hunters sometimes become engulfed in this type of scenario but usually recognize the situation as it develops, drawing on past examples to find practical, workable solutions to the problem.

Either a wooden or reactionary response, if allowed to become chronic, will sooner or later lead to the participants giving up deer hunting altogether. Really successful, well-tuned deer hunters often do not provide much assistance to novice hunters working their way through the syndrome because it tends to make deer hunting look too easy.

Novice deer chasers often find that they must go a season or perhaps two or three before they see a shootable deer. Then, as likely as not, they will have no experience to, or they will not be adequately familiar with their rifles nor good enough shots to reduce to possession the deer they finally spot. A few of these points are illustrated in this case.

The hunters involved in this scenario were a retired husband and wife newly moved into a small, rural community wherein virtually everyone agreed that whitetail hunting was the premier national pastime. The locals knew from watching television that other Americans in places such as New York City, Miami, and San Francisco did not hunt deer, but certainly they could not understand these people or their culture.

The novice couple befriended one of the area's legendary old deer chasers who had hunted in the region for many years. This old-timer knew every patch of cover, deer run, bedding area, and water hole. He was getting on in years, so he now found it was more enjoyable to make every move through the bush count rather than engaging in long-distance patrolling.

Together the newcomers and old-timer conspired against the deer, the couple to supplement their meat supply and the old-timer to engage in the delight of his life—filling yet one more deer tag.

The country over which they hunted was characterized as hilly to steeply hilly. Differences in relief in many places were four to six hundred feet. Ponderosa pine, grand fir, and Douglas fir filled most of the deep ravines as well as covered the domelike hills. Besides the deer hunting tales that they had heard, the retired couple knew from their experience driving rural roads at night that numerous deer lived in the region.

Temperatures were about 25°F, with a strong eight- to ten-knot wind blowing from the west to northwest. Dense, fast-moving dark gray and black clouds covered the sky. Snowstorms looked as though they could start at any time.

In some places, incessant winds blew all of the six to eight inches of snow that fell the previous week from the open ground, but piled it into drifts eighteen to twenty-four inches deep in sheltered places. Most areas in the deep woods were covered by at least a light layer of snow, making it possible to determine if deer were present and/or moving.

The experienced hunter decided to take his friends out into a deep, sheltered draw covered by second- and third-generation pine and fir. Winds in that place were muted, and conditions would not be unreasonably tough for the novice hunters.

The draw in question was actually a side drainage on a steep hill that might have been taken for a mountain in some places in the United States. Sides of the draw were at least three hundred feet high top to bottom. The ridge looked down upon the next draw running off the same mountain. Either might have sheltered deer from the approaching storm, but the old-timer selected the one he did because it was slightly more open. Sight distances were often eighty to one hundred yards.

A graveled county road cut through the base of the draw on the north end. At that spot, about a hundred yards of grassy, open meadow lay between the road and a line of trees extending to the top of the hill.

This draw petered out at the top of the hill at an open meadow of eight or ten acres surrounded by other patches of timber. Given the wind, the generally nasty weather, and imminent snow, the old-timer felt that deer would likely lie in the draw, and that his friends would enjoy the tramp up through the somewhat sheltered area more than making other, more rigorous hunts in larger, more open spots.

The experienced hunter used a .338 bolt-action rifle with 6X scope. His friend carried an older .308 bolt-action with open sights, while the woman carried a 12-gauge pump shotgun loaded with buckshot. All wore wool coats, pants, and shirts. The couple wore wool because that's what the salesclerk told them to wear. The older hunter wore wool because he knew it would enable him to slip through the woods more silently. Boots were wet-weather pacs with cleated soles.

Using the little meadow at the road as a staging point, the old-timer sent the couple up the draw, one on each side. It was just after lunch, with dark expected about 4:30 P.M. He climbed up to the ridgeline, where he walked on through to the top clearing as fast as he could. He intended to push deer coming up to the top back down to the couple so that they might get a shot. He figured that the deer would try to walk through the woods rather than run on such a miserable day. Winds blew across the north/south canyon from the west and really were not a factor.

The experienced hunter got on an old game trail that ran up the steep ridge, pushing along as fast as available energy allowed. Without this trail it would have been difficult to get uphill as quickly as he did. The two drivers worked up the valley at their own speed.

About two-thirds of the way up the hill, she called him on their walkie-talkies, saying that she saw two deer in the bottom of the draw to her left. They were sneaking, "not running," uphill on an angle toward her husband.

The experienced hunter quickly cut over to a place where he could see down into the draw for several hundred yards. He hoped to see or hear the deer and cut them off so that they circled back toward the other two, but to no avail. Continuing on, his pace was slowed a bit without the convenience of the game trail.

After ten or fifteen minutes, he assumed that the deer had heard him and circled over to driver two to the far east, where they stopped till he walked past them. In a few more minutes, he came out as planned at the meadow on top of the hill. In the interim, winds picked up measurably. They were blowing across the top of the clearing at least fifteen knots, and they now contained snow. Visibility in the snow was under a hundred yards. On the plus side, the racing winds made it tough for deer to wind the stalkers.

Top hunter walked all the way out into the little meadow and then cut east toward the other side of the draw. By radio he confirmed that the other two were halfway or more up the draw and still working through the woods in an effective manner. They could no longer see each other but were okay, he assumed, as long as they continued to move uphill.

A small bowl-like landform lay at the southeast corner of the draw. The old-timer knew from past experience that deer often lay in the tall canary grass and brush in the bowl and that their usual route of escape when jumped from above was to run down the steep hillside, a pattern that would put the critters in the middle of the couple's territory.

He moved north with the blustery wind and snow now beating against his left side. He came up on the bowl and walked the rim, peering down through the tangled brush and grass. Almost immediately he jumped a whitetail doe, which ran downhill toward the northwest. The hunter assumed it would run into his two companions, preferably the man with the .308.

He called on the radio, determining the fellow's position and advising him to hold still at the ready for a few minutes. The old-timer also stood rooted in his spot, wanting to see if the stalkers started shooting, but like the first two deer, this one just disappeared. He had no clue as to where it went.

After a brief wait he was so chilled that he had to start moving again. He slowly moved northeast to the very edge of the bowl's eastern rim. Clumps of leafless vine maple grew there at the edge of the bowl. As he moved behind one maple thicket, an old whitetail doe jumped up

161

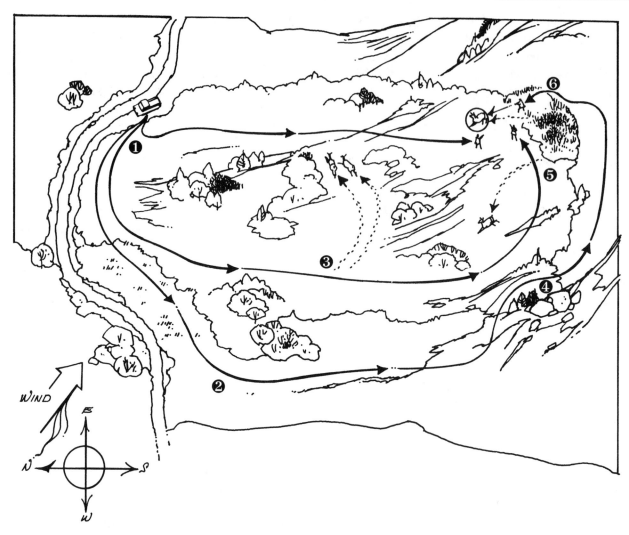

1 - COUPLE DRIVE UP EACH SIDE OF DRAW
2 - OLD-TIMER WALKS ALONG RIDGELINE
3 - FEMALE HUNTER JUMPS TWO DEER
4 - OLD-TIMER LOOKS FOR JUMPED DEER
5 - FIRST DOE SPOOKED OUT OF BRUSH AND DISAPPEARS
6 - OLD-TIMER JUMPS, SHOOTS SECOND DOE

out of the grass, running toward the main body of woods. He caught only fleeting glimpses of it through the heavy growth.

The hunter called on the radio, alerting the other two to the second deer running from the same piece of cover. They called back, suggesting that under the circumstances, he should shoot the deer if possible. He shifted to his left along the rim, searching for a break in the brush. When he found one twenty feet away, he looked out to

the other side and saw the doe at the edge of the trees sneaking along through another set of brush.

He placed the crosshairs of the scope on the middle of the deer and pulled the trigger. It was about 175 yards total, but the tangle of branches covered the animal for only the last ten yards or so. The shooter plainly observed the deer pitch over sideways.

The critter regained its feet and started to run downhill. The hunter was at the point of taking another shot when he saw large quantities of blood thrown over the snow behind the deer's position. It slowed to a crawl and moved another thirty feet downhill before dying. The heavy round punched through the deer broadside, throwing pieces of lung and ribs out its right side and into the woods.

The shooter climbed down to the deer and started to field-dress it. Of his two friends, she was the first on the scene. It was the first deer she had seen dead in the woods.

As sort of a eulogy, she commented, "Oh, Mr. Deer. We are sorry. We don't hate you, but you are really good to eat." The story of that hunt and her comment made the rounds of the little rural community, becoming something of a slogan for many of the deer hunters there.

With their help, the successful hunter shouldered the critter and carried it downhill to the truck. They finished the hunt with the deer at the road about thirty minutes before dark.

The old-timer attributed his success to knowing the country extremely well, to matching the country to weather conditions, and to using a rifle heavy enough to chop through the brush and down the deer. His two companions were impressed and motivated enough that they continued on in their pursuit of the wily whitetail, eventually becoming sufficiently skilled to get their deer every year.

CHAPTER 31

MISSED WHITETAIL

HUNT CHECKLIST

Weather
Crisp, dry, cold in the mid-teens. Only limited snow remained in a few sheltered draws.

Terrain
Gently rolling prairie country surrounding a few rocky, swampy, or hilly terrain features. Cover was second-growth lodgepole pine with occasional groves of aspen and some dense vine maple ground cover.

Wind Direction
Out of the northwest, 6 to 8 knots.

Conditions Previous Day
Cold, dry late-fall conditions before severe winter storms rolled over the area.

How Hunters Move
Stalked through a 350-acre patch of cover more or less parallel till a deer jumped far ahead.

Clothes
Heavy wool pants and jackets for quiet stalking.

Rifle Caliber and Scope
Shooter used a .338 Winchester Magnum bolt-action with 6X scope.

Sex of Deer
Coming 2-year-old buck.

Time of Day
Hunt started with two-man stalk at daybreak. Deer dropped about 8:30 A.M.

Length of Hunt
Entire day. Deer was downed within the first hour and a half of the hunt.

Length of Shot
Estimated at about 100 yards.

How Deer Moved
Deer moved downhill from right to left ahead of hunter, who could just barely see it through the trees.

Skill of Hunter
An accomplished deer killer who hunted this country often.

When researching these deer hunting accounts, I found it prudent to discuss the events leading up to the kill with more than one of the participants. By so doing, one of the tellers was not nearly so likely to be swept away by misplaced pride, foolish rhetoric, or just plain retelling of tall stories which could easily and hopelessly color the event. This case is an excellent example of a situation so strange that the key elements had to be be verified by more than one witness/participant.

Some hunts are so totally strange that their usefulness as real-life examples might be questioned. Nonetheless, experienced deer hunters consistently counsel that successful hunters must learn to expect the completely unexpected at all times. Those who adapt quickly and smoothly are usually the ones who hang the most deer on the meat pole, they say.

The two hunters in this example were experienced deer shooters who often went into the woods as a team. They claimed to always have bagged their deer. It helped that they hunted over the same basic country for thirty or more years. Neither of the two made a ritual of getting out into the woods every weekend during the year to watch the deer, as is true with many successful hunters. Yet, when fall season rolled around, they were almost constantly out chasing deer with wife, son, daughter, neighbor boy, or whomever. In this instance they hunted with each other, although it meant using their own tags, thus ending the season.

It was an extremely cold, crisp day, virtually the last full day of the season. Temperatures were hanging in the 15°F range. Some snow had accumulated in the sheltered draws over the last few weeks, but on the more open ridges the ground was brown and bare. Frozen leaves in the woods crunched underfoot, making a credible stalk very difficult.

Tree cover consisted of groves of dense aspen, birch, and some extremely thick dog-hair stands of lodgepole pine. On the ground itself, the hunters contended with patches of ninebark, vine maple, and small aspen and pine. There were a few open places in the area in which they hunt-ed, but other areas were grown shut in snarly, tangled thickets. Visibility varied from 40 to a max of 120 yards. Because it was so late in the season and so miserably cold, the pair did not expect to see anyone else that day.

They hunted over severe, weather-worn hills. Some areas in the region contained steep, soil-covered hills cut through by deep ravines. Generally these "rough spots" were covered with second-growth stud and pulp-grade timber. A few of the acres, particularly those with stands of aspen, were low and boggy. Hunters tended to work these somewhat isolated rough patches of between 40 and 350 acres as well as the fringe agricultural land surrounding them.

The woods worked by the pair in this situation were about three hundred acres total, surrounded on three sides by cutover grain fields. To the east, the patch connected to other forests. In its center a high hill of almost six hundred feet rose out of the rolling farmland. A low, boggy area of approximately thirty acres lying at the western base of the hill was impossible to farm. No standing water lay in the hole, yet it was impossible to drive a tractor across it at least eight months of the year. During deer season, hunters usually skirted the spot for fear of breaking through the frozen crust into oozing mud below.

Winds blew out of the northwest at six to eight knots the day of the hunt. Varying ground cover, along with irregular terrain features, made hunting the winds properly something of a challenge.

The two hunters parked their truck about 6:30 A.M. perhaps thirty minutes before daylight. A cutover oat field separated them from their targeted hill by about half a mile. Little puffs of frost blew from the kicked stubble as they walked silently through the gray predawn to their starting point.

They spread out in the woods about two hundred yards apart, moving in as much of a straight line as was practical. They attempted to hit small internal patches of especially dense cover lying along their route, hoping to either drive a deer out that they could shoot at or at least run to a partner.

The men recall that they seldom kept to a straight line for any appreciable length of time.

Either the terrain suggested some deviation or it became necessary to come up into the wind to hunt an especially likely thicket. To some extent, fairly brisk winds in the treetops masked the *crunch-crunch* of the hunters walking over the frozen leaves.

While the hunt itself was often difficult and convoluted, the men kept somewhat coordinated by use of their two-way radios, their many years' experience, and the fact that they often hunted that country together. They both knew the terrain well enough to explain to one another exactly where they were at any time.

The hunter to the west started contouring around the hill almost immediately while his companion stalked into the woods at its base, keeping the steep ground to his right as he circled. Not considering the curvature of the hill, both hunters traveled basically north. Winds that could reach them generally hit them on the left cheek.

Inside the woods, they detected traces of recent deer sign in the frozen pine needles and leaves, leading the two to believe that some deer had passed through earlier in the week. Resident deer, they agreed, were not common.

The hunters wore heavy wool jackets and pants. The gloves they wore might have been a hindrance had a quick jump shot been necessary. Their boots were leather pacs with cleated soles.

They continued stalking through the forest, alert to any possibilities for little one-man drives or to deer jumped by the other guy. After about eight hundred yards, the west hunter came to the south edge of the bog. For the most part, he could see across the sparse shrubbery and trees to the opposite side. He called his partner on the radio, whispering that he intended to move around the hole on the uphill side.

His partner responded by saying he would move uphill a bit more to maintain their two-hundred-yard separation. Both again agreed that deer did not seem to be in the immediate area in any great abundance.

The lower hunter skirted the bog as planned, coming up on an old logging road cut on top of a small rise. He stopped on the road for about

five minutes, waiting and watching. Nothing moved that he could see.

When he talked to his partner again, he realized the guy had not stopped and was now at least a hundred yards ahead and perhaps farther up the hill than was prudent. The lower hunter immediately started walking again, heading north of the logging road and down a shallow slope into a creek formed by the tiniest trickle of water. It was about twenty-five feet down into and up out of the little gully.

At the top on a relatively level piece of ground, he spotted a deer running from right to left down off the higher hill.

The animal was out at least a hundred yards in the brush and timber. He could only see its tail and part of its body for brief moments as it passed open places in the cover. He scoured the area through his 6X scope, finally locating the deer moving with slow, calculated bounds at almost right angles in front of him. He does not recall lining up the crosshairs on the deer—all he remembers was shooting through some small brush at a place where he thought the critter might be. He was using a .338 bolt-action rifle.

After the shot he called his partner on the radio, letting him know that he had taken a shot and that he was certain it had not been successful. He did not see the deer fall to the ground or run off. Nevertheless, he set off straight ahead and slightly to his right to check for blood and/or tracks. He took the shot at about 8:30 A.M. after an hour at most of hunting.

As he walked, he again broadcasted a pessimistic assessment of his chances on that shot. The uphill hunter interrupted the call to tell his partner that he could see a large doe running below and between them. The lower hunter instantly assumed it was the deer he shot at. The uphill hunter did not try a shot. The lower hunter never did see that deer.

At the carefully noted spot where the shot was taken, the shooter found to his utter amazement that a nice, coming two-year-old buck was lying dead. It was on its left side with neck outstretched. He called his partner with the surprising news that they did, in fact, have a deer down. While

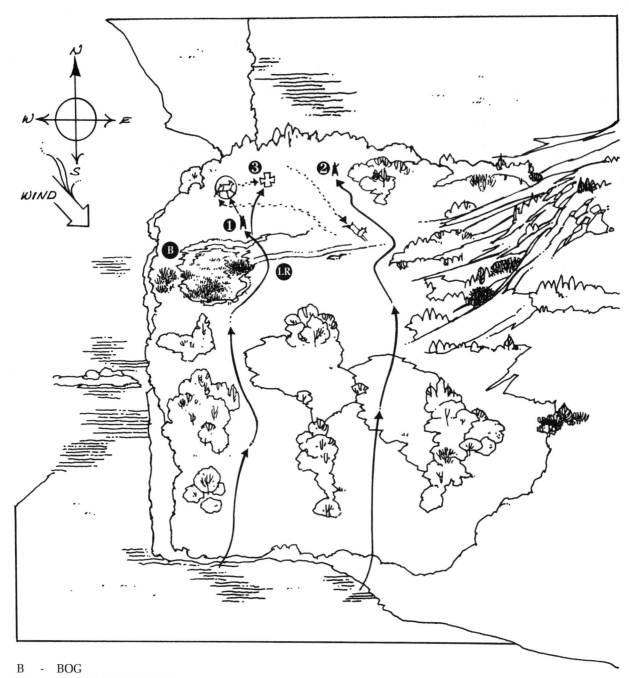

B - BOG
LR - OLD LOGGING ROAD
1 - LOWER HUNTER SEES, SHOOTS BUCK COMING OFF HILLSIDE
2 - UPHILL HUNTER SPOTS DOE ESCAPING BETWEEN THEM
3 - LOWER HUNTER FINDS DEAD BUCK

waiting for his friend to get there, the shooter rolled the deer over and over looking for the wound.

Despite a careful search that became almost obsessive, he could not discover a bullet hole.

There was not so much as a scratch or mark on the entire deer. He carefully examined the head, the chest behind the leg, the bunghole, and every other likely and unlikely spot. There was also no hole in the ground that he could discover.

After his partner arrived, they field-dressed the deer carefully, looking for the wound that caused its demise. They found absolutely nothing. Meticulously, they inspected every inch of the neck and head again. Still nothing.

After finishing, they hunted around the hill to the east where the woods connected via a long ridge to a major tract of timber beyond. No other hunters worked the woods that day, so leaving the deer hanging in a tree was not a concern other than finding it again toward evening.

They stalked the remainder of the hill that showed sign of deer but saw no actual critters.

At about 3:30 P.M., the two hunted back to the one deer they had bagged. The shooter draped it over his shoulder and carried it out to the truck. At home they found it weighed 128 pounds—not a huge deer, but a good-eating critter, especially since there was no wasted, bloodshot meat.

The two hung and skinned the deer with extra caution, yet they still failed to find even the slightest wound. To this day neither hunter can explain exactly what killed that deer. Some theories suggest that it spooked, running into a solid tree, or that the fast heavy round whistled by its head so close that the deer died of fright. They know it didn't die of old age, and its heart, which they saved, looked normal. All theories and explanations leave a lot to be desired.

The hunters concluded that strange things happen out in the woods, especially if one spends enough time there. The shooter was an excellent running shot, but obviously shooting skills and practice with a rifle counted for little in this case. He does believe that his skill at positively marking downed game helped that day.

The best the two can do to explain their unlikely success is to say, "We went out in the woods hunting that day."

HUNT CHECKLIST

Weather

Warming up for a major snowstorm after a week or more of bitter cold. Temperatures up to the low 30s the day of the hunt.

Terrain

Mountainous, rugged terrain with some obscure logging roads cut through the hills.

Wind Direction

Out of the west, 8 to 10 knots.

Conditions Previous Day

Snow started about sundown, continuing all night. Hunters drove through about 8 inches of new snow to the place where they started walking.

How Hunters Moved

Walked up logging roads to an area of low brush cut through by 8 or 10 small side drainages. They hunted across these downhill valleys, jumping the deer out of them.

Clothes

Worn, old wool pants, shirts, and jackets over several layers of flannel. Boots were high rubber pacs.

Rifle Caliber and Scope

She had a bolt-action .270 with 2-7X variable scope. He had a .300 Winchester Magnum bolt-action with 3-9X variable scope.

Sex of Deer

One doe and one 3-point (western count) buck.

Time of Day

They shot the deer about 10:30 A.M. Hunt started with a 20-mile drive at 8:00 A.M. and ended after a 6-mile walk and truck pick up at 11:30 A.M.

Length of Hunt

Hunters walked about 3 miles in, then drove to the downed deer after putting chains on the 4WD truck.

Length of Shot

No more than 90 yards each shot.

How Deer Moved

Deer ran up out of a small valley ahead of hunter.

Skill of Hunters

He was an avid hunter, having a profession that often took him into the woods where he could observe game. She enjoyed hunting but did not go out as often as he did, although she had killed numerous deer.

One of the problems that compilers of deer hunting stories must face is the virtual lemminglike propensity on the part of really good deer hunters to do little more than brag about their accomplishments. Not only is incessant bragging tiring after awhile, it tends to divert one from the core issues of the specific hunt under study. In that regard, it becomes extremely difficult to winnow out the essential details that made the hunt successful from the superficial dross in which hunters often wish to wrap their cases.

This particular hunt meets most of the above criteria. On the surface it was a simple event that netted the hunter two very nice whitetails. Because the skills involved included simply knowing which day to go out and on which specific piece of real estate to hunt, the participants both tend to dismiss the events as being noninstructional. Like many hunters the world round, they wanted to recount a more exciting, glamorous incident that would better, more graphically illustrate their prowess as Mighty Hunters. However, this case wonderfully illustrates the fact that many of the key elements that make deer hunts successful are not particularly glamorous in their telling or even in their on-the-ground undertaking.

The hunter was a seasoned deer chaser. He had killed his first deer on his first hunt some twenty-five or more years ago at the age of eighteen. She hunted with him when they were courting. For both of them, there was enough positive reinforcement to keep at deer hunting more or less regularly through the years. He made his living in the woods as a professional forester, providing numerous opportunities to observe game in the field, and was especially knowledgeable regarding weather and changing conditions on the ground as it influenced the movement of deer.

The territory over which he shot most of the deer was rugged to mountainous. Twisting, tortuous roads cut through the region a minimum of every two to three miles, providing at least theoretical access to large amounts of rough country that, in reality, was actually quite remote. Even limited access into these areas was directly related to the number of obscure, often rock-and-log-strewn logging roads that one personally knew of.

While many roads had been cut through the mountains in years past, it was impossible and perhaps foolhardy to attempt to negotiate them without a four-wheel-drive vehicle, chain saw, wheel chains, shovel, jack, and perhaps a winch. It was principally because of his profession that the hunter knew of these obscure, treacherous paths and how to navigate them as well as having the necessary equipment at hand.

The countryside was comprised of second- and third-growth fir and pine. Some bushy, young conifers obscured the ground, but the limiting factor to seeing game in the many draws on the mountainsides were vine maple, red alder, ninebark, snowberry, and elderberry bush. Dense stands of poplar and birch grew in some of the draws. Clumps of brush obscured otherwise open ridgelines and gully slopes. Visibility ranged from 40 to 150 yards with maddening frequency.

Temperatures had dropped down into the high teens for a full week before the hunt. Little snow covered the drab, brown, late-winter countryside. Starting the day before, weather reports for the region called for warming to the low thirties by midweek as a major winter storm rolled in. The hunter walked out on his deck Tuesday night, concluding that, in this case, the forecasts were accurate—it was impossible to see across the street because it was snowing so hard.

He rolled out of bed at 6:00 A.M. the next morning. Six to eight inches of soft, wet snow covered the ground. It was still snowing but on a more intermittent basis. Sunup that morning would arrive no earlier than 7:00 A.M. Even then, one could only expect a soft, diffused gray overcast.

In recounting this adventure, the hunter maintained that a key element of any successful deer hunt is flexibility—flexibility when planning, when picking a day to hunt, and when walking out in the field.

People tied to 9-to-5 jobs far from their hunting territory are at a distinct disadvantage. As a rule, they cannot drop everything to go out hunting on a day when everything suddenly looks perfect. Professional hunting and fishing guides are famous for telling their clients, "You shoulda been here last week. The weather was perfect and the critters were everyplace." Apparently there is more to this explanation than a guide trying to explain why he can't find game at that particular moment.

By 7:30 A.M., the hunter had all of his day's appointments canceled. He rearranged his entire schedule as well as that of his wife, who was also able to hunt that day. She used a .270 bolt-action with a 2-7X scope. He had a .300 Winchester Magnum with 3-9X scope.

They climbed into their four-wheel-drive truck and motored along a county road. Their track was the first one out that morning in about eight inches of new snow. They observed few fresh deer tracks in the road on their way up the mountain twenty miles from home.

They took a right onto a slick, narrow, muddy logging road and headed west. This particular road had seen relatively recent use, so no fallen trees or frost-heaved rocks obstructed their passage. The hunter motored in, quickly cutting through the snow to slick, yellow clay that oozed up the tire rims. It was about 8:30 A.M.

About four hundred yards in, the logging road stopped abruptly at a log deck. An even more treacherous skid road came down off the snow-covered mountain on an estimated 22-percent grade. The hunter and his wife stopped at the log deck below the steep skid road and parked. The only way up the slick, snow-covered track was to chain up all four wheels on their truck. Given the amount of work involved, they elected to walk the last three-quarters of a mile.

Winds out on top were fairly brisk at eight to ten knots out of the west to northwest. Snow showers came and went, plastering their faces and scope sights with large, watery flakes. The couple wore older, worn, heavy wool pants and shirts over several layers of flannel. Boots were high rubber pacs, made especially to deal with sloppy mud and snow.

They climbed up the skid trail to an old wagon road running along a hogback ridge above. They followed the wagon road west into the cold, wet wind to a place where the road broke out of

bigger timber into another ownership that had been harvested more recently.

Eight to ten small gullies, a maximum of thirty-feet deep, ran down off the ridge to the south. About seventy to eighty yards separated the gully bottoms, which ran off the ridge almost parallel to each other.

Clumps of brush grew quite thickly in some places in the gullies and on the slopes. However leaves were long dropped, creating a situation where the hunters could see virtually everything ahead from one gully ridge to the next.

The hunter's wife walked down off the main ridge about three hundred yards, where she turned west into the wind. He moved down about eighty yards, stopping on an overlook to wait for her to get into position.

Their plan was to hunt into the wind straight across the series of gullies. It is an old trick of mountain hunters. They hoped to jump deer as they walked down slope, shooting them as they ran uphill across the draw.

New snows made it easy to see the most recent deer tracks. They were pleased to note that a number of deer seemed to be moving. It was possible to count three or four trails at almost any place in the gully. Because of the nasty day and the lateness of the season, they expected to see no other hunters in the area.

Staying as coordinated as possible, the pair stalked down through the first gully and up the other side. She had more country to cross getting to the other side than he did, so he waited in the snow and wind on top of the next ridge for several minutes before entering the second gully. As he did so, a big whitetail doe trotted up out of the gully to the top of the other side. He wiped his scope on a cloth he carried in his pocket and took careful aim at the top of the shoulder where the flat shoulder bones lay next to the spine.

His round smashed through both shoulders down about four inches from the spine, taking out both front legs and the spinal nerve. The deer dropped like a pound of lard hitting the pavement from the fourth story. He watched it for a moment. Apparently it went from life to death instantly.

As he stood there, a fat three-point buck ran up

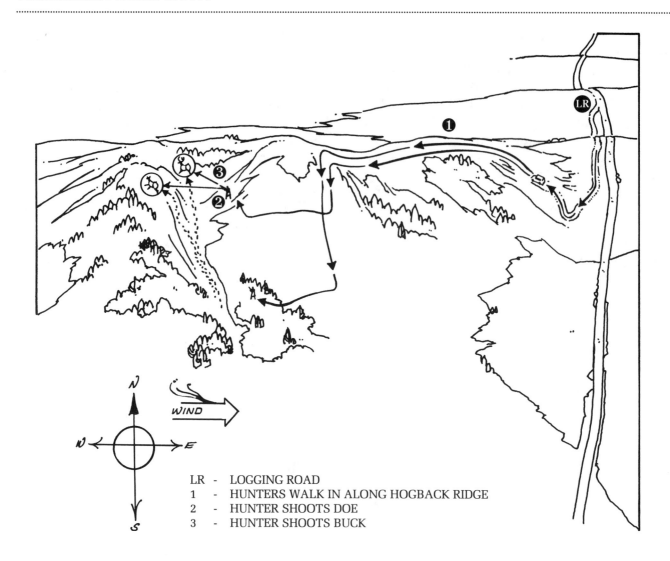

N

WIND

W ← ↓ → E

S

LR - LOGGING ROAD
1 - HUNTERS WALK IN ALONG HOGBACK RIDGE
2 - HUNTER SHOOTS DOE
3 - HUNTER SHOOTS BUCK

out of the draw. It probably had been bedded down as much as eighty to a hundred yards below him in the bottom of the draw. If not that, it had been feeding with the doe on the new aspen shoots. In retrospect, he is not certain why the deer moved. He does recall that—other than the two actual animals he shot—there were many tracks suggesting deer were moving through that area.

The buck ran up the bottom till it passed the hunter. It then contoured the hill, climbing to a location beyond the downed doe about forty yards. The hunter now looked at the deer from the side. He placed the crosshairs of his scope on a spot four inches down in the middle of the shoulder. Because the wind blew fiercely at the top of the gully from deer to hunter, the buck had

no idea from which quarter the danger lay.

The bullet struck the buck about where the shooter aimed, perhaps a little lower. Little meat was ruined in the process, and, again, the deer reacted as though lightning had hit it. Both shots were no more than ninety yards.

After the second shot, he yohoed his wife. She chugged up the hill as fast as possible. Together they field-dressed the two deer, leaving the buck's head in the woods. Its horns were small, but she knocked the little forks off the critter with a hand ax they carried in the truck. Eventually the horn became fancy buttons on a homemade woolen shirt.

It was about 11:30 A.M. as they walked back to the truck. Snow continued in fits and starts.

Other than the warmth from a successful hunt, gusting, wet winds on the ridge made being outside very miserable.

Dutifully she watched him chain up the wheels on their four-wheel drive. With chains and a low gear, plus the winch, they powered themselves up the steep hill to the place on the ridge to which they had dragged the deer. After loading the bodies, they did not encounter one other vehicle on the trip home. Snug in their garage, they happily spent the remainder of the day skinning and quartering the critters.

The hunter attributed his success that day to three deceptively simple elements. He knew the country extremely well; he was willing to drop everything on a day that showed promise (though he realizes this is often not possible for many deer hunters who must plan their yearly excursions months in advance), and he believed it was important to use an adequate rifle and to be able to place one's shots correctly. Owning and using special equipment such as a winch and truck chains was convenient but not essential. The hunter thought he could have packed the critters to the road, but the hunt would not have been as easy as it otherwise was.

CHAPTER 33
HILLSIDE BUCK

HUNT CHECKLIST

Weather
Lower 20s in the morning, rising to the mid-20s by noon. Snow was light and puffy.

Terrain
Rolling hills with patches of scrub brush interspersed with high wild grass.

Wind Direction
Out of northwest, 4 to 6 knots.

Conditions Previous Day
Heavy early-season snowfall for 3 days prior to the hunt.

How Hunters Moved
Crossed a rolling brush field across the wind. Hunted with the wind, then circled a little draw, where hunter jumped the buck. Tracked the buck for another hour, when he jumped it again out of another draw.

Clothes
Heavy wool pants, shirts, and jackets. They wanted to stalk the deer so they wore no cotton or nylon.

Rifle Caliber and Scope
Hunter remembers he used a 6X scope but has forgotten which rifle he had that day.

Sex of Deer
Big-bodied 5-point (western count) buck.

Time of Day
Deer was jumped at about 10:00 A.M.

Length of Hunt
Hunters were out the entire morning, walking about 3 miles in heavy snow.

Length of Shot
Hunter saw deer twice at about 40 to 60 feet.

How Deer Moved
Deer stood in small draw hidden by trees, then ran out across brushy field into another small draw, where it was jumped up out of the area.

Skill of Hunters
Both were older, skilled deer killers who had been over that country many times.

In real life, successful deer hunting requires that one competently put together a string of events leading up to the actual kill. Individually these events are not particularly complicated or difficult to accomplish, but they must be done in the appropriate sequence without a significant glitch. Failures can occur when just one part of the plan is executed improperly. New deer hunters quickly discover that if they miscue on one element, the hunt for the entire day is blown. There are not many key elements, but they are critical.

Unfortunately, many new deer hunters fail at the first of the critical endeavors—organizing a hunt that takes weather, wind, terrain, and game movement into consideration. This fact often discourages the neophyte when he learns that he will be lucky to even *see* a deer the first few seasons of his hunting career. "How can I learn to shoot deer," he asks, "when I seldom if ever see any shootable deer?" A good question, raising an issue that the following hunt goes a long way toward addressing. In that regard, it is vital to note that the participants in this affair were two seasoned deer hunters who had killed hundreds of deer during their lifetimes. Yet even these people found that nothing can be left to luck or choice. The hunt must be put together correctly.

As mentioned, the hunters in this case were, by any reasonable measure, experts. They knew how to kill deer on their own—and virtually anybody else's—territory. One man hunted in three states a thousand miles apart in one year, bagging deer in all three.

It was the tail end of the season in their home territory when this hunt took place. By this time, the two veterans saw children, grandchildren, spouses, and even nephews all fill their tags. The two hunted the difficult end of the season for the sheer delight of being out on the country matching wits with the deer when it was generally considered to be too foul to kill the critters consistently.

They hunted over gently rolling land. At one time the entire area was cleared for farming or for pasture, but it had been neglected for forty years. Scrub maple, ninebark, snowberry, and scrub aspen crept back over the land to reclaim it.

In a few places, dense, high prairie grass grew so well that the brush and scrub could not secure a toehold. Agronomically, it was a constant conflict between tall grass and low brush. At this time the situation was stabilized; it was only when the established grass or brush was burnt or scarred that it was possible for the competitor to gain the upper hand.

Whitetail deer thrived on this mixed, rolling land, which provided both abundant cover and a ready supply of winter browse. So many deer populated the area that there was even talk of issuing a second annual tag in an attempt to hold their numbers in check.

Snow fell more or less continuously for the three days prior to the hunt. About two feet had accumulated, with drifts of three feet and more in places where the wind could stack it. The first major snows in that region were usually light and puffy; walking in it was more tiring than on bare ground, but not as difficult as later in the year when it took real endurance to march across country through the deep snow for even a mile. These early, puffy snows tended to dampen forest noises, allowing skilled hunters to do some extremely sophisticated stalking.

Winds the day of the hunt settled a bit with the passing of the storm front. They blew gently and consistently out of the west to northwest at four to six knots.

The two hunters knew that as the storm passed, the deer would be out moving around in an attempt to refill their bellies. They agreed on the phone the evening before to be in the field first thing in the morning.

They selected a typical scrub-infested spot over which to hunt. At 6:30 A.M. they parked their truck on a county road at the edge of the vast field. They sat there drinking coffee till 7:00 A.M. when it became sufficiently light to shoot. As they had supposed, literally hundreds of deer trails were evident in the new snow, crossing and recrossing the road. They sat discussing the trails but concluded that it was impossible to determine for certain which direction the deer were headed. There were simply too many different sets of tracks.

Temperatures were in the low twenties, with

prospects that they would rise to the mid-twenties at most. The men wore old, worn, heavy wool pants, shirts, and jackets. Not a square inch of nylon or polyester was exposed to scratching brush. Boots were high rubber and leather pacs with cleated soles. Both hunters claimed that mock-toed boots caught more brush and were needlessly noisy—they wore the ones made with rounded toes.

Their plan was to do a coordinated hunt, including some standing and some stalking along with little drives to each other.

Their first hunt was almost due south through the brush field. They spread out two hundred yards apart, putting themselves just out of sight of each other but in position where a deer would have had to exercise great caution to sneak between the two.

The plan was not the best in the world, given prevailing northwest winds, but the hunters concluded that by moving silently across wind they could watch to their left for moving critters. After crossing the first eight hundred yards they reasoned they would be in a better position both from a cover standpoint and relative to the wind.

As they suspected, deer were moving everyplace. Tracks were so numerous it was tough to tell where the maker came from or where it was going. Still, the hunters did not observe a single actual animal on this first leg of the hunt.

The most easterly hunter was first to come through the brush field to a large, grass-covered opening. On reaching the open area, he called his partner on the walkie-talkie, suggesting that he would stalk to within fifty yards of the edge of the brush and then turn left. He would stay in the woods while his partner turned into the open field, keeping parallel to the brush while heading east.

They would now be working even more with the winds than against them, but they hoped to jump a deer into the opening from the fringe, where the guy in the clear could get a shot. They agreed on the plan. Both turned east, working the grassy field and the edge of the brush together.

Somewhat synchronously, they walked east for another eight hundred yards till the now

northerly hunter was almost to a north/south farm road. The hunter in the grass below started coming up on patches of scrub brush again.

The north hunter suggested that they turn left again, heading north across the wind. He continued to report numerous deer tracks while the man in the open saw no sign of deer. He turned north and walked parallel with the old farm road, still hoping to jump something out of the fringes.

The south hunter in the field started down a long, shallow, gentle draw toward the farm road. For the first time that day he encountered a few small pine trees growing in the draw. He made a mental note that this would be a fine place to cut a Christmas tree.

About two-thirds of the way into the depression when the field behind was just above eye level, the south hunter got a feeling that it would be wise to cut sharply to his left, skirting a small patch of trees on the hill's north slope. As he rounded the four or five little pines, he came upon a huge five-point buck standing knee deep in the snow.

The buck was at most forty feet away, standing broadside to the hunter. He immediately brought his rifle up from its slung position and tried to get a sight picture in his scope. As he did so, he removed and dropped his glove to operate the trigger. As it fell, the buck snorted a long, steady, steamy blast and jumped up the hill directly away from the hunter. He recalls the huge size of the buck's rear quarters when viewed through his 6X scope. He did not fire, not wanting, as he said, "to take a Chicago neck shot."

The buck jumped six times through the deep snow and was out of sight over the top of the draw. The hunter retrieved his errant glove, vowing never again to hunt with heavy gloves. As fast as he could, he took up the track.

He followed the deer's track into the big brush patch, over the top of his partner's track, and back in the general direction from which they had come. He informed his partner of the unfolding fiasco, telling him he intended to track the buck for at least an hour or so till it crossed the main road or he got a shot at it.

Tracking the buck through fields covered with

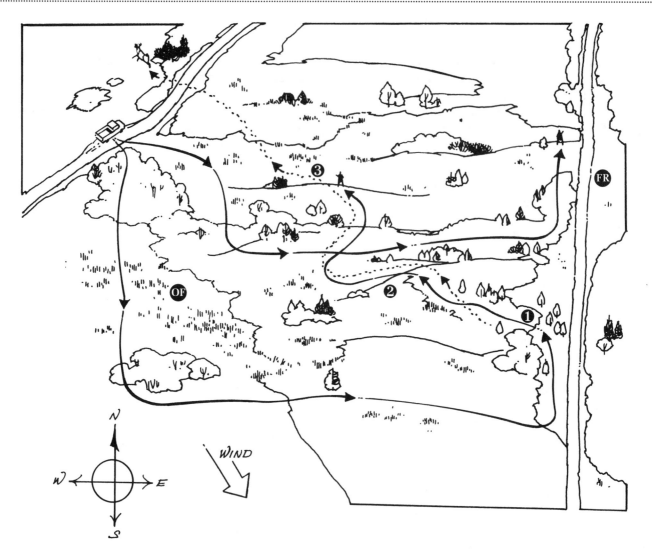

OF - OPEN FIELD
FR - FARM ROAD
1 - HUNTER SKIRTS PINE TREES, SPOOKS BUCK
2 - HUNTER TRACKS BUCK THROUGH SNOW
3 - HUNTER SPOTS BUCK AGAIN; BUCK ESCAPES

recent deer tracks was much more difficult than one would normally suppose. Yet the hunter had the deer moving into the wind through snow so deep that it was usually easy to keep the trail. He was an excellent tracker with many years' experience on trails of wounded game. The only difficulty, the man recalls, was when the buck moved along on the tracks of another deer for any length of time. Then he had to decide which track was made last.

After the initial jumps that took it out of sight, the buck slowed to a steady walk. It was about 10:00 A.M. when the hunter first jumped the deer. He kept on its track for about an hour, pushing it through some rough and wooly brush patches. By radio he learned he was five hundred yards west of his partner, who saw nothing but tracks and was tiring from the effort of stalking through the deep snow.

Silently but as swiftly as possible, the west hunter stalked down another shallow roll in the land. He was about six hundred yards from the place he had first seen the deer. About two-thirds of the way down, he thought he saw movement perhaps sixty feet ahead on the opposite uphill slope.

Like before, he threw his rifle up, attempting to peer through the scope. This time he had even less success. Snow plugged most of the tube, and a great mass of brush stood between him and deer.

The hunter quickly cleaned the lens with this shirttail. He might have seen enough of the deer to shoot were it not for the dense brush that obscured his sight. He knew the buck was standing there but could not be sure of the shot. Since he often killed the deer he pursued, he did not feel a strong compulsion to abandon all caution and rush into the shot.

He stepped sideways as quickly and silently as possible. As he did so, the big buck jumped from its hillside position up over the top of the swale. Like before, the hunter watched it take three or four quick bounds before it was out of sight. He tracked it to the top again from where he could make out its trail racing across country for at least a hundred yards. There was no deer in sight.

Over the radio he suggested to his partner that this particular deer had outfoxed them. He further suggested that he had enough of the deep snow and that they meet on the road and call it a day. They climbed into their truck at about 11:30 A.M. As far as they knew, that buck survived hunting season.

The hunter who stalked the buck concluded that they had picked a perfect day to hunt and that they hunted some very good country correctly. He saw the buck the first time because he played a hunch, but the animal got away because of the dropped glove. The second sighting came as a result of a careful stalk on the part of a skilled tracker. He was not successful principally because he was overcautious with the shot.

In retrospect, the hunter feels he could have fired through the brush, but then he may not have hit the deer. It may not actually have been a deer; better to be certain of the shot, he maintained. He was sorry for not getting the buck, but his sorrow was temporary. A foolish, ill-planned shot could have made him sorry for life.

HUNT CHECKLIST

Weather

Early fall, with highs in mid-30s, lows dropping below freezing at night. It was quite dry in the hills.

Terrain

Steep, rolling, soil-covered hills with numerous old roads cut through them. Hills covered with Douglas fir, ponderosa pine, and heavy red alder, aspen, and hazel underbrush.

Wind Direction

Out of the west into the drive at about 5 knots. Strong canyon updrafts tended to obscure and confuse the wind's movement.

Conditions Previous Day

It had been warm and dry, characteristic of the early fall season.

How Hunters Moved

Walked along an overgrown logging road till it crossed a steep hillside. They shot the deer when it stopped running downhill to look back.

Clothes

Denim pants and shirts, no jackets, low-cut leather work shoes, and canvas chaps to shed the burrs and sticktights.

Rifle Caliber and Scope

.30-06 bolt-action with 6X scope.

Sex of Deer

3-year-old doe.

Time of Day

It was about 4:00 P.M. when they jumped the deer and shot it.

Length of Hunt

Started about 2:00 P.M. and lasted till after dark, covering about 2 1/2 miles total.

Length of Shot

About 80 yards through quite a lot of brush.

How Deer Moved

Deer was lying in brush along logging road, ran downhill and stopped, where hunter shot it.

Skill of Hunters

Two of the hunters were skilled deer chasers. The third man was on his first deer hunt.

This account involves two older, experienced men who took a young whippersnapper with them for his first deer hunt. The younger fellow was an acknowledged excellent shot, a skill he acquired in the military. Yet all three knew a world of difference existed between shooting whitetails and shooting in the military.

The old-timers were intimately familiar with the country over which they intended to hunt, having been on it scores if not hundreds of times. Both had killed dozens of deer in their lives and could certainly write a considerable volume related to the lives and times of deer.

The young man wanted to bag a deer in the worst possible way. In his mind he attached more glamor to the event than was ever appropriate. The old-timers felt confident they could spot him in a place where they could drive a critter, which he could at least shoot at.

Probably the biggest single hurdle they faced was finding a time when everyone could get together for a hunt. There was also some concern whether the young guy would exercise sufficient patience and stay at his station till the drivers got set up and came through. Performing the duties of a stander is much more difficult than one who has never tried it would suppose, they reminded each other.

The two experienced hunters agreed privately that it did not necessarily follow that someone who shot hawkeye in the military could also spot game moving stealthily through the brush. While they were certain they could find deer and drive them through to the stander, they were not certain whether the young man could actually bring them to bag.

The terrain over which they hunted was steep, rolling, soil-covered hills. Some observers might refer to them as mountains, but the maximum elevation was three hundred feet at most, ruling out a mountainous classification. Numerous logging and mining access roads cut through the hills, providing reasonably easy access to places as much as two miles from the county road.

Scrubby second-growth alder, hazel, ash, and maple grew on the older road cuts, restricting even foot access at times. Yet lush, tall, sweet clover, perhaps seeded forty years ago by loggers and miners, grew wherever the woody brush did not dominate. Deer in the region always seemed anxious to come down to these patches for a good feed. Often the clover persisted bright and green till the first snow of full winter.

Cover on the hillsides themselves was comprised of Douglas fir and ponderosa pine in the upper story. There were also clumps of grand fir growing here and there. In many places the grand fir had matured and died, creating a unique situation wherein groves of twenty to thirty dead trees were standing.

All of the needles were off these trees, depriving game of cover they might normally have expected in such places. On the other hand, hunters working the area found that the dead clumps were difficult to get past, although one could see game through them. Dead branches cracked, scraped, and snapped when touched by even the most careful person trying to work through them.

Although it was early in fall in an area characterized by early deer seasons, there were few deer hunters in the woods. About the only others one could expect to see were errant pheasant hunters who might wander into the area from the distant grassy fringes.

Temperatures were in the mid to high thirties during the day, dipping below freezing at night. Some broadleaf trees still held their leaves, obstructing long-range shooting in places, but the promise of better times ahead was in the air as cool, dry, fallish weather encouraged them to drop.

It was a delightful warm fall day. Frosty temperatures at night killed the bugs and cooled the draws, but virtually anyone would agree that under these conditions, "hunting was indeed easy."

The hunters left the county road at about 2:30 P.M. They reckoned that they had about an hour walk to the far east end of the patch of wooly undergrowth, patches of dead trees, and the few lofty pines they intended to drive.

Their overall plan was to leave the young guy on a mostly abandoned, overgrown farm road cut along the west edge of a reasonably deep draw. High bushes and a few trees grew along the side of the road, providing numerous hiding places for the stander, who was to slowly and carefully move back and forth on the road watching. It was about two hundred yards straight across to the opposite hillside from which they hoped to drive deer. The maximum extent of the skills needed by the stander involved being able to move quietly back and forth on the road to a place where he could best see game coming from the opposite hill. Then he had to find the deer in his rifle sights.

Even after spending several minutes explaining the operation, including how to move silently and unobserved on the road, the old-timers had some doubts regarding the fellow's ability to pull it off. They pointed out the faint ribbons of trails contouring the opposite hill and strongly suggested that any jumped deer would probably use these, the easiest paths. In addition, they warned against moving once the deer came into sight, suggesting that he stay hidden behind clumps of brush whenever possible.

The senior deer chasers assumed that the gentle five-knot winds would swirl and mix sufficiently to dissipate stander's scent as they blew across the canyon to the east. Considering the prevailing winds alone, the drive was far from ideal.

The drivers intended to work their way into the wind as they contoured around the hill on the opposite side. They expected numerous changes and shifts, but generally they were going to try to push deer upwind to the stander across the large, fairly open canyon. This separation, along with the stander's elevated position on the road as well as the past propensity of the deer to follow the old trails on the hillside, provided the only hope the two could muster that the drive might actually work. In retrospect, it was not an unreasonable hope.

They finally left the young fellow alone on the road about 3:15 P.M. They knew they now had a mile hike to the place where they could climb the hill, spread out, and push back through. Both were still quite confident that they would jump a deer at which the young stander could shoot.

As was possible and practical, the two drivers walked along side by side, discussing hunt plans past and present in hoarse whispers. At times, brush on the road narrowed it to the point where they had to proceed single file.

Due to the pleasant warmth of the afternoon, the hunters wore cotton denim work pants and shirts. They may have been mistaken for armed auto mechanics strolling through the woods. Boots were regular low-cut leather work shoes, and they wore canvas chaps to help shed the numerous burrs and sticktights.

It had been dry for the last three weeks, with warm air moving continuously over the hills. The drivers expected dust rising from the path to be more of a problem than mud or moisture on the grass and underbrush. Given the gentle rustling breeze overhead, the time of year, and the type of hunt they were doing, noise in the woods was not a factor.

There were many tracks in the dusty trail. The drivers were impressed by the number but—given the small sampling they saw on the road—were uncertain how, exactly, to interpret what they saw.

On and on they walked as the serpentlike path wound around the hills and across little draws. They hoped the young stander was not discouraged and that he would still be there when the deer came through. At times their hike carried them downwind while at others it circled sufficiently that they were moving crosswind. As in all hilly country, nothing about the wind was predictable except in the most general sense. Twice their path took them into fairly deep side gullies where no air moved at all. At these places, even the dust kicked from the path hung indolently in the air.

A single large, deep canyon marked the east boundary of the hillside. Their rapidly petering-out logging road ran one more time around the hill before plunging to its terminus in the last canyon. As the pair rounded the last curve, the land fell sharply away from them down into the draw. It was about an eighty-foot drop virtually straight down through several patches of pines. Little understory obscured their view.

As the pair, walking two abreast, turned the

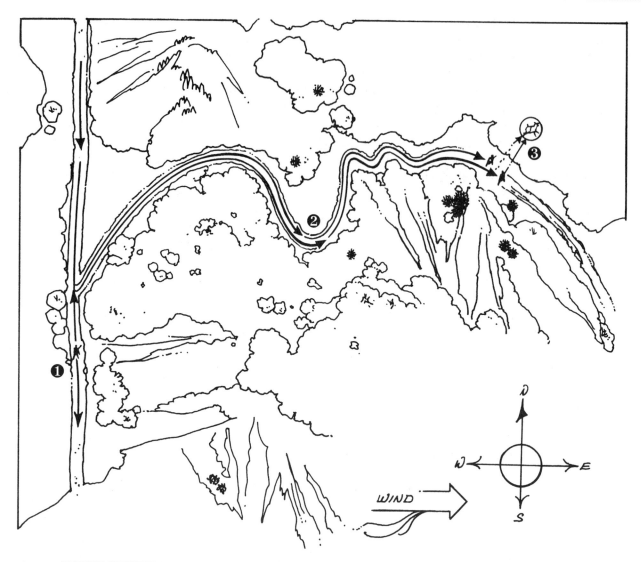

1 - YOUNG HUNTER TAKES UP STAND ON FARM ROAD
2 - HUNTER WALKS ALONG LOGGING ROAD
3 - HUNTER JUMPS, SHOOTS DOE

corner, the outside man saw a jumped doe and large fawn run out of the brush growing at the road's edge. The doe ran downhill about eighty yards, stopping dead still in the only available clump of small leafless aspens. It no doubt thought it was hidden.

The fawn simply disappeared. The hunter did not see it again till after the shot. For some reason no wind moved in that particular place.

The hunter on the inside of the road did not see or hear the deer. He walked on about six feet

until he realized his partner was frozen in his tracks with rifle raised, looking through the scope down over the road's edge. He used a .30-06 bolt-action with 6X scope.

As the inside man turned, the first hunter fired at the doe through the tangle of branches. Even though sundown was still an hour away, the shooter had problems seeing the deer through the brush in the shaded draw.

The deer was hit with a downward shot through the middle. It tumbled over and over down the hill. The shooter assumed he got the deer but was not absolutely sure. Quickly they turned downhill, searching about twenty yards apart. The body was soon found lying on the steep slope. The shot had entered just behind the left shoulder, raking down through the lungs and stomach and exiting just in front of the right rear quarter.

They pulled the deer head up into position for field-dressing. While removing the head, feet, and entrails, they discussed how the hunt might continue. As it was, should they have continued with the original plan, they would have finished the drive back at the stander at full dark. Then they would be faced with walking all the way back to the kill to carry the deer out after dark. Neither hunter wanted to disappoint the young fellow, but they also did not want to pack a deer through these rough hills after full dark.

Field-dressed, the deer weighed about 115 pounds. One of the hunters hoisted it on his shoulders. They discussed buttonholing the deer but had the legs off before realizing that they had to make a decision.

As they packed the deer, they made extra noise calling to the stander as they emerged from the west end of the logging road. They were not certain if the young guy could distinguish between a packed deer and one proceeding on its own power.

They regrouped on the farm road about fifteen minutes before dark. As a partial sop, the noncarrying hunter took the young guy up the farm road for the last fifteen minutes of daylight. They hoped to spot at least one deer moving voluntarily from its bed on the hillside but were disappointed in the endeavor.

Later in the year they did manage to drive a big buck out on basically the same kind of hunt in the same type of country. The young hunter fired twice with his .308 but was unable to connect at the two-hundred-yard range. As far as the old-timers know, the young man still has not killed his first deer. In that regard, the reconnoitering hunters are not certain that this was really a successful case for one to study, even though they did get a nice eating deer out of it.

They concluded that they got the deer because they were alert even when traveling over country they did not think would produce a deer. The shooter used a big, powerful cartridge, firing through heavy brush. The shot may have been successful only because of a fortunate opening in the brush and because they knew from past experience where the deer might be.

Start to finish, this hunt did not meet the experts' expectations—which may be the entire lesson.

CHAPTER 35
REFORMED MEAT HUNTER

HUNT CHECKLIST

Weather
Coolish, 40°F, with last real rain about 3 months prior.

Terrain
Steep hill on edge of rugged, deep draw. Country was used for grazing cattle, sheep, and horses. Surrounding areas were farmed occasionally.

Wind Direction
Out of southwest, 4 to 5 knots.

Conditions Previous Day
About the same. Deep canyons mitigated and tempered the weather.

How Hunters Moved
Walked up open ridge, spread out in center of slope about two hundred yards apart, and walked through in a line for several miles.

Clothes
Cotton jeans, flannel shirts, good quality leather hiking boots.

Rifle Caliber and Scope
Model 740 Remington semiauto rifle with two 10-shot magazines and 6X scope.

Sex of Deer
Doe. Hunters cannot remember if it was a mule deer or whitetail. Both ranged over that country.

Time of Day
About 1:30 P.M.

Length of Hunt
Hunt started about first light at 6:50 A.M. after they walked half a mile uphill into position. Then they walked about 1 1/4 miles across the slope on the drive itself.

Length of Shot
Estimated 250 yards. Last missed shot was at least 300 yards.

How Deer Moved
Deer was lying in small brush patch, ran through a little draw, scaring out another deer, which hunter missed. When it ran up a small rise, hunter got it.

Skill of Hunters
Younger men were little more than foot soldiers directed by older man who knew the country well.

Put enough ambitious people together who can walk over the hills, let a person who knows the country and who understands deer direct them, and I will get you a deer or two every time they go out, one especially philosophical old-timer explained. He went on to recount in detail several hunts that illustrated his supposition. One of these especially "notorious" hunts that occurred many years ago contains some concepts that may be of interest to the student of deer hunting today.

It is material to this case to understand that the events occurred right at the time Remington brought out their Model 740 sporter semiautomatic rifle. The then younger hunter had purchased one of these rifles in .308 and installed a 6X scope and aftermarket ten-shot magazine. He figured the package would assist him mightily in his endeavors to speedily reduce deer to possession. As an afterthought, he also carried a spare ten-shot magazine as backup.

All of this is pretty tame by current standards, but, in its time, it was the subject of much curiosity and conversation. The man now admits that this was part of the pride of ownership he enjoyed at the time. As the case unfolds, it will become evident that little thought was given to marksmanship or to really hitting the target properly. As the raconteur suggests, it probably was an early example of attempting to scare deer to death by carrying a big magnum rifle, similar to techniques used today by owners of 7mm Magnum rifles.

The hunter and gun owner was in his late twenties. He was in the field with at least one old-fashioned deer getter who really knew his business. At this modern day retelling, everyone—including the hunter—admits that he was trying to substitute fancy equipment for skill, an endeavor he now knows was doomed to failure.

Their informal group of miscellaneous farmhands, ranchers' boys, school kids, and self-employed construction workers went out in the woods and hills hunting deer about three days a week during the season. They were orchestrated and directed by old-timers who really knew the country in detail for twenty miles in every

direction. Little skill was required on the part of most of the participants in the hunt. They simply lined up and bulldozed through the brush, shooting whatever they drove out. Although it was not always obvious to the young men, the key to their considerable success lay in the vast knowledge and experience of the senior organizers of these massive deer chases.

Generally, the crew worked over mixed agricultural land close to home. However, given seasons lasting three weeks or more at three days a week hunting, they soon ran all of the land around them once and all of the especially good areas two or three times. In summary, they were tired of the country around home, and the neighbors were tired of them.

During this time, one senior organizer "refriended" a farmer/rancher/owner of a large tract of land lying on the slope of a huge, steep canyon. The rancher was forced by economics to get out of the cattle business a few years prior. As a result, deer by the score lived and thrived on his two sections of land totaling 1,280 acres. The slope lay about a mile between pasture and farmland on a plateau and the main road running up the valley floor below.

Sage and chaparral covered the open section of the hill. In the draws and hollows, thickets of thorn apple, sumac, alder, elderberry, and some snowberry grew. Dense stands of cheatgrass covered the many open spots on the hills. The grass greened only briefly for three months in the spring, growing to about knee depth except where livestock grazed. By fall hunting season, no beast—domestic or wild—ate the grass, feeding instead in the little draws, some of which held a trickle of water.

Deer pushed off the wintry plateaus ate the cheatgrass with relish in early spring when everything else was brown and dormant. Depending on the number of domestic livestock, the deer summered in the heavy brush in the draws or went up to the plateaus above. Based on the fall and hunting pressure above, they could be strung out anywhere on the slope.

Even given the hundreds of patches and clumps in which deer could hide, thoroughly working 1,280 acres of property was not particularly difficult for the eight or ten men who showed up for duty. They hunted not only the friend's ranch but most of those adjoining. The original property became a springboard from which they ranged.

Their plan for that day, which had worked nicely at least two times before, was to move noisily through the brush in an attempt to jump any deer in the area. When one or more ran ahead, two or three concentrated their fire on the critters. Most shots were taken at relatively long ranges of two to three hundred yards. As often as not, most of them missed, but everyone had a feeling of participating in an especially enjoyable hunt.

Weather in the canyon was tempered to some extent by the high surrounding landforms. The few winds reaching the area came from the southwest, blowing down the hill and across the area at about four to five knots. Rain fell mostly in the late fall, winter, and early spring. At the time of the hunt it was crispy brown and dry on the slopes. If silence were critical, the hunt would have been a bust. Temperature was about 40°F.

Drivers all wore cotton work pants and flannel shirts. Few bothered to wear jackets other than as a utilitarian collection of pockets. Boots were of much better quality than one would otherwise suppose from the ragtag look of the crew. They knew they would be climbing great distances, requiring their best, newest leather work boots.

The hunters reached their destination ranch at least thirty minutes before light, about 6:30 A.M. They parked their vehicles in a neat row in the barnyard between house and shop.

After BSing with the rancher for a few minutes, they started off up the hill. They climbed about half a mile of steep, difficult country till they arrived at the midpoint of the ranch. First gray was just showing in the east. By full light they were in position for the massive push south to southeast.

Maintaining a long line as much as possible, they pushed through without standers. Fortunately, full light enabled them to see the men to either side and thus keep coordinated on the drive, although hunters two or three men away seldom caught sight of their companions scattered out on the massive piece of real estate. Generally, it was possible to see around the hillside—up, down, or across—from three to four hundred yards. They expected to see no other hunters in the area. It was midweek, and the slope was too tough to negotiate for the casual deer chaser.

The strung-out crew pushed through about a mile of slope by 1:00 P.M. Intuitively they felt they may have massed some of the frequently shot-at deer that elected to hold tight rather than break cover, but they saw nothing but one coyote, which three or four shot at without effect. One nice buck did run over the hill at a place so distant that no one could shoot.

Most of the drivers were too inexperienced to be reliable trackers given the dry, lifeless soil. But the old senior organizer reckoned that there were still numerous deer in the draws they were running.

At 1:00 p.m. they gathered to eat their lunch as well as talk about the best plan for the afternoon. After lengthy discussion, it was decided that they would push on another mile before descending to the road below, from which they could walk back to the ranch and their vehicles. This plan put them over several hundred yards of new country not driven in prior outings.

Again they lined up on the slope about two hundred yards apart. What little wind blew still crossed their intended path. Theoretically, deer in the draws should have been jumped by the hunters noisily busting through the grass and brush.

The hunter with the Model 740 concentrated on staying upright on the steep hills. He was somewhere in the middle of the pack. After walking two to three hundred yards, he angled slightly down a small draw toward a clump of red sumac. As he did, he jumped a full-sized doe. It was the only shootable deer he had seen so far that day.

Unfortunately, he had his mind in neutral when the deer jumped. It took him the first eighty yards to get his slung rifle ready to shoot.

Two drivers—one below and one above—spotted the deer as it ran. Each fired twice without ef-

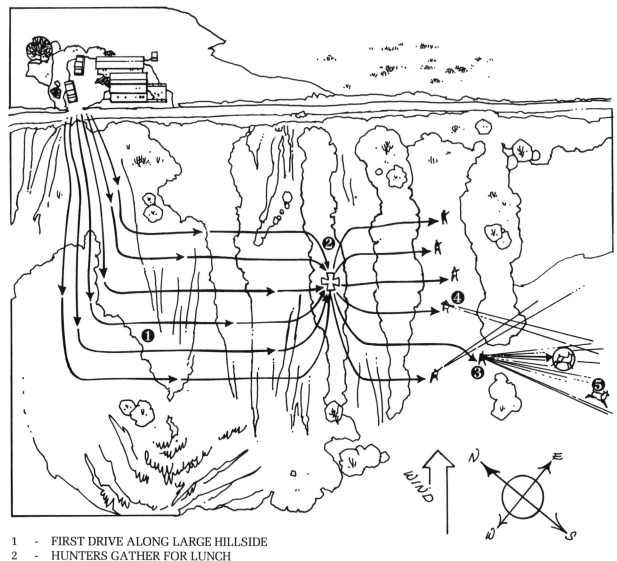

1 - FIRST DRIVE ALONG LARGE HILLSIDE
2 - HUNTERS GATHER FOR LUNCH
3 - HUNTER JUMPS DOE ON SECOND DRIVE; BEGINS FIRING
4 - DRIVERS ABOVE AND BELOW TAKE TWO SHOTS EACH
5 - REAR DEER FINALLY HIT

fect. From their angles and at that distance, it was extremely difficult to hit that kind of target.

The hunter moved onto the crest of a little rise, watching the deer from almost directly behind. He started pulling the trigger on his semi-auto in a regular cadence. Range was about 180 yards. He could not see the rounds hitting but assumed—because the deer continued on its original course—they were landing behind it.

He fired eight times total before the deer ran down an old, unused cattle trail into a small, brush-choked draw. For an instant, the critter completely disappeared from sight. The hunter used the pause to cram his fresh magazine in the rifle. Anxiously he peered through the scope, trying to locate the deer in the bush.

He couldn't see the animal but decided to fire into the spot on the hill where he had last seen it. He was now about two hundred yards away and perhaps fifty feet above the critter. At the first shot into the brush, a deer broke cover, running perhaps twenty yards before a second deer also broke cover, following the first out on the same cattle trail.

The hunter resumed his rhythmic fire, trying to adjust after each round. On the third shot at the front deer, he hit the rear deer between the shoulder blades. The sound of the bullet hitting the critter was audible. It fell immediately in the trail. Range, he guessed, was about 250 yards.

The hunter moved his 6X scope to an area way ahead of the lead deer. He fired three more times as it ran up the gentle side slope. Apparently the deer was not bothered by the shooting—it stopped dead still at the top of the next rise, looking over its shoulder at its tormentors.

The shooter sat down on the ground, took a rock-steady hold, and fired one more time. At the shot, he and two of the drivers watched the deer kick out involuntarily to the rear with its left hind leg. The shooter was not sure, but it appeared that the shot burned across the deer's rump, causing little damage and no reaction other than the kick. At the shot, the critter jumped three times and was out of sight. The hunter estimated range to the second deer to be at least three hundred yards.

Deer one started to squirm around on the trail. It flopped end over end, rolling and crawling back downhill into the heavy brush. In a few seconds it was completely out of the hunter's view. He feared the deer would crawl away and be lost in the heavy brush.

With a sense of urgency, the hunter called to a companion, who worked his way down into the center of the brush strip. The shooter made sure his companion was below the deer, preventing escape downhill. He continued to urge the fellow lest the deer run down into even heavier cover. In spite of the confusion, his companion worked up the brush strip slowly and methodically.

Finally, the searcher located the deer peering up over a clump of dry grass. He carefully placed a round from his .22 pistol in the animal's head. Range was about twenty feet. Later, when butchering the deer, the hunter found that the spent .308 bullet had passed through the top of the shoulders and spine, penetrating about six inches into the body cavity.

During the interval, two other drivers, including the experienced deer hunter, walked over to the spot where the hunter had last shot at the leading deer. They were directed to the exact spot by the shooter, who kept his position on the hill. They managed to find the critter's tracks, but there was no blood or hair. They tracked it a quarter of a mile before concluding that if the shot touched the animal, it was nothing more than a scrape.

Various members of the group dragged the animal down to the road, where they left it for later pickup. It was now coming up on 2:30 P.M. By mutual consent, the crew agreed that they did not wish to hike back up on the hill. They gave up hunting for the day, electing instead to start the forty-mile drive home while daylight remained.

The shooter endured hours and hours of comments, criticisms, and suggestions from his fellow hunters regarding his rifle and hunting technique. Comments were made about his poor marksmanship, volume of fire, militarylike attitude toward deer hunting, and incessant hollering for help when the deer was down.

As a sequel to this case, the hunter sold his semiauto rifle, purchased a bolt-action, and began to hunt with rounds in the magazine but not in the rifle chamber. He practiced constantly under various conditions of light, range, and cover until he became one of the region's best shots and most accomplished deer getters.

His empty rifle—which he had to load when he saw the deer running—encouraged him to take his time when contemplating a shot. For years after, he always got his deer with just one well-placed shot.

As a result of that experience, the hunter concluded that jump-shooting deer can be effective under some circumstances, but the shots will likely be long or hurried. He learned that superb marksmanship is a must for any consistently successful hunter. Finding this out is often traumatic, especially for a young man.

CHAPTER 36

MOST MISERABLE HUNT

HUNT CHECKLIST

Weather

Cold, miserable rain that cycled on and off all week. Temperatures in mid-40s.

Terrain

Fairly heavy, steep mountains with 600 to 800 feet differences. Many large pine and fir covered the area, with aspen and birch as intermediate cover. Ground cover was very dense.

Wind Direction

Out of east to northeast, 1 to 5 knots.

Conditions Previous Day

Rained off and on all week with varying intensity. Started raining the day hunters arrived.

How Hunters Moved

Drove up an old fire lane to a place where they knew three deer trails converged. Stalked these trails in the rain till one man got a close shot at a standing deer.

Clothes

Wool pants and shirts, nylon rain slickers, knee-length boots.

Rifle Caliber and Scope

.338 Magnum bolt-action with 6X scope.

Sex of Deer

Probably a doe.

Time of Day

About 11:30 A.M.

Length of Hunt

All day.

Length of Shot

Not more than 40 feet.

How Deer Moved

Deer stood up out of bed but was obscured by brush. Hunter estimated the deer's position and took an unsuccessful shot.

Skill of Hunters

Shooter was a skilled weekend deer hunter with some measure of past success.

It is often said that the average hunter is happiest when he is most miserable, certainly a piece of country wisdom that applies to every duck hunter.

As a rule of thumb, one must conclude that deer hunters who venture out in truly awful weather do so because it is one of the easiest times to bag a deer, not as a result of a subliminal need for self-flagellation.

Deer, the good hunters have found, may move if they sense a storm coming, departing, or settling in to cover the country for an extended period of time. Sometimes deer are better weather forecasters than the lady in the little box. Without benefit of TV, they seem to know not only when the storms are moving but how much snow will be dumped on their feeding areas and how long the suspicious weather will last. The problem for most hunters is that the deer seem to know more than they do. Yet skilled old-timers who have been out in the country a great deal know where deer will bed, where they will eat, and how best to approach them under these conditions.

Most of these people have many incidents to relate about shooting deer right in their beds in really crummy weather. The problem with these accounts is that there is little the novice can learn from them. The hunter simply goes out where he knows the deer will be lying and shoots one.

The case in question was a deer hunt in the far reaches of some very rugged backcountry and involved knowing where deer would bed during a storm. The three hunters had planned and schemed for the event for at least six months prior to actually undertaking it.

The territory was worn-down mountains. Most were soil-covered, but severe, tough rock outcroppings were strewn about the region, giving it a rough, mountainous look. Reliefs ran to roughly six to eight hundred feet from rivers below to windswept ridges above.

Ground and upper-story cover in most places was thick to virtually jungle. The high trees were comprised of tall pines and firs mixed with a few ash and maple. Aspen and birch grew in clumps here and there, comprising a sort of intermedi-

ate-level cover. On the ground a tangle of stunted maple, alder, and thorn brush choked off most of the sunlight.

The participants in this case were accomplished weekend deer hunters who had killed a satisfactory number of deer in the past. They were not highly skilled old-timers, but they spent enough time in the bush to begin to learn about deer. Equally important, they had spent enough time on this specific piece of country to begin to know how the deer moved. As a result, they had something of an advantage over the run-of-the-mill hunter who might occasionally walk over the area.

In retrospect, this advantage seems to have been only marginal. The men did not speak with confidence about their ability to always find deer. They continued to hunt these mountains mainly because in past years they often saw and/or killed deer there. Through the years the country was kindly disposed to them and they to it.

Upon arrival at their motel about twenty miles away, it started to rain. At first they were pleased that they didn't have to deal with heavy snow, but when the rain continued on in torrential quantities, they seriously discussed calling off the hunt. As a practical matter, however, they were committed to the week of vacation from their offices and could not reschedule easily.

Perhaps in one last supreme effort to look on the bright side of things, the three partners agreed that it would be easier to stalk through the woods quickly in the drenched state they now found it in than if it were dry. There would be little danger of crackling twigs and sticks, and the constant patter of drops would help obscure noise. They also liked the lack of strong winds.

Having concluded that they had little other choice, they got up at 5:00 A.M. and drove out to the mountain they intended to hunt. Thick, indolent clouds hung on the ground in many places. Mud, even on the graveled country roads, was horrible. As in times past, they were able to maneuver their four-wheel drive truck up an old, now mostly overgrown fire road, but they slipped and slid the entire trip.

Three traditionally active game trails converged on this old fire lane near the place where they parked their vehicle. Fortune smiled on the hunters in this regard, as the heavy red mud made it questionable if they could have gone farther except on foot.

As per their long-agreed-upon plan, each hunter took one branch of the game trail, still-hunting through it in an easterly to northeasterly direction. Winds, such as they were, came out of the east at from one to five knots. They did not believe winds would be much of a factor.

The game trails were the result of perhaps centuries of deer traffic. Rumor had it that livestock had run on that country in years past, but the hunters never did see a domestic beast or tracks. Deer tracks in the moist soil were there in the thousands.

The hunters probably were overdressed for the weather, which was admittedly miserable but not particularly cold for deer season. Temperatures ranged from the low to mid-forties. They wore wool pants, wool shirts, nylon rain slickers, and slouch hats. Boots were knee-length rubber. The clothes they wore somewhat reflected their needs from the prior year rather than being the best for that day, as after an hour of hunting, they were soaking wet and hot from exerting themselves.

Gray, wet, miserable dawn came at 6:45 A.M. With far less spring than normal in their steps, the crew left their vehicle. Through heavy rain and sometimes pea-soup-thick mist, they hunted the mountain ridgeline. They made it along the game trails for about three miles.

Their stalk along the game trails took them east somewhat parallel to each other but diverging into a fanlike pattern. The man in the middle was especially confident, thinking the other two might run game to him. The hunter to the right found his trail wound along the edge of a creek which, because of heavy underbrush, he could hear but not see. He moved through several draws and pockets. All three hunters found that visibility varied greatly, from twenty yards in some thickets to a hundred when peering downhill into heavier stands of timber. As a general rule, visibility stayed at the lower end of the

range. They had not seen or heard each other since daybreak.

As they hunted, it absolutely poured down rain. Except under sheltered brush, new tracks on the trail were gone in five minutes. The men were soaked cruelly by brushing against soaked bushes. Chances of seeing other hunters in that remote area were virtually nil. It was not a place where people were likely to hunt, and it certainly was not a day in which the locals were likely to be out.

By about 11:00 A.M., the three hunters were so miserable they must have really been having fun. One man stood under a tree, where he lifted his slicker a bit and watched steam pour out from his clothing. Water squished in his boots.

At the far east end of the saddle ridge in which they stalked, the middle hunter came onto two small, rocky projections. They stood alone, rising at most sixty feet from the land. To the east the ridge petered out, falling steeply to a creek some five hundred feet below.

Silently and carefully, the middle hunter climbed the first of the two domes. He reasoned that deer might be lying in the thick aspen covering at the top. Exercising as much caution as possible, he checked among the brown ferns growing among the aspen for signs of deer beds. He found nothing, not even gouges in the soft earth suggesting past tracks.

The hunter knew in a general sense where his two companions were at that time. Again as carefully as possible, he stalked from the first nob toward the second. The cold sapped his energy enough that he did nothing in a big hurry. To make matters worse, no game or even recent sign of game appeared to fire his enthusiasm.

As he climbed to the top of cone two, it started to pour again. He got to the top, pulling up under a spreading pine. As he peered out, he saw a steady stream of steam rising from inside an especially tangled scrub maple thicket not more than forty feet away. The steam just hung there in space for a few seconds, as little to no wind moved in that place.

He fumbled around for a rag he carried with which to wipe the lens of his 6X scope. The rag

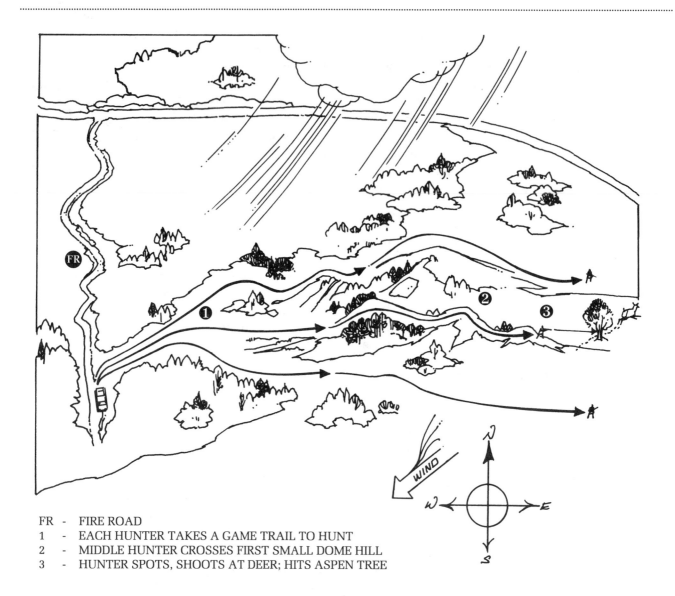

FR - FIRE ROAD
1 - EACH HUNTER TAKES A GAME TRAIL TO HUNT
2 - MIDDLE HUNTER CROSSES FIRST SMALL DOME HILL
3 - HUNTER SPOTS, SHOOTS AT DEER; HITS ASPEN TREE

was so soaked he simply smeared the water around, sufficiently breaking up the drops so that he could see ahead.

The hunter focused his scope on the steam. To his absolute amazement, a critter was defecating right there in the brush ahead of him. Other than the steam, he could not make out the deer through the tangled brush.

He waited patiently for perhaps two minutes for something to happen. It obviously was a deer, yet it did not move another hair that he could see. He realized that if he jumped it, all he would get was a split-second glimpse as it ran off. Looking back now, the hunter believes he should

have whistled softly, stomped his foot, or otherwise caused the critter to look around for him. However, he didn't. He simply stood there soaking up cold rain. Range to the deer was, at most, forty feet.

Finally the hunter pushed the safety forward on his .338 bolt-action and, using the scope picture of the brush, estimated the location of the center of the deer. When he had the theoretical place where he thought a round would punch through the body cavity, he fired.

On doing so, he got his only look at game all day. The deer wheeled around and ran almost instantly out of sight.

Crawling on his hands and knees, he carefully checked the place in the brush where he shot, thinking that there had to be some blood and hair. There was absolutely no sign of the deer except a pile of recent pellets. Looking even closer, he found a five-inch aspen tree with a fresh bullet hole. The hunter was amazed to see that he hit the trunk dead center and that the relatively small tree stopped the big, fast bullet completely. As far as he knows, his bullet still resides in the tree.

He finally gave up and walked down the steep grade at the end of the saddle to the creek. A path along the creek led out to a county road. On the path, the hunter encountered his two buddies. They were tired and dejected, having seen no game.

They walked two miles to another county road, where they hitched a ride with a logger to the fire trail. It was 2:30 P.M. and still raining when they got back to their vehicle. Their energy was entirely used up.

Although they were a bit unspecific, the hunters claimed that they all got their deer later in the week when the weather cleared and the game moved.

The hunters concluded that, because they lived in the city, they had to plan their hunt at least six months ahead. As a result, they were at the mercy of the weather. They felt they knew the county well enough to hunt it, but no game was moving on that miserable day. They also agreed that being miserable on a deer hunt is not all that much fun.

CHAPTER 37

OLD BUCK

HUNT CHECKLIST

Weather
   Cold rain, turning to snow when hunters got into woods. High trees broke up precipitation and wind, sheltering hunters to some extent.

Terrain
   Flat area abutting a knoblike hill that rose sharply to the east.

Wind Direction
   Mostly from the east. Area was sheltered from winds by the high landform and some mature timber.

Conditions Previous Day
   Cold and gray with little rain as front moved through.

How Hunters Moved
   Stalked through woods together, then walked back around, picking up an old logging road that they followed till they jumped the deer.

Clothes
   Green army parkas over wool pants and shirts. Boots were rubber knee-length variety more suited to duck hunting.

Rifle Caliber and Scope
   .308 bolt-action with 6X scope.

Sex of Deer
   6- or 8-year-old 10-point (eastern count) buck, obviously past its prime.

Time of Day
   Hunters started about 8:00 A.M., walked about two miles, then shot the deer around 10:30 A.M.

Length of Hunt
   Hunt started in one man's kitchen when they figured out which piece of country would be productive on the type of day they faced. They drove about 30 miles to the woods, then walked about 2 miles. Time elapsed was about 4 hours.

Length of Shot
   Estimated at 60 to 70 yards.

How Deer Moved
   Deer apparently was lying in the woods between stalking hunters. It tried to get up and walk away quietly.

Skill of Hunters
   Both men had hunted extensively but in recent years hadn't been in the field much because of the press of business.

It was toward the end of deer season when two otherwise preoccupied businessmen finally succeeded in scheduling a few days together in pursuit of whitetails. They would have enjoyed going out earlier in the year when the deer were more numerous, less wary, and the weather less inhospitable, but other events intervened.

As it was, the press of duties related to a successful, growing business kept the men out of the field until it was almost too late to organize an effective hunt. The two deer chasers, in this case, were excellent sport hunters who, as younger men with fewer responsibilities, had spent considerable time in the fields and forests learning deer. As people commonly do when they grow older, the hunters found that their interest and energy levels changed to the point that it was too easy to ignore deer season.

As fortune would have it, the Saturday they finally selected to go hunting turned out to be awful—torrential fall rain mixed with snow. Little of the heavy, wet snow accumulated as temperatures fluctuated in and out of freezing, allowing the rain to wash it away.

At 6:00 A.M., the men gathered in a warm, dry kitchen to discuss their folly. Having finally committed the time to hunt, they were somewhat piqued that Mother Nature dealt them such a poor card. They sat drinking coffee, not really wanting to abandon the hunt but not wanting to get soaked to the skin in the miserable, cold rain and snow either. Secretly, both wished a deer would run through their backyard so they could shoot it from the shelter of the porch.

After perhaps fifteen minutes of meaningless discussion, the hunter who lived in the area the longest recalled a wooded area in the lee of an almost cylindrical cone mountain where, as a young man, he often killed deer during periods of foul weather. He suggested that they drive to the place about thirty miles distant and give it a try.

East winds blowing through the region at fifteen to eighteen knots tended to obscure noise in the woods. They thought they might get a deer in spite of noisy rain slickers and knee-length rubber boots needed to maintain some semblance

of comfort in the bush. The trick was to find the place where the critters were taking shelter till the front moved through. They agreed that this ancient hunting ground might be the place.

The targeted patch of woods lay about four hundred yards from a blacktop road. It was covered by a fairly heavy stand of older pine mixed with popple and aspen. The land had been logged in the 1920s but now was regrown enough to constitute a veritable forest. The pines grow sufficiently close and tall to shade out any potential understory; they also sheltered the men from the full fury of the falling rain and snow. Clumps of aspen and popple grew thick enough to preclude a pheasant from running through, much less a man or deer.

Leaves, such as they were, lay on the ground in a soggy, spongy layer. Although it was a tight squeeze through the timber in places, the lack of leaves as well as the masking wind in the treetops all contributed to the possibility of doing a credible stalk. If one moved around slightly so as to line up sight distances between the trunks, visibility was in the 80- to 120-yard range.

The actual topography of the land over which they planned to hunt was gently rolling to quite flat. The tree-covered knob rising sharply to the east was extremely steep. However, the two planned to stay over on the flatter ground abutting the knob on the west. After the hunt they had wondered why that land had never been cleared to farm.

Encountering other hunters on that miserable day was unlikely. Deer hunting was relatively easy in that region; most hunters who wanted one often had gotten their deer the first week of season.

It was a dreary, depressing 8:00 A.M. when the hunters parked their truck on the county road some four hundred yards from the targeted wood. Snow had fallen continuously for the last thirty minutes and was piling up in the more sheltered places. The men speculated that they had either gained a tiny bit of altitude or a cold front was moving through. Conditions in the woods shifted from poor to reasonably okay with the passing of the torrential rain.

They wore heavy army surplus parkas over

their thick wool jackets, shirts, and pants. Boots were a rubber knee-length type more suited to duck hunting than hiking through the woods. Other than the funny green boots, they looked more like refugees from a national guard maneuver than deer hunters.

Walking across the sticky, plowed, muddy field to their starting point was probably the single most difficult part of the expedition that day. Had they known about the thick yellow mud that stuck to their boots in great globs, it may have been impossible to get them out of their vehicle.

In the woods they spread out about two hundred yards, turned left, and started stalking through. Because the incessant rain and snow wet the forest thoroughly, trunks of the tall pines were stark black, contrasting against the whitewashed popple and aspens. The beauty and color renewed the hunters' spirits. Also, they found that the winds that howled about their ears when they walked across the farmed fields bordering the hunting area were relatively benign and of little consequence once they were in the timber. They monitored the winds on a continuing basis by means of the falling snow.

The first hunter walked in about eighty yards from the edge of the woods. His companion stalked through an estimated two hundred yards beyond his buddy. They hunted for about eight hundred yards before concluding that there was nothing in that section that was willing to expose itself.

The hunter who had worked the property as a young man recalled an old logging road running against the high hill at its base. He would not have remembered the path had he not walked these woods again, stimulating his powers of recollection.

At the end of their first drive, they decided to walk out to the plowed field again and swing all the way around to their starting point. Boot mudding was kept to a minimum by walking in the grass at the edge of the field. The hunters do not recall all of the reasons why they went to all of this effort to find a path that ran parallel to their current position, other than the fact that they were unsure as to the exact location of the logging road. The men agreed that they were a bit damp on the outside but far from miserable. It had turned into a halfway nice day to be out in the woods.

It was at least 10:00 A.M. when they arrived back at their starting point, ready to probe deeper into the woods in an attempt to locate the path. Both hunters were confident somehow that the path was their key to success.

At first they walked around somewhat aimlessly looking for the old logging road. Finally, they found two deep ruts running down a steep grade where vehicles once moved. The path was virtually overgrown with trees and brush, but the erosion caused by now extinct logging trucks could not regrow. Once they found the location, it was obvious where the road once ran.

They spread out in the woods again, approximately two hundred yards apart, intending to stalk through to the end another eight hundred or more yards. It was still calm and beautiful down on the forest floor. Somewhat together they walked on through about two hundred yards. Heavy snow filtering through the pine canopy was the main limiting factor to their sight distance.

Suddenly, without noise or other warning, the hunter farthest to the east creeping along the old road saw a chocolate brown movement deep in the brush to his left. He pulled up his .308 bolt-action rifle, peering through its 6X scope and searching for the source of his alarm. He looked over in his partner's direction but immediately realized the possible consequences of his action.

He searched through the heavy timber and steady snow for several minutes till he found a buck whitetail sneaking slowly through the trees. He thumbed the safety forward as he tracked the deer in his scope. It was now hard to his left, almost behind him. The hunter speculated that his partner jumped the deer and it was now trying to sneak between them. Surely, he reasoned, it must have had his scent—winds seemed to be moving directly from hunter to buck.

He continued to swing with the buck till he

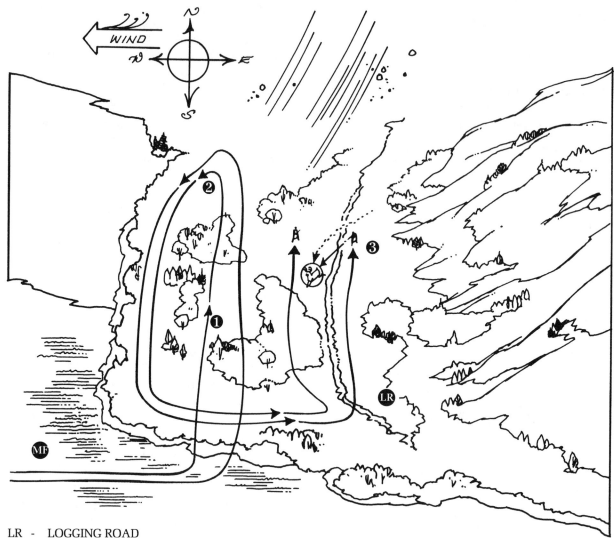

LR - LOGGING ROAD
MF - MUDDY FIELD
1   - FIRST DRIVE THROUGH WOODS
2   - HUNTERS GO BACK TO STARTING POINT TO SEARCH FOR LOGGING ROAD
3   - HUNTER SHOOTS BUCK

found an opening through the tree trunks. When he did, he tapped the trigger.

At the shot, everything went out of his sight. He could no longer see the dark brown critter either lying on the ground or running away. A small patch of scraggly brush and grass stood in the middle of his sight path, something he had not previously noticed. The hunter estimated range to the spot where he saw the deer at sixty to seventy yards. He bolted another round into the chamber and moved around for a better look.

Nothing moved that he could see.

The hunter stood silently and waited in the snow for perhaps five minutes. His period of inactivity ended when his companion called from deep within the bush. They worked their way over to the critter, which they found stretched out on the damp forest floor.

The buck was an ancient ten-point whitetail. Using the worn cusps on its teeth as a guide, they concluded that it must have been six to eight years old or even more. In addition to its worn teeth, great abscesses in its mouth must have made eating very difficult. Its somewhat scrawny rack obviously had been magnificent in years past. The animal was in poor condition, skinny, and with no fat layer stored up for winter.

The round hit it low in the left front shoulder, passing entirely through the critter and out its right side. It tore up one shoulder extensively while the other took considerable washing and trimming before it was edible. Due to its poor condition, the men ended up running the entire critter through their meat grinder.

It was the opinion of the two hunters that the buck was so old and in such poor condition that it would not have survived the winter. Appar-

ently, its poor mouth kept it from storing sufficient body fat for even the current relatively benign conditions. At the first real cold snap, coyotes certainly would have singled it out as a relatively easy meal. The animal was in such poor condition, they later agreed, that it could not even have run from them.

The pair concluded that they got the deer because they knew which piece of country to hunt during a storm and because one of them was familiar with the terrain. They also believed it helped to know how to shoot through heavy timber at a relatively long range. The shooter also felt that less experienced hunters might not have seen the critter trying to sneak away.

CHAPTER 38

OUTMANEUVERED BUCK

HUNT CHECKLIST

Weather
Cool and dry, with temperatures in the mid-40s.

Terrain
Single 600- to 800-acre knob bordered on all sides by farmland. Knob was covered with dog-hair pine and red alder, with only a few large fir and pine trees.

Wind Direction
Out of northwest at 12 knots, hitting the ridgeline on an angle and swirling around in an unpredictable fashion.

Conditions Previous Day
Basically the same. Last rain was a week earlier, with little residual effect.

How Hunters Moved
Walked up small mountain out to end of prominence, then dropped over edge with two driving ridge slope while one watched from top.

Clothes
Cotton work pants, light wool shirts, denim jackets.

Rifle Caliber and Scope
Hunter wounded deer high across the front shoulder with a .300 Winchester Magnum bolt-action with 3-9X variable scope. Stander killed the deer with a .308 bolt-action with open sights.

Sex of Deer
3-year-old fork-horn buck.

Time of Day
Started walking into area at 6:00 A.M.

Length of Hunt
About a mile into hunting area, then a 300-yard drive and tracking job that took about an hour, covering 1/2 mile. Hunt took most of one day.

Length of Shot
First shot with .300 Winchester Magnum was about 40 feet. Second killing shot with .308 was about 80 yards.

How Deer Moved
Deer was jumped out of its bed, where it was shot with a grazing round across its top front shoulder. When pushed, it ran uphill to a patient stander, who killed it from his stand.

Skill of Hunters
All the hunters were very skilled. As fortune would have it, those with the greatest skill in a particular area were called on to use it when pursuing that deer.

Veteran deer chasers most enjoy recounting incidents where they or those they usually hunt with had executed a perfect hunt, one where the game is brought to grass with apparent simplicity and impunity. Unfortunately on close examination, it becomes painfully obvious that the perfectly executed hunt seldom occurs.

When one really gets to digging around for the facts connected to most hunts, it becomes evident that the deer or hunter who made the last mistake, as the case may be, is the one who ended up losing the encounter. Most hunts are nothing more than a grand series of mistakes strung end to end. For the purposes of this book, the deer are the ones who generally make the last mistake.

The following case involves three experienced deer hunters. Only two of them figured materially in the incident. The third man, because of his position, timing, and perhaps unwise decisions, took himself out of the action. The remaining two did things reasonably well, resulting in a nice, full-bodied whitetail buck. However, the outcome was very much in question even after what should have been the conclusion of the hunt.

The country over which the three hunted the day of this incident was quite unusual in some respects. The land was dominated by a large knob (or small, freestanding, tree-covered mountain) rising out of the relatively flat surrounding countryside. The knob covered six to eight hundred acres and was bordered on all four sides by farmland.

Perhaps because of the cover afforded by the wooly, rugged prominence and the feed available in the abutting grain fields, large numbers of whitetail thrived on the hill. During fall deer season, hunters in the region singled out this and similar areas as being excellent places in which to kill a deer.

In the deer's defense, Mother Nature scattered a number of these lone knobs across the countryside, diluting the number of hunters one might see afield in a day. Yet the area was a magnet for men who could not otherwise think of a place to hunt. Although this trio saw no other parties the day of their expedition, the possibility always existed that they could encounter ten or fifteen others.

The little mountain in question was about six hundred feet high, running on a short ridge from northwest to southeast. Two particularly tall prominences provided a footing for microwave towers that generated the necessity for a primitive, seldom-used, double-track dirt access road. The hunters used this road to get on the knob with a minimum of effort.

From afar the landform looked like a simple single dome. From the hunter's perspective on top, it seemed much more like a little ridge with two smallish dimples.

Cover on the hill was an often extremely thick, tangled mess of dog-hair pine and red alder. A few larger red fir still grew, survivors of past logging activity. Down in the brush, visibility was often forty yards or less, but out on the somewhat open edges and the little side ridges, one could sometimes see a deer as far as two hundred yards or more.

Problems arose when the numerous, much-chased deer simply hung tight in the heavy brush or jumped quickly from one patch to the next, offering at best a running shot. Those deer that elected to run out over the open grain fields bordering the area could be taken by hunters accustomed to shooting accurately over long distances.

The weather that day could best be described as benign, cool, and dry. Some rain fell about a week prior to the hunt, settling the dust a bit, but the effects were dissipating rapidly. Temperatures ran in the low to mid-forties.

The men wore cotton work pants, denim jackets, and their regular, tattered wool shirts. Because they traditionally hunted the area by using drives, they did not worry about scratchy, noisy clothing. The steepness of the ground necessitated that they wear relatively high-quality footwear, so all chose Vietnam jungle boots, believing the cleated soles were ideal on the steep slopes.

The three hunters elected to park their truck on the county road and walk the mile or so in and up onto the ridge. It was a long, arduous, mostly uphill grind, but they figured that taking a noisy, smelly vehicle into the area might compromise the hunt. It was now mid-season, and deer on the knob had already been run around a bit by other hunters.

They left the road at 6:00 A.M., fully forty-five

minutes before daylight. First light just showed in the east when they got to the relatively level ridgeline. It lay in a bit of a crescent, making it resemble a mound when seen from the surrounding countryside. About three hundred yards out on the ridgeline, the hill opened up into open grassland. Ahead and below to their left, the first brush patch was evident in the chilly morning gray.

One of their party knew the top of the ridge better than his backyard patio. He knew the exact location of the numerous game trails leading up the hill from the brush patches below. More important, he was aware of the precise location of the few especially advantageous places which he knew from past experience overlooked the trails on which deer were likely to move.

The bottom driver knew from experience. where deer were likely to bed and where they might jump into the open for a few yards so he could get a shot.

The middle hunter had the worst of the drive. If experience was a guide, he knew he had a tough hunt ahead. Most of the deer would try escaping up or down. Any shots he got would be extremely fortuitous, although he agreed to the middle position as a result of killing a nice white-tail from that position on a similar drive several years back.

Because of his past experience, the stander could to some extent keep track of the two drivers strung out below him. His most pervasive problem would be moving slowly along the ridge while keeping alert for any deer ahead and simultaneously keeping track of the hunters below. He also watched his back trail—in twenty years of hunting, he often had gotten deer trying to sneak out behind.

The middle hunter scrambled just to keep up without falling off the mountain. Bottom hunter moved through as quickly as he could to cover the proportionately larger area to which he was assigned.

Winds in that area were always a problem. Generally they came out of the west to northwest, hitting the ridge at twelve to fifteen knots. On the very top they chilled one even on a warm day. Twenty feet over the crest on the south to

southeast side, they were not a factor until one got down almost to the bottom, where they started moving again. Because they swirled and eddied, it was virtually impossible to predict how they might move.

The hunters sifted dust into the air continually but never could keep ahead of the many changes that occurred. They did know from experience, however, that, winds or no winds, the deer would run along the slope side, over the top, and out of the area. The winds were so mixed and diverse, they speculated, that perhaps any sort of human scent would merely confuse the deer.

The hunters worked together nicely through about three hundred yards of country. The east driver had more actual game trails to evaluate. He reported numerous tracks but no sighting of critters. The middle driver saw few tracks and no deer. He had only rocky, hard trails on which to look for sign.

Three hundred yards was something of a benchmark for the drive. At that point, heavy brush closed in on the land, limiting sight distance to twenty yards at most.

The east driver swung down into a small bulge of tree-covered land known to contain hundreds of crisscrossing deer trails. Middle driver plowed through on course, hoping only to jump a deer out of the cover to his friend above. Stander, having stood that area dozens of times in the past, knew he now had to hustle around the ridge to a game trail that ran up through the bottom of a slight depression.

The stander was in the process of moving when the middle driver fired a single shot. Using their walkie-talkies, the shooter confirmed the fact that he had jumped a nice buck out of its bed in an alder thicket. He took a quick shot with his .300 Winchester Magnum bolt but felt that at best he might have scraped the deer.

The east driver assumed that if the buck was wounded, it would come down to him. He slowly and cautiously worked through the drive another fifty yards, coming on a large deer track running straight off the hill. Using the Indian tracking method of swinging off and on the track as he followed the route that experience sug-

1 - STANDER MOVES ALONG TOP OF RIDGE
2 - DRIVERS PUSH THROUGH COUNTRYSIDE
3 - MIDDLE DRIVER JUMPS, SHOOTS BUCK
4 - MIDDLE DRIVER CUTS OFF ESCAPING BUCK IN THICKET
5 - STANDER SHOOTS BUCK
6 - BUCK FALLS

gested that the critter would take, he started after the supposedly wounded deer. While moving off to the side, he positioned himself for a shot in case he saw the deer move ahead. Then he worked back over the track to be sure it was actually in the place he supposed it was. It was a

most effective technique if one was actually a good tracker.

The stander hurriedly arrived at the only spot from which he knew he would see the buck approaching if it decided to head uphill.

The middle driver found the track and a few

hairs and small drops of blood. Of the three, he was far and away the best tracker. He quickly determined that the deer had run fifty feet back behind him through the heavy brush. He also ran back and down, hoping to cut the deer off before it left the large thicket in which they were thrashing around. On working uphill again, he cut the track heading back into the center of the thicket and slightly uphill. Apparently, his driving technique was effective.

The middle driver did not know where the deer might head now. He simply reported his position and the deer's movement to the other two.

The third hunter below was sure he was on the deer's trail. The tracks he was working were red hot, obviously made after the recent shot. After the radio report that the deer had turned back, he redoubled his efforts to get up on the deer he was tracking. He was now about five hundred yards downhill and slightly ahead of his companions.

The middle driver doggedly kept on the track of the buck, thinking that if he were both careful and patient, he would eventually drive it to one of his buddies. The stander, who was famous for his patience, waited rock steady with rifle to shoulder, watching a game trail as he leaned against and behind the lone tree in the area.

The middle tracker pursued the wounded critter for at least thirty minutes, while the bottom hunter followed his track to a place where he could see almost a hundred yards ahead. The stander concentrated on doing the simplest of tasks, but one that few standers can do correctly: waiting patiently in the proper place without moving a muscle.

After a long, long while, the stander heard the *crunch crunch* of a critter trotting through the brush. After about thirty seconds, the noise quit. Obviously, the animal had stopped. Carefully, the stander peered down his rifle barrel. Suddenly, a buck's head and shoulders appeared under a large tree about eighty yards below on the trail.

He swung his .308 bolt-action rifle a few inches over and placed the blade of his open sight square on the deer's brisket. Without further delay, he pulled the trigger.

At the shot, the fork-horn buck jumped quick-ly, switched directions, and headed back downhill on the trail. The shooter thought he caught a glimpse of a bloody wound across the deer's front shoulders before it disappeared. He reported the situation to his companions by radio. Although range was only about eighty yards, he couldn't actually indicate a hit or miss. He just didn't know yet.

The middle tracker dropped the trail he was on to fight his way over to the scene of the second shot. The shooter kept his original position so that he was certain to put his companion at the exact location.

At the place where the deer stood when shot at a second time, the tracker found a few additional drops of blood and some hair. He reported a definite second hit and headed down the trail. Meanwhile, the lower hunter found an open spot on one of the many trails, where he stopped to watch.

It took a full five minutes for the upper two hunters to follow the track down some sixty to eighty yards to the spot where the deer had died. It was an impressive three-year-old buck with nice fork horns, shot cleanly through the center of the brisket. The round smashed through the top of the heart, coming to rest against the inside of the rear right ham. The middle hunter's original shot, they found, hit about one inch down on the front shoulder, cutting a narrow furrow through the top of the shoulder and spine.

Conventional wisdom suggested that the buck should have been hurt by the first shot and that it should have tried a downhill escape rather than up. The hunters concluded that, although the wound looked severe, it probably wasn't.

Little meat was wasted on the critter, but because only two holes in strange locations were evident, they did not know until they skinned the deer exactly how it was hit. At first it looked as though the round through the brisket exited up through the top of the shoulder, an impossible shot from the second shooter's uphill position.

It took the three hunters two hours to carry the deer (which they eventually found weighed 177 pounds, field-dressed) uphill to the jeep trail. Then it was another hour before they managed to drive their four-wheel-drive truck to the deer's location.

The hunters felt they got that deer because they were fairly good shots, could track deer, knew the country, and were willing to actively track the quarry or stand patiently and wait, depending on the best strategy at the moment. In many respects, this hunt was nothing more than knowing where to stand and wait as well as where to jump a deer out of the thicket.

HUNT CHECKLIST

Weather
Cool and dry, with temperatures starting at about 35°F and rising to about 48°F by noon.

Terrain
Rough, soil-covered hills with elevation differences of 400 feet. Pockets and little draws chocked with heavy brush. Occasional pines in the open areas.

Wind Direction
Mostly out of the west. Intensity is not known.

Conditions Previous Day
Rained the previous day, but country was now drying.

How Hunters Moved
Hunted up the steep slope of a hill, mucking around on the hillside for most of the day. Deer was shot as they walked back down to their vehicle.

Clothes
Cotton work pants, flannel shirts, light cotton jackets, and Vietnam jungle boots.

Rifle Caliber and Scope
Shot leg off with .257 Roberts and killed deer with shot to the head with a .308 Winchester.

Sex of Deer
Whitetail doe.

Time of Day
Deer was shot about 4:00 P.M.

Length of Hunt
Hunters worked hill the entire day, walking about 5 miles in the process.

Length of Shot
First shot was an estimated 175 yards. Second shot was taken at about 30 feet.

How Deer Moved
Deer came out of thicket to nibble grass, where hunter shot it broadside. They followed it into thicket, killing it where it lay.

Skill of Hunters
Both hunters were extremely inexperienced and had never been over the country they hunted that day.

At least three-quarters of Americans who do not hunt game animal believe that hunters simply stroll out in the field engaged in some sort of nefarious plot to murder animals in cold blood. No conception exists of the philosophy of the chase, much less the reclusive nature of wild animals.

Deer hunters understand that those not born to it cannot endure the long hours of often boring hard work necessary to figure out how to take game. Often we hear hunters say, "I would never do this for pay." If murdering anything is one's bag, he will never be satisfied with deer hunting.

Honest deer hunters will admit that much of the time spent hunting is simply wandering aimlessly around the countryside with no overriding plan as to what to do or where to go. Little thought is given to what is happening and why. In many respects, the following case bears extensively on this truth. A few points of instruction can be gleaned in what follows. Unfortunately, the incident is probably typical of the vast majority of hunts, reflecting conditions as they actually occur in the field.

The hunter under consideration had bagged two or three whitetails in the past as part of larger hunting parties. He was not a good hunter by any stretch of the imagination. By his own admission, he knew little about whitetail habits and patterns. As a solitary hunter, he had killed a few game animals such as coyotes and turkeys, but this was one of his first outings in search of deer without the guidance of a master hunter or the protection of a large group. He took along a companion who, other than finishing off the wounded deer, did not kill a deer that day or any time in the future.

They decided to hunt over fairly steep soil-covered hills. Elevation extremes varied to about four hundred feet. These hills were part of a larger, rough, desolate topographical complex known for its quality as deer habitat.

The hills were grass covered or only thinly populated with trees and brush, yet extensive pockets of thick brush grew down in the swales and valleys. Some of these patches comprised of rose thorn, thorn apple, sumac, and blackberry

were too thick to walk through. There were occasional pine trees on the hills.

Grass grew on the hills when sufficient fall or spring rain nourished it to life. Cattlemen in the area used the area for fall and winter pasture but were forced to move their herds elsewhere during the summer.

Winds in the region could be out of any direction. The hunter believes that they were predominantly out of the west but does not recall anything more specific. He does recall that it rained quite hard the day before the hunt. Red, greasy mud made it tedious to climb up the steeper grades.

The temperature the day of the hunt started at a crisp, dry 35°F, warming to about 48°F by midday. The ground had dried in most places except in some pockets and draws. Where it was wet, the ground was very slick.

The hunters parked their truck along the side of a county road at about 6:00 A.M. They discussed the hunt for a few minutes, evaluating how they might best work the hill rising steeply to their side. They argued for fifteen minutes till full daylight was upon them, yet not much was settled. Their only emerging strategy was to spread out about three hundred yards and hike straight up the hill.

Once up the hill about a quarter of a mile, they figured they would walk along the edge of as many brush patches as they could, hoping to scare a deer out in the process. Neither one had hunted that hill before. While standing on the road they could only guess as to how many pockets and strips of cover lay out of sight above them.

Youthful enthusiasm carried the two up the steep hill fairly quickly. By 6:45 A.M. they both turned left to contour through and along the targeted brush pockets. Perhaps because it was midweek they could see no other hunters in the area. Unless one were down in the brush, it was common to see 150 to 200 yards or more.

Both hunters kept the other pretty much in sight as they climbed up and then worked along the brush. No logical reason existed for keeping visual contact except perhaps for a misplaced desire to coordinate their hunt. It would have been impossible for them to become disoriented, as any path down would take them to the road running through the valley on which their truck was parked.

Lacking any real hunting plan, they worked around the hillside the entire morning, walking a total of perhaps three miles. Neither man was much of a tracker, but now and then they came across deer tracks in the slick mud, which they thought might be fresh. Neither man knew how to read the sign nor what exactly to deduce from it. They simply assumed there were some deer around, but very little beyond that.

After walking laterally on the hill, they suddenly changed strategies, starting a longer and perhaps even more unproductive walk to the top. All of a sudden, getting to the top became a goal every bit as pervasive as shooting a deer.

By about 1:00 P.M. they topped out on the hill's rim. They sat down and rested, eating their last sandwich. Both men carried binoculars that they used to glass the lower hills for deer. They recall that the fresh wind cooled them at the top when they stopped moving. Even relatively close to noon, temperatures were about 48°F. They were wearing Vietnam jungle boots, cotton pants, and flannel shirts topped with light cotton jackets that retained heat poorly.

Working together, they ran a couple of small drives trying to push a deer out of one of the little brush patches lying at the top or on the lip of the hill, but all they managed to get up were some pheasants. Both men enjoyed pheasant hunting, and, given their success so far with deer, they inwardly wished that they had packed along a shotgun.

One hunter walked over a little roll in the ground when he spotted what looked like a medium-size German shepherd sitting on its haunches in the dry grass. He peered at it through his scope trying to decide if it was a stray domestic dog or a coyote. Range was ninety yards at most.

He was unable to decide what he had till it started running. Then he knew it was a coyote. The hunter decided not to make a noisy, probably ineffective shot at a moving target.

Darkness was expected about 5:30 P.M. By about 2:30 P.M., the pair reckoned that they had had enough fun for one day. Turning sharply downhill, they started a hunt that would quickly take them to their vehicle. It wasn't exactly the same path they took coming up, but it was quite close.

For about an hour they concentrated on zigzagging back and forth downhill, hitting little patches of brush here and there. They had no plan other than getting back to the road before dark.

By about 3:30 P.M., shadows on the hill started to lengthen. Air movement—always minimal—virtually ceased. The only action was gentle breezes generated by warm air rising uphill from lower elevations, bringing the previous day's rain out as humidity. The hunters mopped their brows, concentrating more on putting one foot in front of another than on deer.

One hunter walked down an intersecting old wagon trail cutting precipitously along the side of the hill. It took him hard to his right instead of straight downhill to his vehicle.

As he shuffled along the path, he happened to look ahead across a wooly patch of brush. There, twenty feet from the patch, stood a whitetail doe. Its head was down, nibbling new grass. He might never have seen it had it not been standing perfectly broadside to him.

Range was at least 175 yards, though the hunter admits that he is a poor guess of range and that he did not bother to pace off the distance after the shot. He also had no clue regarding winds relative to the critter. He did stop long enough to think about the position of his partner; three hundred yards above, he recalls.

After having carried his heavy binoculars all day, he did not even use them on the deer. Quickly he unslung his rifle, viewing the doe through his 6X scope. It did not look like a terribly large critter, but it was definitely and positively what they had been looking for all day.

The deer kept on nibbling at the grass, oblivious to the danger. The hunter looked around for a rest for his rifle. There was nothing. If he was anything (besides being only an average deer hunter), he was reputedly an excellent shot.

He placed the crosshairs on the deer's chest, thought about it for a few moments, and then el-

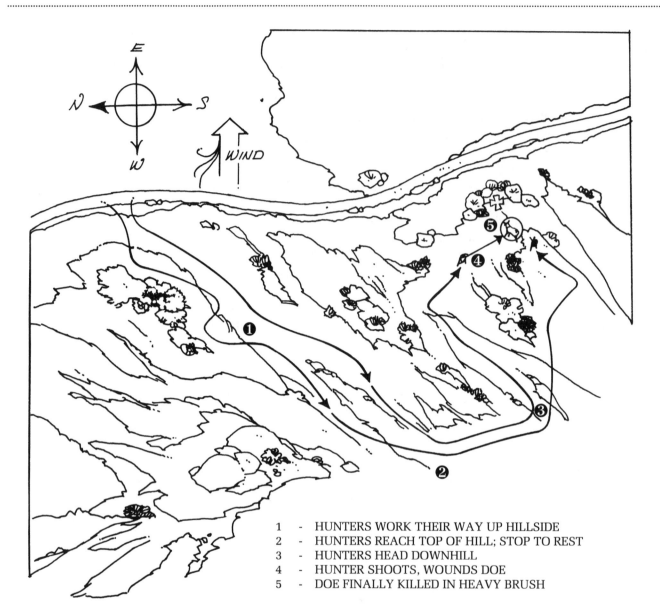

1 - HUNTERS WORK THEIR WAY UP HILLSIDE
2 - HUNTERS REACH TOP OF HILL; STOP TO REST
3 - HUNTERS HEAD DOWNHILL
4 - HUNTER SHOOTS, WOUNDS DOE
5 - DOE FINALLY KILLED IN HEAVY BRUSH

evated them till the horizontal line was parallel along the deer's back. The vertical line centered the deer's left front shoulder. Had this shot been successful, it would have wasted a large portion of the meat.

The deer fell kicking and squirming at the shot from his .257 Roberts bolt-action rifle. It quickly squirmed its way downhill and out of sight. The hunter watched through his scope as long as he could.

He ran at full speed along the wagon road toward the downed critter. As he topped the last little draw, he spotted the deer wildly propelling itself downhill using only its rear legs. It moved so quickly along a game trail in the draw that he could not get another shot off before it disappeared again.

Doing perhaps his only correct thing all day, the hunter ran downhill as fast as he could into the open grass at the edge of the brush that was concealing the deer. He managed to get in below the animal, stopping it from continuing down the hill. Apparently the wounded deer was incapable of running uphill. It was apparent that he hit the deer, but exactly where was still a mystery.

Miraculously, the hunter's friend appeared at

the top of the draw above the deer. He called out, trying to determine what was going on. The shooter suggested that he come down the draw while he stayed below to cut it off. They discussed the possibility that the deer might still have enough energy to run up the hill and away from them.

His companion started down through the heavy brush, walking slowly for about thirty feet. At that time he hollered frantically that he could see the animal's head. The shooter suggested that he quit bellowing and simply shoot it again. His companion then shot the doe in the head at thirty feet with his .308 bolt-action rifle.

On examination, they found that the first shot had literally blown the deer's right front leg off at the knee. It still hung attached by a few strands of skin, but it was bleeding profusely and useless to the critter.

They dragged the deer out of the brush. Field-dressing took an inordinately long time since neither man really knew what he was doing.

Taking turns, they dragged the deer downhill to the vehicle. Even this portion of the hunt was somewhat poorly undertaken. Mud and sand worked its way into the open body cavity, creating very gritty hamburger later.

It was only thirty minutes before dark when they loaded the critter into their truck and headed home.

The hunters concluded that they were successful because the deer was unfortunate enough to crave a nibble of new grass at that particular time and because the shooter was a reasonably good offhand shot. One must also conclude that both hunters could learn quite a bit more about deer hunting, as this doe was the only deer they saw over an entire day of hunting through some excellent deer country.

CHAPTER 40

IT'S OVER WHEN THE FAT LADY SINGS

HUNT CHECKLIST

Weather
Snowed some the day of the hunt, but the major storms that had dropped 2 feet of snow had passed.

Terrain
Long, deep canyon providing food and shelter for deer that historically migrated there during rough winters. Ground cover consisted of intermittent clumps of lodgepole pine, alder, and ninebark with only a few really large trees.

Wind Direction
Out of east at 8 knots, but not a factor in this deep, sheltered canyon.

Conditions Previous Day
Stormed for 3 or 4 days prior to hunt, dropping at least 2 feet of snow.

How Hunters Moved
Two hunters walked about 3 miles into the canyon. Virtually at the farthest distant location they shot a big mule deer doe that they had to drag out.

Clothes
Heavy wool coats and pants topped with nylon slickers. Boots were cleated rubber pacs.

Rifle Caliber and Scope
.308 bolt-action with 6X scope.

Sex of Deer
Large, mature mule deer doe.

Time of Day
It was about 3:30 P.M. when the deer was shot, but it took till 3:30 in the morning to get it out.

Length of Hunt
They did not start terribly early, but the hunt lasted about 18 hours till they got the deer home, covering at least an 8-mile hike.

Length of Shot
About 125 yards.

How Deer Moved
Deer was feeding on hillside when it was shot standing broadside to hunters.

Skill of Hunters
Two old-timers had hunted for many years, killing scores of deer. Young lad killed his first deer on this hunt.

For the purpose of this case, it is important that one keep in mind that the events which transpired did so during the very last hour of the last day of deer season, far back in country so rugged it could be classed as desperate.

The hunters were two hardened, seasoned deer chasers with dozens of years of collective experience behind them. They took along a teenaged boy out on his first season of deer hunting. Although the boy had yet to kill a deer, the two older men must have bagged in the hundreds during their lives and have killed many more since this incident.

Contrary to contemporary wisdom, the lad was not turned off by events of the day. He went on to become a deer getter of local renown. He currently is not a deer hunting fanatic, but he still gets out during the season from time to time. He now admits that his first successful hunt was most rigorous, and that he hopes never to repeat it.

The country in question was a long, deep canyon known as a refuge for deer when weather in the surrounding rugged, tree-covered high country got tough. Driven by deep snows, deer migrated down into this and other canyons, some of which were eight hundred feet deep. There they found shelter from the snowy cold and a bit of grass to eat while they waited for the weather to pass.

Hunters who worked the deep canyons at these times often found deer standing around in an almost dazed condition. They moved about during the day in little groups of three and four with little thought of keeping in the cover. Killing the deer of one's choice was very easy.

Often, gut piles from previously bagged deer dotted the countryside to the extent that a hunter standing in one spot might see three or four hills. Thus harassed, the deer moved down into somewhat thicker cover, but basically they remained in the same general area.

Under these circumstances, it theoretically would have been possible for hunters to reduce the deer herd considerably. However, several factors worked in the deer's favor, precluding their mass destruction.

Snowstorms of sufficient intensity to con-

centrate the deer in the refuge occurred at most every three years. Furthermore, the state department of natural resources set deer seasons so that they were likely to conclude before major snows arrived, thus resident deer hunters were unlikely to hold their tags unfilled in anticipation of a "big snow." Having filled their tags early, most were precluded from taking easy deer if, by chance, conditions of weather and terrain did align themselves.

Ground cover in the deep canyon consisted of lodgepole pine, ninebark, alder, and some maple. These species grew in occasional dense clumps surrounded by large, open patches of cheatgrass. Toward the upper reaches of the canyon and on the upper rim, vegetative cover grew together so that grassy areas comprised only an acre here and there.

With the advent of winter rain and snow, abundant cheatgrass sprung to life, producing nourishing green nibbles for the newly arrived deer. Warmth in the canyon kept most of the snow melted, providing wonderful open pasture for wildlife.

Late-season hunts into the canyon area were frustrated by additional factors besides deep snows, previously filled tags, and closed seasons. There were virtually no roads, tracks, or trails into the canyon that would allow people to drive in close. Successful hunters were faced with a long walk in and then a tough pack out. It was a minimum of a mile to the nearest reliable road.

There was also the challenge of simply walking along the steep slopes in the slick, icy weather. Hunters usually wore heavily cleated rubber hunting pacs in an attempt to maintain traction.

Snow blew in torrents the last three days of the season. On the very last day the weather broke a bit, leaving two feet of snow in its wake. Older hunters learned from acquaintances that deer had been seen moving into the canyon in large numbers. Even during the storm, they were told, fifteen or twenty hunters willing to make the walk had filled their tags. Most did so by taking a wife, girlfriend, sister, or younger son along with their recently purchased tag.

The skilled hunters had taken the teenaged

son of one of them hunting a number of times during the now concluding season. The lad saw a few deer but was unable to get off a proper shot. At that point, he was anxious over his yet unfilled tag.

Damp, nasty 33°F temperatures greeted the three the day of the hunt. Winds blew brusquely at eight knots out of the east when they parked their truck on the closest county road. Melting, semislushy snow was everywhere. In the sheltered woods on either side of the road, it was at least two feet deep.

Numerous vehicles cruised the freshly plowed road, most carrying road hunters watching for an easy deer crossing into the canyon. The hunters picked a wide spot to park their truck, where they knew from experience they were unlikely to encounter other hunters. They started walking into the canyon at about 9:30 A.M. wearing heavy wool jackets covered by nylon rain slickers. Pants were extra-heavy wool that kept the wearers warm even when wet. Boots were the cleated pacs required for that country.

One of the men broke trail for the lad and the other man. Marching in single file, they walked in for about a mile, taking forty minutes to break through the heavy snow and tangled brush. Eventually they came to the canyon rim, where they turned right slightly. After walking down into and up the canyon another half mile, they were eventually able to intersect an old, little-known logging road.

At the road, the hunters stopped to rest and plan. So far they had seen only tracks. They agreed that one man and the boy would follow the path into the canyon while the other circled above, dropping down on the road thirty minutes later. Hunting conditions in the forest were incredibly miserable. They saw no problem with a man following thirty minutes behind on the same track.

The hunter and boy carefully walked into the canyon on the old logging road, covering at least three miles. They saw countless deer trails but not one deer. They often heard shots in the distance, reinforcing their belief that their general plan was a good one. As they continued to walk, the snow thinned out to a few inches in depth. Because the trail led mostly downhill, it was relatively easy to walk. They continued creeping along silently, watching the hillsides both above and below.

As planned, the lone circling hunter dropped down on the trail about thirty minutes later. Although he looked at the same territory that his companions had crossed, he felt his chances were equally good given the migratory nature of the deer. He did not catch up with the first two. Tracks on the road confirmed that they were the only ones hunting the area that day.

Sheltering canyon walls confused and blocked the winds, especially as they went deeper into the hole. Both the older hunters had concluded that they would see deer when they saw deer and not before, regardless of any attempt they might make to work into the swirling, unpredictable winds. Deer up on the hillside or below might never get a human scent, or errant breezes might betray their presence as much as a mile away. There was no way to predict or mitigate the situation.

At 3:00 P.M., his lunch long turned to calories, the rear hunter decided to turn back. His companions' tracks carried on in a wearying patter ahead, but the hunter knew he was four miles from their truck and that he faced a long, arduous hike back.

He did find it a bit easier to walk even uphill through the trail now that it had been beaten down by three sets of boots. He pushed on, arriving at the truck about 4:00 P.M., just moments before dark. He wolfed down a box of crackers while waiting till well after full dark for his friends.

The hunter with the boy in the canyon knew full well at 3:00 P.M. that they were in trouble. However, they kept pushing on ahead on their little logging road.

At about 3:30 P.M., he rounded a prominence on the slope, looked back and up into a large draw, and spotted a huge mule deer standing in the brown, dead ferns up on the hillside. Instantly, he stopped. On doing so, the lad also stopped dead still. The youngster searched the hills where his friend watched till he, too, spot-

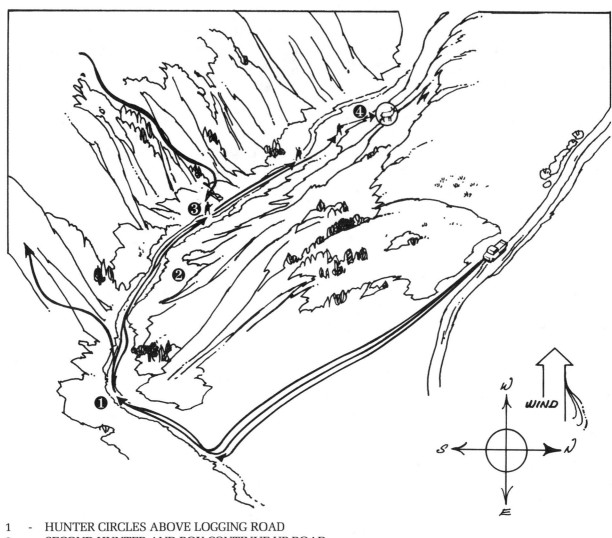

1 - HUNTER CIRCLES ABOVE LOGGING ROAD
2 - SECOND HUNTER AND BOY CONTINUE UP ROAD
3 - FIRST HUNTER DROPS BACK DOWN ONTO ROAD
4 - BOY SHOOTS DEER

ted the dark brown, almost black critter. It stood broadside to them, pawing in the thin snow about 125 yards away.

Without a word, the young hunter raised his .308 bolt-action rifle with 6X scope. As he zeroed in, the deer started walking. Like a pro, the boy tracked the deer, touching off a shot at about the sixth step.

At the shot, the deer blew all of its air, then bounced up and onto the top of the ridge and ran out of sight. The lad thought he might have missed, but the older man knew it was well hit.

"I shot for the ribs," the kid hollered, "and I think it was a good shot! I really took my time—the crosshairs were dead on!"

They walked up on the ridge, intent on looking for blood and/or a trail in the thin snow. Tracking the critter was not necessary. A fat, 220-pound mule deer doe lay dead in a pool of creamy red blood next to an old burnt stump on the face of the ridge. As they suspected and hoped, it was shot through the lungs. The shot blew through from the left, carrying baseball-sized chunks out the right.

They dragged the deer uphill, slit the belly, and pulled out the steaming entrails. They cut the feet off at the knees and the head at the top of the last vertebra. By the time they finished, it was quite dark.

The experienced hunter carried a piece of nylon rope and a small handle, much like those found on lawn mower starters. He looped the cord around the deer's exposed neck vertebra and attached the handle. Dragging the deer uphill on the logging road was slower and tougher than just walking, but it was not unreasonable as a result of the slick snow.

The boy carried the guns and the animal's heart and liver. After a mile or so, he started holding and slightly pulling one rear leg to prevent the deer from flopping around. It made the load much easier for the man to pull.

They carried on through the deepening snow toward the canyon rim. By 4:30 P.M., it was black as the inside of a cow and they were still a mile from the rim. Only because of the white snow and the beaten trail were they able to continue.

At the road, several vehicles had stopped to inquire regarding the hunter's companion. Now forty minutes after full dark, he reported to interested passersby that his friends were probably lost.

Finally tiring of waiting, he decided to walk back down the now well-worn trail. It took him only twenty-five minutes even in the black of night to hike over to the place where they intersected the logging road earlier in the day. There, he decided to holler. He had heard no shot nor had contact with his companions the entire day. He was not even sure that this was the correct place to stand and holler.

The deer-dragging hunters, half a mile down the canyon road, heard the shout and answered. Their companion walked down the path for a third time that day till he met the struggling pair and took over dragging the deer. As they labored along, they discussed their options. Everyone was very tired.

Initially, the fresh hunter reckoned he could drag the deer out to the road by himself. However, on reaching the canyon rim, he also was played out. They agreed that they were fortunate that this was the only deer they saw that day. They also agreed that it would be extremely desirable to get the deer to the road and home, it being the last day of the season. Yet everyone was so tired from walking long distances in deep snow, some of which included dragging a really big deer, that they now felt they would be fortunate if they could get themselves to the road.

With apprehension they stashed the deer in a deep, fluffy pile of snow. It was 6:45 P.M. when they got to the road and the forty-mile drive home.

They made it home to a roaring fire and a giant meal. Eating was geared more to taking on fuel than dining. Despite clean, warm clothes, they were still chilled. All three lay on the floor in front of the fire.

Warm fire and full bellies had their effect. At 1:00 A.M., one of the older hunters woke from his deathlike sleep and roused the other man to talk about their situation.

Both were concerned about possible unpleasantness if they were to bring the deer in the day after season. They were also concerned about the meat, which could taint under the deer's heavy winter coat even when surrounded by snow. They did agree that the chance of theft was minimal since they had not seen one other hunter off the road that day. They finally decided that they were sufficiently recovered to go back out for the deer.

It was 2:00 A.M. when they got back to the parking area along the road. Night winds seemed colder and more biting as they walked in. All of the trails were most familiar by that time.

Working together, they rolled the deer out of the snowbank and skidded it to the road. By 3:30 A.M. the deer was safe in their truck. They drove home and skinned it. About an hour before sunup, both hunters changed to dry clothes again, threw another long on the fire, and went back to sleep on the floor.

They attributed their success to knowing where the deer would likely be under specific circumstances and being persistent in searching those areas. They were in reasonably good phys-

ical condition, able to withstand the grueling abuse of walking miles and miles through the *cold, wet snow. Shooting the deer was well done by the boy but anticlimactic in this case.*

CONCLUSION

So what is to be learned from all of this, one might ask. Hopefully, quite a lot. Some obvious truths along with some that are more subtle. I did prove, for instance, that my phone bill could reach new astronomical heights as I searched for accounts from really good hunters throughout more than twenty-five states. But other, more practical conclusions are possible.

It did not, for instance, really make much difference which caliber an expert deer hunter used. It could have been anything from a .22 Long Rifle to a .338 Winchester Magnum. Perhaps strangely, no one used a pistol, and no one would admit to regularly using a .270, which I thought would be the most common deer hunter's tool.

Really successful deer hunters, as illustrated in these cases, tend to use either a larger, heavier magnum or the extremely standard .30-06 type rounds. Several hunters who shot the six or eight deer required to actually test a caliber's effectiveness depreciated another supposedly popular deer round, the 7mm Remington Magnum. Like the .270, this round may have passed its peak popularity for those who use a deer gun as a tool. "Tears the meat up too much," I was continually told regarding 7mm mags.

Hunters who used them tended to favor 6X scopes on their rifles. Yet we know 6X scopes make up only 9 percent of annual scope sales in the United States. My conclusion is that neophytes who reason that 6X scopes are the cat's paws for deer just because most of the experts use them delude themselves. These people certainly could have gotten most of their deer with open sights once everything else had fallen into place.

Good, consistent hunters really know the country over which they hunt. Repeatedly, hunters emphasized that large chunks of time must be invested checking out the territory. Most old-timers suggested four trips per year: in late winter, spring, summer, and early fall. Based on the information collected, I can say that scouting out the land carefully during all four of these periods would almost guarantee a perfect hunt.

One must also conclude that unflustered, unhurried marksmanship plays a major role. Not one of the many deer hunters I talked to mentioned long hours on the range. Some talked about their companions being good shots, and one hunter did reckon that shooting robins out of the neighbor's cherry trees with .22 Shorts was excellent practice.

"By the hundred and fiftieth cherry-robbing robin, I could hit anything offhand at a hundred yards," he boasted. That man felt that he got his deer as a result of the weeks of fast-action, offhand practice he received in the summer. Yet most deer getters merely assumed that they or their companions would simply shoot deer wherever they saw them. Tales of skunked hunts were tough to draw out of most old deer hunters.

Particular sections of the country did not seem to matter, but techniques one learned while growing up did play a part. Wisconsin deer hunters, for instance, were used to shooting from a stand, yet they easily translated that method to similar terrain and ground cover in Oregon, Texas, or parts between, even though it was a method not otherwise practiced in that area. For this and other reasons, specific states in which the hunts took place were not identified. It seems important to be able to adjust one's method to the terrain and ground cover, regardless of which section of the country is being hunted.

Although it was impossible to quantify exactly, weather played a major role in all successful deer hunts. Although on some days the critters were moving everywhere, and on others it was impossible to locate even one deer, old-timers with thirty or forty years of field experience seemed to be able to sense in their bones when the deer were out there. Yet when I questioned them closely about weather and its relationship to numbers of shootable deer seen, it became apparent that they were correct only 75 percent of the time. Many of the cases include examples wherein hunters assumed the weather was perfect for deer when, in fact, it proved to be far from ideal out in the field.

If one were to take all of these cases at face value, one might conclude that hunting was usually best on days when the weather was worst. During these times, deer tended to move, but it was never certain. It was certain, however, that hunter noise and scents were effectively masked by wind, rain, snow, or combinations of the three.

In retrospect, it seems odd that I found no one who would tell me about shooting deer over bait, that remarkably effective new device causing so much controversy in some states. Also, I did not come up with a believable account regarding rattling deer. This method seems to rise and fall perhaps in symbiosis with the stock market. At this time, as a method of deer hunting it seems to be in remission.

So what is the bottom line?

It appears that no matter what equipment is employed, the user must be able to bring it into action quickly and flawlessly.

Hunters must thoroughly know their country and the deer habits therein. They must never walk through the woods without a definite plan, their minds in neutral.

Consistently successful hunters watch the weather. Over the years they develop a feel for the times when conditions provide the greatest promise.

It helps to be able to mentor an old, experienced hunter. Not always possible, but valuable if one can put it together.

Finally—although this exact concept was never articulated in so many words—it appears that deer hunters who can frequently and easily drop everything to get out onto their territory for numerous little half-day hunts enjoy an enormous advantage over those who live in cities and can get out only a day or two per season.

After spending hundreds of hours talking with these old-timers, many of whom had never "opened" to an outsider before, and following these conversations with analysis by real sharp technique people, I know exactly what I will be doing next deer season. I will be on the ground early, scouting the country. I will pay much more attention to weather, hunting for a few hours when conditions are ideal far more often than I have in the past. I will learn to work more effectively with my partners, and I will shoot a couple boxes of ammo on the range before the season starts. Most importantly, I will walk through the woods thinking about the hunt at all times.

My feeling is that I, for one, will be a far better and more confident deer hunter this upcoming season.